Welcome to Our
Nightmares

Welcome to Our Nightmares

Behind the Scene with Today's Horror Actors

Jason Norman

McFarland & Company, Inc., Publishers
Jefferson, North Carolina

LIBRARY OF CONGRESS CATALOGUING-IN-PUBLICATION DATA

Norman, Jason, 1979–
Welcome to our nightmares : behind the scene with today's horror actors / Jason Norman.
pages cm
Includes bibliographical references and index.

ISBN 978-0-7864-7986-3 (softcover : acid free paper) ∞
ISBN 978-1-4766-1724-4 (ebook)

1. Horror films—History and criticism. 2. Motion picture actors and actresses—United States. I. Title.

PN1995.9.H6N557 2015   791.43'6164—dc23   2014042762

BRITISH LIBRARY CATALOGUING DATA ARE AVAILABLE

© 2015 Jason Norman. All rights reserved

No part of this book may be reproduced or transmitted in any form or by any means, electronic or mechanical, including photocopying or recording, or by any information storage and retrieval system, without permission in writing from the publisher.

On the cover: Don Shanks as Michael Myers in *Halloween 5*, 1989 (CBS/Fox/Photofest)

Printed in the United States of America

McFarland & Company, Inc., Publishers
Box 611, Jefferson, North Carolina 28640
www.mcfarlandpub.com

To all my colleagues in the horror film fan world.
It's because of them—it's because of *you*—that our favorite
genre has become its own outstanding cinematic standout!
Throughout the course of this book, I kept feeling a sense
of pride: the pride that those who entertain us have
from doing it, and the brother- and sisterhood that
run through the camaraderie of fans like us that
keep giving them so many chances to do so!

Table of Contents

Introduction	1
Michelle **Argyris**: *Devil Seed*	5
Blythe **Auffarth**: *The Girl Next Door*	7
Belinda **Balaski**	9
Tim **Balme**: *Dead Alive*	11
Ashley **Bank**: *The Monster Squad*	14
Michael **Berryman**: *The Hills Have Eyes*	17
Doug **Bradley**: The *Hellraiser* films	26
Jonathan **Breck**: *Jeepers Creepers, Jeepers Creepers 2*	33
Jamie **Brewer** and Naomi **Grossman**: *American Horror Story*	36
Stacy **Chbosky**: *The Poughkeepsie Tapes*	41
Noelle **Coet**: *Mischief Night*	44
Lora **Cunningham**: *The Book of Eli*	46
Fiona **Dourif**: *Curse of Chucky*	47
They Came from *Elm Street*!	50
Katie **Featherston**: *Paranormal Activity*	58
Hannah **Fierman**: *V/H/S*	68
Friday the 13th: Their Name Was Jason (Voorhees)	70
The *Friday the 13th* Family	80
Sid **Haig**	90
Celebrating *Halloween*!	93
Danielle **Harris**	99
Legend Alert: Rondo **Hatton** and The Creeper Films	104
Legend Alert: Jackie **Joseph** and *The Little Shop of Horrors*	107
Michael **Karnow**: *Incident at Loch Ness*	110

Table of Contents

John **Kassir**: *Tales from the Crypt* — 112
Camille **Keaton**: *I Spit on Your Grave* — 114
Nick **King**: *Sinister* — 117
Brandon **Lee**: *The Crow* — 119
Michael Reid **MacKay**: *Se7en* — 125
J. **Mallory-McCree**: *Cloned: The Recreator Chronicles* — 128
Meet Some *Massacre* Men — 129
Chris **McGinn** and Ted **Levine**: *The Silence of the Lambs* — 136
Pollyanna **McIntosh**: *Offspring* and *The Woman* — 139
Zoe **Naylor**: *The Reef* — 145
Lyla Hay **Owen**: *Interview with the Vampire* — 147
Katie **Parker**: *Absentia* — 149
Elizabeth **Pena**: *Jacob's Ladder* — 151
Nick **Principe**: *Chromeskull* Films — 153
Lorna **Raver**: *Drag Me to Hell* — 157
Silje **Reinåmo**: *Thale* — 160
Julianna **Robinson**: *Wasting Away (Aaaah! Zombies!)* — 163
Felissa **Rose**: *Sleepaway Camp* — 166
The *Saw* Films — 169
Susan **Swift**: *Audrey Rose* — 177
Pat **Tallman**: *Night of the Living Dead* — 180
Tony **Todd**: *Candyman* films — 183
Dee **Wallace**: *The Howling*, *Cujo* and *The Frighteners* — 186
Virginia **Welch**: *Prosecuting Casey Anthony* — 189
Ian **Whyte**: *Aliens vs. Predator/Requiem* — 192

References — 197
Index — 203

Introduction

Over the decades, horror has established a full-blown following unmatched by any other area of film. Put together a meeting of performers in the horror neck of the movie woods, and fans will most certainly come. Why does this happen? What sets the horror world apart from other aspects of cinema? What makes horror not only its own genre, but seemingly, its own private culture?

Actors quite often find themselves in the scary world at the beginning of their careers. We will never forget Jamie Lee Curtis' turns in the first two *Halloween*s, just as even the least hardcore fans of Kevin Bacon and Johnny Depp are quite aware of the pair becoming two of the first victims of the *Friday the 13th* and *A Nightmare on Elm Street* franchises. Chances are that Jennifer Aniston probably still gets teased once in a while about *Leprechaun*.

But before Amy Adams racked up five Oscar nominations from 2005 to 2013, she was in *Psycho Beach Party* (2000). Leonardo DiCaprio's 1993 Oscar nomination for *What's Eating Gilbert Grape* would light the match that set the inferno still burning under his career, but his cinematic debut was two years earlier in *Critters 3*. Before she was winning an Oscar for showing us the realistic side of horror with *Monster*, Charlize Theron walked past the cameras of *Children of the Corn III*. George Clooney rocked the horror world in 1987 and 1988 in *Return to Horror High*, *Grizzly II*, and, wait for it … *Return of the Killer Tomatoes!*

And in 1980, a struggling actor managed to snare his first film role as a shrink in the slasher flick *He Knows You're Alone*. He wouldn't hit the big time for a while, but today he's a household name—two Oscars and about a bazillion dollars in box-office revenue can get someone there. The fellow? Tom Hanks.

What is the common thread between performers and their fans?

Well, definitely the creative aspect. Conventions are a chance for fans to forget about our daily lives and become the characters we see on screen, to step even further away from creativity and sometimes all the way near to transformation. How often do we go to these conventions and run into fellow fans in costume and full-blown character (language included) as these people? Or even become them ourselves?

It probably has a great deal to do with loyalty. Perhaps even camaraderie between not only the fans who crowded into a theater to be puzzled and terrified, but the fans and the actors who did the scaring itself. We get a chance to be around people who know what we think, and who understand, if they don't necessarily agree. They may not like the same films, characters, or series as we do, but they know *why* we like them.

When I was young, if someone had asked me why I liked to be scared when I was a kid—I thought that *Thriller* was the scariest "film" of all time until I was about 13—I would probably take the easy way out: "I dunno, it's just fun to be scared!" But what makes a person stay a member of horror's fan club into adulthood?

Looking back to my graduate school years at Old Dominion University, one favorite class and teacher were found in American Pop Culture 101, and as a longtime horror buff, I can remember one lesson in particular.

"There are three types of horror films," she explained (I'm paraphrasing, as time has erased the exact quote). "There are the uncanny films, where situations are unusual, but not impossible, like *Jaws* or *Psycho*. There is the marvelous category, in which situations are impossible, like *Night of the Living Dead* or *A Nightmare on Elm Street*, where the villains keep coming back to life. There are fantastic films, in which we, the viewers, are never really sure what's going on, even after the film. That includes *The Shining* and *The Sixth Sense*."

Sitting in her class, I started thinking about what exactly goes into making a good horror film. How can a filmmaker get together a screenwriter and a few actors and put on something that makes people walk out of theaters saying, "Man, that's going to keep me up for the next month!"

I've always believed that uncanny films are the scariest, if they're done right. They don't have an aura of fantasy; they could truly happen. They're unlikely, but the small margin of possibility makes them that much more terrifying. There's not *much* of a chance that Hannibal Lecter could sneak up and make us into dinner ... but it's possible. We *probably* wouldn't get found by Leatherface and his family in the backwoods of Texas ... but we might end up getting the wrong side of the chainsaw. Along the pages of this book, you'll meet quite a few people who agree.

Something else that makes the uncanny films the most horrifying is that many are based in reality. One part or another was in some way true.

In the winter of 1957, police in Wisconsin followed a van seen near a store whose owner had recently disappeared. They were led to a house owned by Ed Gein, known to his neighbors as a quiet but decent sort who never took much of an interest in women, or close friends in general. The contents of Gein's house would shock, disgust, and (cinematically) inspire many. The store owner was found hanging by her heels, her heart in a coffee can, her head gone. But this wasn't the end; before the police had finished searching Gein's home, they had come across fifteen more bodies, or at least sections thereof. Gein had killed at least two, and had stolen the rest from graves.

The Gein story was an inspiration for Robert Bloch's novel *Psycho*, which in turn inspired one of the cinematic world's monumental achievements, the 1960 movie adaptation. In 1974 came the first *The Texas Chainsaw Massacre* flick, partially based on Gein. In 1991, film fans were shocked by the actions of Buffalo Bill in *The Silence of the Lambs*: Like Gein, he had a mother fixation from hell, and tortured, killed, and skinned innocent women.

Gein wasn't the only bit of realism incorporated into the Best Picture of 1991. Just as serial killer Ted Bundy attracted his victims by pretending to be injured, then pulled them into a car, so did Bill. Just as Bundy helped (or pretended to help) police detectives search for Green River killer Gary Ridgway, Hannibal Lecter (Anthony Hopkins) "helped" Clarice Starling (Jodie Foster) search for Bill.

When we look at the horrific acts of Gein, Bundy, Ramirez, Dahmer, Gacy, Berkowitz,

Introduction

McVeigh, D.C. sniper John Muhammed, and others, it's often far beyond anything we've seen on the screen. This is nothing new; Bram Stoker based his novel *Dracula* on Vlad the Impaler, who ruled over Transylvania in the late 1400s, slaughtering thousands, usually in the manner that earned him his nickname. These things remind us that the most horrifying acts happen far from, and far before, they're ever on screen.

Sometimes, even the marvelous and fantastic films can have a certain basis in reality. Stephen King, whose works have gone from page to screen for decades, based the story of a telekinetic woman named Carrie on two girls he'd known in high school. With her family in the grip of poverty, one of the girls wore one outfit per year; another lived in a trailer adorned with a huge crucifix. *Pet Sematary* sprang from an incident in which a feline friend of King's daughter was killed by a truck and buried in a nearby animal-exclusive graveyard. He turned a hotel he'd visited on a trip to Colorado into the *Shining*'s setting of the Overlook.

Several actors interviewed for this book cited the uncanny as the worst things they had seen. This book covers one of the most notable of the uncanny in recent times with a chapter on the *Saw* series; Betsy Palmer, both the best and worst of mothers as Pamela Voorhees in *Friday the 13th*; the many men who will tell us how they got ready to become a man named Michael Myers in the *Halloween* movies; and a couple of Leatherfaces from Texas (home of the *Chainsaw Massacres*).

Blythe Auffarth, Noell Coet, Rochelle Davis, Danielle Harris, and Camille Keaton will describe their preparation to face down horror and torture of the painfully realistic sort, and some women who battled back Freddy Krueger and Jason Voorhees get to take a look at those fights. Pollyanna McIntosh got to play both hunter and prey with the same character in two movies.

Horror may have a larger cult following than any other film genre, but there are still *far* too many wonderful offerings that haven't quite gotten the credit they deserved. Let's give it to them. Let's learn about how the stars of *Absentia, Wasting Away, Thale, Cloned: The Recreator Chronicles,* and so many other underrated and underappreciated flicks, learned to take their first steps into a frighteningly welcoming world.

Of course, we won't forget the people who have kept horror in the cinematic mainstream for so long, the people who find a way to tell the same story over again and still make us want to watch several chapters of *Friday the 13th, Hellraiser, Paranormal Activity,* and others.

So many of us have seen these people hard at work and have been terrified of them. But now we'll ask a new question: How did *they* get ready to meet *us*? What did these friendly, normal folk do to transform themselves into killers or victims? How did they become agents of innocent good or pure evil? What did they do before the camera rolled to prepare on their own? How did they get ready to become a part of the film world's most (in)famous genre?

Meet those who have so terrified and fascinated us through the years. Those who battled evil from outside life, outside this world, outside reality. Those who have become such evil. Those who got to kill, got to torture, and even watched themselves and hoping they'd lose the battle, along with the audience.

Read on ... and fear...

Michelle Argyris: *Devil Seed*

If we really want to find the enemy that always comes back, we have to look beyond the Jasons, the Freddys, and everyone else who sticks around for remake after sequel. We have to look for the enemy that truly straddles the line between the uncanny and the marvelous.

It's the eternal down-dweller. The he, she, or it that lurks in the fiery pits below (say the religious folk) and keeps sneaking up to unleash its wrath through one individual at a time, in fact and fiction.

These battles are nothing new to the movies, and have kicked off more than one horror film career. Linda Blair's Oscar-nominated work in *The Exorcist* set the bar high, putting her square on the acting map. Three decades later, Ashley Bell shined through demonic darkness in her first two top roles in the *Last Exorcism* flicks.

Then in 2012, a longtime model became the devil's playground and enemy in her new jaunt before the cameras, stepping into the genre that had nearly pushed her into sleep deprivation as a kid.

"I was the little girl who would turn her dolls around at night, because I felt like they

Michelle Argyris became the latest reluctant possession of evil in *The Devil Seed*.

were staring at me," recalls Canada native Michelle Argyris. "I couldn't remotely leave my hands or feet dangling off the bed—I'd tightly wrap them up in my blankets. I was more afraid to see a ghost than have a burglar rob my parents' house."

Dark irony, then, that the supernatural helped her move from commercial performances to the cinema.

"The beauty of being an on-screen character is, you can be anybody: a knowledgeable doctor, a sneaky detective, a psychopath killer, or I guess in my case, a student struggling with demonic possession." In 2012's *Devil Seed*, Alex (Argyris) and a friend, on the way home from a night out in the adult beverage world, take a break from worrying about the first weeks of college to hang out with a local psychic. The lady knows a bit more than the stereotyped soothsayer, describing the passing of Alex's mom and illness of her grandmother. Then she looks toward the future, and clams up. It's a good sign that something bad's going to happen when your psychic is too afraid to speak.

"Although being the lead in a film seemed beyond exciting," recalls Argyris, "the idea of possession sat so uncomfortably with me that I initially turned the role down. But after sitting on it for three days and chatting with family and friends, I decided to face my childhood fear, and become a real on-screen character struggling with the devil himself." Struggling both physically and emotionally, as the psychic's prediction starts to come true. Alex see weird signs in her schoolbooks and on walls. Marks appear on her body.

"My reasoning was that any great actor should not be afraid to dive into many different types of roles," she says. "Acting is never comfortable and if an actor sits too comfortably in a role, then the scene may become dull. Especially for horror, we want to sit at the edge of our seat feeling the pain or discomfort the 'character' is truly feeling. Acting is a commitment to reveal the uttermost real character you can possibly portray."

Poring over the script dozens of times before and after cameras started rolling, Argyris kept looking for Alex inside the words. Just as Blair's Regan and Bell's Nell had learned the hard way, the devil tortures his way inside his vessel before barreling out in voice and action. She hallucinates, blacks out, and can't remember anything. Soon her possessor starts to creep out, dangling her above a bed (still the landmark scene for exorcism films) and dropping her voice into evil monotone in the third person.

"Having done gymnastics prior to landing this role also helped with preparing for it," says Argyris, nationally ranked in gymnastics and cheerleading in her youth. "We had scenes where I was harnessed from the walls, being dragged up the stairs, backwards bridge walking, and basically doing my own stunts.

"It is ironic that the easiest scenes to shoot, taking into consider[ation] my childhood fears, were those as a full-blown demon," says Argyris, who spent hours in a makeup chair to become the dark representative and aerobicized to stay tired between takes. "There's something about being someone, some*thing* else that sits more comfortably than being yourself.... Acting strips you: [You are] very vulnerable. It can be both invasive and exhilarating."

Emotions like that, Argyis hopes, will keep carrying her deeper into the acting world, frighteningly or otherwise. "In order to succeed in this business, actors have to face a lot of rejection," she says. "But what you can do is make a committed character choice when walking into the audition room and owning it.... You can't just wake up one day and expect to run a marathon; it takes steps to build up your strength and stamina, much like acting.

But I would like to emphasize that with passion, determination and persistence, anything is attainable. Dreams do become realities and hard work does pay off."

Argyis, Michelle. E-mail interview. June 14, 2013.

....

Blythe Auffarth: *The Girl Next Door*

Anne Frank, who saw and underwent some of the worst humanity ever offered in a life that never got to be fully lived, said in her diary that she still truly believed people were naturally good inside.

Sylvia Marie Likens might disagree with her.

Right around Independence Day of 1965, the young Indianapolis woman was sent to board with her neighbor after her parents took their concession stand out with the local traveling carnival. The kindly Ms. Wright, the mother of several kids, seemed like a fine caretaker to the parents.

But Wright wasn't really Ms. Wright. She was Gertrude Baniszewski, an unemployed, hard-drinking chain smoker who'd been through several abusive relationships and at least six miscarriages. But no one could have guessed what would happen next.

Sylvia quickly became a target for Baniszewski's other children, and visitors. Rumors were spread about her imagined promiscuity (one of Baniszewski's daughters had become pregnant as a teen), and the older woman believed them, physically disciplining her for offenses never committed.

Before long, the young woman's life became nightmarish. More and more local youths—

David Moran (Daniel Manche) tries to comfort Meg Loughlin (Blythe Auffarth) in *The Girl Next Door*, tragically based on a true story.

even some pre-teens—were turned against her, convinced by Baniszewski that Sylvia was no good. She was beaten. Burned by cigarettes. Tied up in the cellar, nude for days at a time. Letters and words branded into her skin. Forced to eat vomit and excrement. Raped.

By the time someone finally got up the nerve to let someone know what was going on, it was too late. Just before Halloween, the local cops got a call that the young woman had died.

Far, *far* too late, Baniszewski was revealed. To the shock and anger of many, she got life in prison, rather than the chair. She did about twenty years, was released in 1985, and died of cancer five years later.

As Blythe Auffarth arrived at the set of *The Girl Next Door,* her obligation went beyond following the director's "Action!" request. Of course it was about trying her hardest as a character (renamed Megan Loughin), but there was much more here.

The performance was about, in her own small, subtle, but very special way, standing up for someone who never got the chance to stand up for herself. Someone who almost no one had ever stood up for, until it was too late. And to do what she could to ensure that this wouldn't happen to someone else—watching the film might give others in such a situation the guts to stand up for themselves and let someone know. Sylvia would never know she'd done it, but Auffarth still could help her make a difference.

"I was drawn to the writing," she explains. "The screenplay was incredibly on point—and Meg's character arc. I knew a lot would be demanded of the actress who took on the role. It was daunting and intimidating."

Not surprisingly, the story has inspired other adaptations, both true and creative (*An American Crime* first cinematized the story in 2007, with Ellen Page in the lead). Told from the perspective of a young man who witnessed the abuse but never spoke up, Jack Ketchum's novel *The Girl Next Door* put a creative spin on the piece. Light years away from her role as Molly Ringwald's sister in *Sixteen Candles,* Blanche Baker became Baniszewski in Ruth Chandler, who begins a mindless barrage of torture against Meg.

"After researching the true story of Sylvia Marie Likens, I almost felt an obligation to honor her and tell her story," says Auffarth, who, ironically, played Anne Frank in a small theater production. "I'm always looking for challenges and brick walls. I prepared right up to the first day of filming. I spent days poring over Sylvia Marie Likens' case files and accounts from her trial. I read up on her background, the crime scene, and the horrible abuse she endured. I looked through countless photos of her."

Realistic horror might be the scariest of all—not just because of what could happen but, as in the case Auffarth researched (and too many like it), what already has. "The stuff horror films are made of is happening around us every day," she says. "Just turn on the news. Just open the paper. Look at the JonBenet Ramseys of the world. It's truly frightening. And that's what originally attracted me to *The Girl Next Door.* There was a real Meg in 1965. She experienced those things in the book, only a hundred times worse ... I did this film because I think it could make an important statement: show the 'horrors' that humans are capable of committing. Me? I guess I'm just interested in the horror of life.

"As part of my staple preparation, I always create a character spine for the character I'm playing—just simple 'Who am I?' stuff. Meg's character wouldn't stay on the page. She was amazingly real for me."

The film pushed the envelope farther than many have ever tried, even those in the horror genre. Young performers plied their trade torturing an adult actress, who often was forced to appear not only ("only") tortured, but unclothed as well. One of them had to act out a committal of arguably the world's worst crime.

"The rape was hard," she says of the scene. (She and the actor were the only performers in the room during filming.) "The other actor was only a boy. Though I looked his age in the film, I was many years his senior. I found myself wanting to shelter him, to keep him from exploring the psyche needed for such a ghastly act."

Unfortunately, it was a journey which Auffarth had to take herself throughout filming. Meg's prison wasn't the only cellar in which she'd be trapped.

"Playing Meg was a challenge, in that I was asked to visit the 'basement' of my being every day, deep, dark and dripping with vulnerability. Having to imagine and experience some of the most ghastly crimes you could commit against an individual was a daunting undertaking."

In the midst of filming one scene, Auffarth stepped even farther into Sylvia's world. The young woman had been kept seemingly forever in the dark, storyline-wise. After being cosmetically transformed that morning, Auffarth left Sylvia's mask on until stepping all the way into character. "[That was] so that my initial reaction to the light would be as real and truthful as possible," she explains. "It was also an attempt to remove myself from the bustle of set and create a more controlled, focused environment where I could prepare. The circumstances surrounding the scene and the scenes leading up to that moment were so intense, I couldn't just jump into [them]."

"Actress Blythe Auffarth Featuring The Girl Next Door." *Killer Reviews*. 2009. Retrieved Oct. 18, 2011, from http://www.killerreviews.com/dispinterview.php?intid=1572.
Auffarth, Blythe. E-mail interview. Oct. 18, 2011.
Noe, Denise. "The Torturing Death of Sylvia Marie Likens." *TruTV*. 2012. Retrieved Oct. 19, 2011, from http://www.trutv.com/library/crime/notorious_murders/young/likens/1.html.

••••••••••••••••••••••••••••

Belinda Balaski

No matter where she goes or what she does on the screen, someone's always chasing Belinda Balaski.

Actually, it's usually some*thing*.

Mutant rats and other animals in *The Food of the Gods*. Ravenous carnivorous fish in *Piranha*. Weird little green monsters in the *Gremlins* films. Werewolves in *The Howling* and *The Werewolf at Woodstock*.

Balaski's usually the girlfriend or best friend of the main characters in horror and sci-fi films, and that's never been a safe place to be in the movies: Those are the people who usually get the brunt of the creatures' cruelty, introducing the villains to the audience before the hero(ine) has a chance to create a new extinct species.

There's more to her acting life than the realms of terror; her career gained some serious firepower before horror even touched it: Her performance as a scared, diabetic teenager who runs to the streets from her stepfather in the 1974 afterschool special *The Runaways* nabbed the show an Emmy. And even before that, she took home several Best Supporting Actress awards for theater work.

Her horror debut in *Gods* turned a bit scary in itself, as the shoot on a Canadian island was plagued by days of snow, making the shooting of a foggy summer break beyond difficult, and forcing the cast to actually use blowtorches to melt the snow.

But she recovered, and stole more than her share of scenes in *Piranha,* even adding some scene-writing of her own to the film, which ironically would sow the seeds for Balaski's future career.

Balaski plays Betsy, the caring counselor helping children learn the basics of safe swimming at a summer camp. But downstream, a group of mutated and extremely hungry fish have just been released from a military base, and they're literally out for blood. Under attack in the midst of a lesson, Betsy helps some of the kids and her fellow counselors onto a raft as the fish start their meal.

"I got to take scuba-diving lessons," Balaski says. "There was a lot of underwater stuff that I had to do. I was a really good swimmer, but they have to take precautions." Reaching out for help, the desperate young woman is sucked down into the black depths, the definitive first victim in such movies.

"They tied the rubber piranhas to me so when I fought them underwater, they bounce back," she says. "Then it looks like I'm being dragged underwater, but I'm really being dragged from one end of the pool to the other. There were about ten guys on one end of the pool pulling me through the water, with a rope tied around me."

As brief as her appearance was, however, it helped form one of the biggest links in the network that would give her a steady film career over the next few years. When they were putting together *The Howling* in 1981, Joe Dante, who'd worked with Balaski in both *Piranha* and the action-comedy *Cannonball,* and writer John Sayles decided to add to the werewolf flick the new character of Terry Fisher, one based on the Betsy she'd played in *Piranha.* Terry was a colleague of TV newswoman Karen (Dee Wallace). With Karen confined to a rustic mental institution after encountering a serial killer, Terry goes on the hunt for Eddie Quist, the man who escaped from a morgue and is now in lycanthrope form.

But something's hunting her as well. As Terry arrives at the camp, she's suddenly attacked by a wolf-human creature. She fights it off with an axe and keeps searching, but just as she discovers the secrets behind everything (i.e., why just about all the residents are morphing into werewolves), another pursuer corners her and comes out on top.

Here's where continuity become a bit of an issue for the close-eyed. Some may notice that Terry's hair suddenly shortens and lengthens during her fatal battle; it grew in the two months between shooting the singles and close-up shots with the creature.

"We never saw werewolves when we shot all of our close-ups," she says. "We came back three months later and did the other scenes." Balaski had no idea what the werewolf looked like or what it could do. "As an actor, I had to put him there, in my mind. If you don't believe what you're doing, how can anyone else? It's what I say to the kids when I'm teaching." (More on this in a bit.)

She and Dante worked together on several more projects through the '80s and '90s, including both *Gremlins* films, *Small Soldiers,* and eleven television shows.

"Once you begin to work and people like you," Balaski says, "you can go from job to job, which makes it difficult for other people to cut in front of you. When you're auditioning, you may not get the part you're auditioning for, but if they like you, your name will come up again. 'Hey, I remember that girl that came in for an audition….'"

If someone were to create a time machine, actors and actresses would probably be amongst the top customers; time and again throughout the research for this book, I've run across performers who turned down certain roles and had to be dragged kicking and screaming into others, only to have that film, and performance, begin their ascent to elitehood.

Just after *The Food of the Gods,* Balaski was called in to audition with two young directors who had just finished film school and were looking for young ingénues to help them make their marks on Hollywood (each was trying to cast his own film). Armed with her book of pictures, Balaski arrived and the three started to chat.

Then one of the fellows, George, turned to the other. "She winked at me!" he said to his partner. "I said that I didn't," Balaski recalls. "He said, 'Yes, you did! Did you see her wink at me?' I said, 'No, I didn't' again, and eventually said, 'You guys are into playing, and I'm into working.' I picked up my briefcase and walked out."

George's last name was Lucas. The other fellow's name was Brian DePalma, and the films that came from that interview were *Star Wars* and *Carrie.*

"I'd like to know if they said that to Carrie Fisher!" Balaski laughs. "He was probably trying to get my reaction. I certainly acted like an indignant princess, huffing and puffing and storming out."

During her college years, as acting research for various characters, Balaski and a girlfriend made a habit of hanging out at airports. They'd notice people coming off a plane and go into private investigator mode, following them and personifying them.

"I'd take on one person's walk, and [the girlfriend would] take on another," Balaski says. "We'd create these people. When I got to Hollywood, I had multiple characters in my 'back pocket,' and I was using them in theater, in auditions, in workshops, everywhere. You need a place to create all the characters you end up with. Acting is all about making choices and observing other people."

Ever since starting her own acting school in the early 2000s, Balaski has been observing and facilitating a slightly younger group: BB's Kids has helped hundreds of youngsters obtain roles in commercials, films, theater, and TV. Miranda Cosgrove of the Nickelodeon show *iCarly* and on the big screen in *School of Rock* and *Despicable Me* has passed through her school, as have Vanessa Chester (Jeff Goldblum's gymnast daughter in *Jurassic Park: Lost World*) and others who have hit both size screens and Broadway stages.

"It's amazing what these kids can do," Balaski says. "They never cease to surprise me. I believe that if you believe what you're doing, everyone else will. You must put yourself in the situation, because when you're on a set, it's do or die."

Balaski, Belinda. Phone interview. June 11, 2010.

•••••••••••••••••••••••••••••

Tim Balme: *Dead Alive*

The first time he reads a script, he looks for what it *doesn't* have.

Take away the death, take away the fear, take away the buckets of blood, the guts, the destruction, and what's still there? If it's enough, Tim Balme is in.

"A good horror film is a script that reads well without the horror bits," Balme explains.

Battling the undead can call for the most unorthodox of measures, as lawnmower-wielding Lionel Cosgrove (Tim Balme) found out in *Dead Alive*.

"That is, it must work as a story with relatable characters who are interesting and/or funny, independent of being characters in a horror. The horror is the icing on the cake that makes the film have a destination on the DVD shelf. The gore or thrill factor is what sets it apart from being a straight drama."

One of the first performances on his acting résumé was as a man torn between two women: one, his dear but domineering mother, who he was convinced would always need him. The other, a gorgeous find, with the potential key to open the door to his heart to a land of love that hadn't really been explored. Having an in-your-face mom can do that to a guy.

How many storylines have started this way? Some take the romantic comedy route: The mother and girlfriend battle throughout, only to have their final confrontation—usually in a very public place—end with a hugging war, with the mother tearfully letting go as the boy and his babe walk off into the sunset, or to the altar. Others have taken a much darker route. Generations of audiences have been traumatized and filmmakers inspired by the story of a young man and the drill sergeant mom who made her way so deeply into his mind that she controlled his destruction of at least one lovely young lass and others who attempted to help them both (the family name was Bates, which should the only hint anyone needs here).

Balme's film, however, would end up going another way. With a ninja-kicking priest and zombies galore, one of his first film works would set unofficial records in gore and hilarious massacring.

Balme wanted to be an actor right from his teenage years. "I was dabbling at school and I had a lot of inspirational people around me during that time," he recalls, "so [acting] was an interest that quickly became a 'habit.' The sci-fi–horror thing was never on my radar and to be fair the horror genre wasn't really one that was part of the New Zealand cinema landscape in any great part." But then a director showed up with his newest play for the screen.

It had death, live amputation, some heads torn off, a jugular vein entered here and there—par for the course for the sort. Looking for the male lead, Balme tried to see this director.

"The key thing about that part is grabbing hold of the truth that it's about a young man who is socially repressed due to an overbearing mother," he says. "The zombie killer is simply a by-product of that." He'd never even seen a horror film, but this wasn't just about the horror.

"I'd read a fair few screenplays at that early stage," Balme says, "and although I'd never read a splatter-horror one, it didn't matter. The screenplay still read like a classic."

With the help of the director, Balme got a crash course in craziness, ready to become Lionel Cosgrove in *Brain Dead*; the film was renamed *Dead Alive* when it played in America. He sat through *Night of the Living Dead*, *Dawn of the Dead*, and *Evil Dead 2*, all landmarks in the art of zombifying. Balme got ready to blend blood, fear, and the occasional zinging one-liner into a cocktail of Lionel. But he'd need to go much farther than any of the viewed predecessors.

With Lionel's mom turned into a zombie early on, the devoted young man can't bear to say goodbye all the way, instead locking her in the cellar. Repeated escapes result in the deaths of one innocent neighbor after another (including the black-belted father) and the warp-speed pregnancy and childbirth of a kid that makes Rosemary's baby look cute. Lionel manages to keep the news of these events from spreading, with an extra special reason to do so in the form of a new girlfriend. With the aid of a soporific (he thinks), the zombies are buried, and it's time to throw a party.

But that wasn't euthanasia he gave them—it was a stimulant. The dead are back alive, and they bring some friends. Soon Lionel, his girlfriend, and the party guests are in the midst of a bloody battle royal with a mob of zombies, or at least parts of them (undead severed heads and limbs can cause just as much damage as those still attached). While his monstrous mother supervises the invasion from the roof, Lionel and his guests battle the party crashers. One particularly hilarious scene has him slipping in blood while trying to run away from them.

It appears that the undead will prevail until Lionel pulls out an uncommon but incredibly effective weapon: the family lawnmower. It would actually be the toughest part of the storyline for both the actor and character. In take after take, Balme slashed his way through the zombies, with literally hundreds of gallons of fake blood pouring all over him. His determination gave way to fatigue. His shouts of aggression turned to those of exhaustion.

Finally, when he couldn't have been more soaked in blood than if he'd swam in it, when a new standard had been set for blood and guts around the globe, he heard the director's merciful shout of cut.

"He had his final moment," Balme says. "Interestingly, though, all the special effects were done on the floor—as in, there was no CGI then. But the miniatures and forced perspective were an eye-opener." As the film won a place in the hearts and DVD collections of devoted horror fans around the globe, Balme knew that he'd done something special. The

Dead director moved across the water and terrified Old Glory with the underrated *Frighteners*, then shifted to a different genre, three times over: *The Lord of the Rings* trilogy.

Yes—it was Peter Jackson.

"It's easy to write sequences of horror-splatter and string them together as an excuse for a story but it will never stand up as film of note," Balme remarks. "The tip (for actors) is (to) make sure the script speaks to you on more than one level. If it doesn't, chances are it will be very lonely on the shelf at the DVD store."

Balme, Tim. E-mail interview. Oct. 8, 2012.

•••••••••••••••••••••••••••••

Ashley Bank: *The Monster Squad*

When you're still at a golden single-digit age, it's sometimes tough to tell the difference between fantasy and reality. How many parents have had to reassure their little ones that the monster on TV wasn't coming to have them for a midnight snack, or that something wasn't trespassing in the closet or under the bed? Confession time: A certain writer spent six years sleeping under the covers after watching ghosts fly out of the tomb and melt everyone in *Raiders of the Lost Ark!*

Of course, adults are hardly immune to this sort of thing; surely at least a few of us hesitated before going for a swim every time a new *Jaws* flick came around.

In one of her first major roles, Ashley Bank wasn't sure where the real world ended and the reel world began. Being surrounded by a wolfman, the black lagoon's featured resident, the film world's most famous fanged one, and a doctor's monstrous creation probably didn't help matters much.

Phoebe (Ashley Bank) calls *The Monster Squad* to action.

"At three or four, you don't really understand that the people you see on television are real people, but not the people that you see them as," Bank recalls. "I really thought that I would have to get shrunk in order to fit into everyone's television and go to everyone's house."

Two lucky breaks rolled her way in the mid–80s. The first was to spend a few weeks hanging around mysterious critters (human and otherwise) in *The Monster Squad*. The second was *Fatal Attraction,* scary in many different ways. She would have been the proud owner of that legendary ill-fated rabbit.

"*Monster* made me an offer first," Bank says. "Had *Fatal Attraction* shot in Los Angeles, I probably would have done both, but it was in New York, so I had to do *The Monster Squad*. My parents wanted me to have more fun. It was a bigger part, and it would be a kids' movie that I could actually see. There was no way they were ever going to let me watch *Fatal Attraction*. It was more fun for me to do something I could understand and be a part of. I never regretted it at all." (Ellen Latzen got the *Fatal* call.)

In *The Monster Squad*, Bank was Phoebe, whose older brother Sean leads a group of social outcasts known as the Monster Club, dedicated to kicking hell out of any creatures that dare step into town. In typical older sibling fashion, Sean can't stop labeling his sister "jerkoid," "Phoebe the Feeb," and other terms of endearment.

"My mom had the idea that when they say mean things to me, I should just stick my bottom lip out and look up and them and pout," Bank says. "I think that that's what got me the part, looking so cute and pitiful. How could they *not* give me the part?

"A lot of times as an adult actress, you get into your character, and you ask, 'Okay, why are they screwed up? What's wrong with them? What did they go through? What have they gotten used to in their lives?' But at five, you're already the character. You know what situation you're going to be in. You do a little thinking about it, but you always finish on set. It's about your interaction with the director and the other characters. That's the part that really stays with you."

In the movie, Sean's mom, a garage sale connoisseur, finds a diary of legendary vampire-whacker Dr. Van Helsing, and a local concentration camp survivor translates it to find out that every 100 years, evil comes to town—and its next arrival is scheduled for the following night.

Soon, a wolfman shows up at the police station. A mummy walks out of the museum. Dracula (Duncan Regehr, in a role Liam Neeson almost snared) is around, and he's thirsty.

"The role took me back to my childhood, watching Bela Lugosi," Regehr says. "That stuff was a lot of fun to watch. The big challenge for myself was to make it different somehow. It's been done so many times, and to take out some of the melodrama, but to use some of it too, to make the character have a sense of humor about what he was doing, to retain a kind of direct approach to exactly what he wanted, as a sociopath.

"Most villains know what they want. The hero doesn't know what he wants, the hero (only) knows that he wants to stop the villain. The villain, in this case Dracula, knows what he wants, and nothing was ever going to stop him."

"It's every kid's dream to be able to play make-believe," Bank recalls. "It was just about getting the chance to be with a bunch of kids and having a great time. You do it because you enjoy it, and how much fun is it to run around and scream and be scared? But the best part about being on set was that we only had three hours of school."

Learning her lines, however, was even tougher than multiplication tables. "I didn't read yet, so I had to memorize the lines," she says. "I'd memorize my lines before work, with my mom, my acting coach. To this day, sometimes I wish I could have her on set and at auditions; she gets me going, creatively and in a lot of other ways. She'd read the material with me, and we'd work on how to say it. Sometimes she'd say it, and I would try to copy her." This is a practice that Phoebe herself would use at a critical moment.

One line in particular stood out for everyone. Running into the boys in a park, Phoebe introduces them to her new friend—who just happens to be Frankenstein's Monster (Tom Noonan, playing a different kind of horror than his role as a serial killer in *Manhunter* the year before). The boys can't get away fast enough. But Phoebe, faring much better than Maria, the Monster's flower-throwing companion from the 1931 film version, just takes his hand.

"Come on, guys," she says nonchalantly. "Don't be chicken shit!"

"I remember being afraid to curse," Bank says, "because I was afraid I'd get in trouble."

Just before midnight on the fateful day, the Club and its enemies meet in the center of town. There's an amulet there holds evil in check, and a magic spell, read by a virgin from Van Helsing's writing, will send those creatures right back where they came from.

Phoebe's got the amulet. Dracula wants it. Here's where those old lines got crossed again.

"I was terrified of [Regehr]," Bank says of the new vampire. "I saw him once, and I wouldn't go near him. My mom told him not to put in his contacts or fangs. As adults, we try so hard to get into character, and to try and go through and really get into what the character is feeling, but at five, you don't have the same sense of reality that you do as an adult. It all seems very real."

That's why, when Dracula grabs Phoebe and yanks her into the air, Bank wasn't acting: The first time the young girl screams, it's the sound of real terror. "I was so scared that it went out a little scream, and then went silent," she says. "We did two takes, and they asked me to scream a little longer on the next one. [Regehr] felt so bad about it. It didn't do any permanent damage; it's how movies are made."

The Monster comes to her rescue, but there's another problem: The sister of one of the boys reads the spell, but the cyclone to another world doesn't appear. Turns out, she wasn't all pure. But another person was far away from that way of thinking.

Just as her mom had shown her before the show, Bank now did the same act in character. Helped along by the old translator from before (longtime character actor Leonardo Cimino), Phoebe had to say the spell. As brawls erupt around her between the Club and the Monsters, she's speaking German before she could read English.

Recalling the cyclone scene, Bank says, "Everyone was being blown away. There were these huge six-by-six fans, five or six of them. I was on a bench with a string tied on it to pull away, to look like it was falling over. The first time we shot it, they pulled the string too hard, and I felt like I was being blown away. I weighed about forty pounds, and I was clutching the grass."

If *The Monster Squad* had a flaw, it was that it didn't appeal to any particular audience. *The Goonies* (1985) had sent a group of kids on a cartoonish wild goose chase that everyone could enjoy; *Stand By Me* (1986) showed exactly how to make a grownup-aimed film that happened to be about kids; but *The Monster Squad* got stuck in the middle between the two, and never got where it wanted to go at the box-office. It had enough juvenile humor for a young audience, but there was too much that parents didn't want their kids to see. The main storyline is a couple on the edge of an angry divorce; kids play around with huge guns; and Dracula coldly blows up the club treehouse and some cop cars and then calls a kindergartener a bitch.

"They gave it a bit of reality that a lot of kids' movies don't really have," Bank says. "[The Club] weren't caricatures of kids. They were real kids that felt like they didn't belong. Especially, unfortunately, kids that are into monsters and comic books when they're growing up can also feel like they don't fit in. It was like having friends, a group of friends that you felt connected to when you didn't feel connected to other people."

After some steady work in television for the next decade, Bank headed to college, and came out with a new career in the same business. She went into producing and casting—but the acting bug lives on.

"There are always tons of interesting people on set, and everyone's doing different things, and you've never seen anything like it," Bank says. "I fell in love with acting. Once you've bitten, even if you're being held by a vampire, you never go back."

Bank, Ashley. Phone interview. April 24, 2010.
Dekker, Fred. *The Monster Squad* [DVD]. Santa Monica, CA: HBO, 1987.

....

Michael Berryman: *The Hills Have Eyes*

"I believe through art, society can be improved upon," says Michael Berryman. "We can take issues and concepts and deal with them in a story, song, play, film, or a book and allow people to negotiate through their conscience, I'd say their moral register."

One day as a young man, making deliveries for his gift shop, Berryman ran into a fellow named George Pal, who'd been producing features for 25 years. Soon, Berryman was playing a role in Pal's *Doc Savage: The Man of Bronze*.

Pal introduced Berryman to actor Michael Douglas. Douglas' dad Kirk had owned the screen rights to Ken Kesey's novel *One Flew Over the Cuckoo's Nest* for quite some time, and played the story's lead on Broadway for over two months. Now Michael wanted to bring the moving story about overcoming the stigmas of mental illness to the screen.

For years, America had been unwilling and/or unable to see the difference between the mentally handicapped and the evil of society, between those who wouldn't function in everyday life by choice, and those who simply couldn't. Their addled minds manipulated by others to enter the life of a recluse, the afflicted, often by their own volition, spent their lives in ominous, confusing, even frightening institutions, pumped full of worthless medications and zapped into catatonia by electroshock therapy.

On gift delivery trips, Berryman had been to several such places. He'd seen sanitarium residents strolling around outside, the welcoming warmth of sunlight a heavenly gift from their dark (emotionally if not physically) normal existence inside. At Oregon State Mental Hospital, he and the rest of the cast got a closer look at the inadvertent mental outcasts of society, ranked next to or even lower than criminals by too many for too long.

Berryman looked perfect for the role of those that society just loved to look down

Michael Berryman's ominous Pluto still terrifies today, decades after *The Hills Have Eyes* hit the big screen.

upon—but in this case, that might not have been a full-blown positive. He'd been born too early, before his hair, teeth, and sweat glands had reached functioning level. His skull and facial features weren't fully developed. Doctors had used grafted bones from his hips to finish out his skull, but Berryman would never develop the ability to sweat, leaving him in lifelong danger of heatstroke and keeping him home as America fought in Vietnam. Cast in *Cuckoo's Nest*, he'd become Ellis, a quiet, frightened patient who receives an out-of-nowhere source of inspiration.

In an active ward, surrounded by guards on duty, the *Cuckoo's Nest* cast spent months around the residents. The son of a neurologist (his dad had helped in his cranial operation), Berryman had spent enough time around members of the medical field that this wasn't an entirely new world.

"The days I had off, I was still on the set watching so I could learn my craft," he says. "I wanted to learn as much as I could about the lighting and the blocking, how you do coverage." He and the rest of the performers watched the residents get more and more accustomed to the actors and crew members.

"We would ask them specific questions," he says. "One gentleman was committed, in his early 20s, for burning a church. We looked at his artwork, and it was very disturbing—it was pictures of people on fire. To him, it was a step into his particular world. But some of the patients weren't violent, just really lost souls. We really felt some sympathy for the patients.

"It was a very strange place with these individuals whose lives weren't like yours and mine. But it gave us a nice insight into what really goes on." Some of the patients would make their way into the film, milling in the background as Jack Nicholson's legendary Randall McMurphy riled them into inspiration.

The sad, depressing world that Berryman had seen so many mental patients live in was the same one that enveloped Ellis, Chief Bromden, Billy Bibbit, and so many others. Away from the cameras, it was the same world that patients had lived in for so long. But *One Flew Over the Cuckoo's Nest* wouldn't just end up named one of the ten greatest films of all time (many have it right at the top); it would get credit for revolutionizing and lightening the everyday world and treatment in mental facilities across the nation.

As the *Cuckoo's Nest* crew drowned in accolades, another director found his eyes snared by a new story, one that had morbidly fascinated millions for centuries. It was the story of the Beane family of Scotland. Outcast by society into the caves of Galway, a man named Sawney and his wife brought up a family that never knew any world, any normalcy but their own. Surviving by robbing and cannibalism, existing through incestuous reproduction, pleasuring themselves via torture and murder, the family, often hunting as a pack of mothers and daughters who were sisters, of men who'd fathered their brothers, sons, and grandsons, made short work and dinner of anyone unlucky enough to wander into their personal Utopia. Hunters, travelers, even subjects of the reigning King James I disappeared into the Beane land. Some estimates range as high as a thousand falling victim to the clan over a quarter century.

But was it really like that at all? How much of this was real, and how much of it was dramatically exaggerated or improvised? Is it all folklore, edged only by the Loch Ness resident as Scotland's most famous saga?

Wes Craven wasn't worried about answering those questions. He had more than he'd need for his next frightening feature. It wasn't entirely different from his recent trip to the *Last House on the Left,* as these villains had at least *some* justification. They were much farther from everyday society than the *Last House* crew, but there was now something of a monster-ish tone to them and their violence. Despite being based on fact—again, *maybe!*—there was enough of a break from reality to appeal to full-blown horror film fans.

"My agent called me, and told me about Wes Craven and [producer] Peter Locke," Berryman says. "He said that they were making a movie in the desert—and good luck!" After hiding a kind heart behind his disfigurement in *Cuckoo's Nest*, he was now going to be an American Beane man, part of a group more than content to live in their own little world in the middle of nowhere—except when it was time to venture out for dinner.

As jammed and overpopulated as America can seem at times, especially in the big cities, there's quite a bit of space to run wild and free, to live a secluded lifestyle. The deserts of the central and eastern states of this nation would provide such a place. Craven took his creations away from the Beanes' cave hangout and stuck them into the midst of sweltering sand.

The movie title was at first the ghoulish *Blood Relations*. Eventually it was changed to *The Hills Have Eyes.*

"I actually lived in Big Bear, a town just south of where we filmed [Victorville, California]," says Berryman. "I used to spend a lot of time in desert, mostly in the winter and fall. We would go desert camping twenty miles into the desert. We went into an area where practice bombs had dropped during World War II. Spending time out there is very quiet. You can just get into the mindset that if you break down out here, you're in some jeopardy."

In the movie, the vacationing Carters are stranded in the desert when their car breaks down.

But that's the least of their problems; early on, an old man at a gas station spoke of a family he was ashamed of being related to, one that patrols the barren lands ahead, one that kills and feasts upon all those unlucky enough to have their cars break down.

Not out of malice, or greed. Just of survival. It's normal for them to eat others, and procreate from within. It's just the way they've always been. It's the life they know. Now the Carters are the hunted.

Berryman was Pluto, one of the deformed cannibal brothers. They kill one of the Carter dogs early, so we *know* that these people are evil!

While Craven doesn't make a habit of doing walk-bys in his films, Locke stepped in to become Mercury, Pluto's slow-witted brother. A second dog avenges his four-footed friend's death, shoving Mercury off a cliff.

"The makeup got me into character," recalls Locke. "It made me feel like a feral person. I decided to play the undereducated, the genetically inferior. He wasn't the brightest-sounding person. It was fun getting into the makeup and the costume. It wasn't really a speaking part. I ran across a field and got pushed off a mountain by a dog!"

To play the young cannibal Ruby, Janus Blythe tossed hygiene out the window, dirtying herself up and smearing black matter all over her teeth, which she'd put to use when Ruby chows on the murdered canine.

Getting in the shape that enabled Ruby and her family to chase down their unwilling prey, she recalls, "We ran footraces in the parking lot. We all lined up. I stood there, then bypassed everybody. Temperatures went from sweltering to freezing and back again, through twelve- to fourteen-hour days."

Contrary to looks and popular Internet belief, temperatures during filming weren't *that* changeable. Stories of Berryman's condition causing him torture from the heat and cold throughout filming have found their way into popular lore, but he says climate wasn't much of a problem. "We were not in the middle of summer, so it was just vaguely hot during the day," he says. "We had to make sure that if I got confused or started to overheat, first aid was near. The first aid people [aware of Berryman's condition] would occasionally just speak to me to make sure I had mental clarity. I wasn't slipping into heat exhaustion. They kept cold liquid and a fan near me."

There wasn't much time between Berryman getting the role and playing it. As Pluto, he beats up young Brenda Carter for his brother Mars to rape her, then steals her baby niece, intending to turn the infant into a family snack, perhaps between himself and Papa Jupiter.

"I was really into what Pluto would do on a day-to-day basis," Berryman recalls. "He had a lot of time. As a cannibal out in the desert with not a lot to eat, in your down time, you'd make sure your equipment was prepared. You could beat Pluto in a fight, but he'd stab you. I wanted him to be efficient and not prone to making emotional mistakes, especially when it came to what the family did. Everybody had to do their part, and Pluto was certainly good at it."

Craven asked him to do a scene where Pluto frightens a Carter by drawing his blade across a rock. Berryman saw it as out of character. "I argued that Pluto wouldn't do that, because it would dull the knife. Pluto's knife would be razor sharp at all times."

During filming, lines of communication weren't exactly rock solid either, he continues. "When we were working, those of us playing the cannibals didn't associate very much with the other actors," he says. "We roughed them up a little bit, and it turned to our advantage. During lunch, our cannibals would hang in a separate group than them."

"I was just beginning and it was a great break!" says Dee Wallace, who played Lynne, the Carters' eldest daughter. "I prepared for it the way I do all my roles: read it, let my subconscious work on it, and then be in the moment and allow the character to be born. It's kind of like I channel it. All of it is pretty tough to watch, because it was tough to shoot: hard conditions, one trailer, long drive, and hysterical scenes."

After Lynne and her parents are slaughtered, Brenda, her brother Bobby (Robert Houston), and Lynne's husband Doug—and their last dog—are the only ones left, aside from the baby girl, who probably wouldn't be much help in a knife fight. If they're going to get away, they're going to have to do things that seemed impossible just days ago. But Brenda's been physically and sexually assaulted, and Bobby's pissed too; the justification is there in abundance.

New to the film world (she'd done quite a bit of TV and theater work), Suze Lanier-Bramlett tried to channel the spirit of the legendary Vincent Price and others who had intrigued her so much back in her days as "just" a fan.

"If you're going to do horror," says she who was Brenda, "I think it should have some class to it, not a film filled with monsters and blood. Have a story and hopefully allow your character to be more than one-dimensional. Brenda … was bratty, funny, and curious at the beginning; then after the rape and the death of her mom and sister, she becomes vulnerable and defeated. Then she realizes nobody's going to save her but herself. She rises above the situation and becomes strong and comes up with a plan to save herself and Bobby. She survives and sort of grows up at the end. As an actor, you have to commit to all of those colors. It's what makes the work fun."

With Pluto incapacitated by the same dog that killed his brother, and Lynne's husband off retrieving his daughter (Mars is also taken out), Brenda and Bobby blow up their trailer to take out Jupiter. (Done in one take, it was one of the last scenes filmed.) But years of living in the desert have toughened him up, and they're forced to beat him all the way out.

"This was one of the last scenes we filmed," remembers Lanier-Bramlett, who calls it one of her favorites to film. "When Bobby and I finally finish off the worst and most evil member of the 'desert family,' the joy and exuberance was very real and truly heartfelt. Robert and I felt very connected during the shooting, and being close friends personally, made us in real life care about each other on film. I think that really came across in that scene."

Pluto was down but not dead, and with his own family to avenge, he came roaring back in the flick's sequel seven years later. With the help of his uncle, Pluto stalks after Ruby and her friends before that mangy dog knocks him clear off a cliff.

"The fact that [the sequel] was greenlit and ready to rock and roll," Berryman says, "I said, 'Yeah, let's do it!' I liked the wardrobe even better for Part Two, with different lighting and cameras."

Many credit Craven with reigniting interest in American horror cinema with the *Scream* films, so few were surprised when Hollywood decided to venture back up the *Hills* in 2006 with Alex Aja in the director's chair and Craven and Locke producing.

"If you live long enough, there's a new audience for the films," Locke says. "When we did the remake, an entirely new audience was available for it. The terror genre is a strong genre, and it seems to come in waves. The waves, like any other hit, Hollywood likes to follow. If you're in a place where someone has pitched out a successful terror movie, you can bet that other terror movies in the works that nobody has greenlit will go forward because of the success of something that has come out."

The role of Pluto now went Michael Bailey Smith. Smith, who'd showed up briefly in *A Nightmare on Elm Street: Dream Master* and *Men in Black II* knew what to do … and what not to, like watch Berryman's work.

"I didn't want to 'try' to do an imitation of what Michael Berryman did," Smith says. "That would have been impossible. Second, Alex, the director, and I wanted to bring a different approach. The first film has some camp to it. The remake has no camp. It's in your face, raw and brutal."

That's the mindset in which Smith places himself when he needs to *become* such characters.

"When I have to be an intense maniac, I have to put myself in that space," he says. "I'm normally a quiet, laid-back kind of a guy, but when I need to kick some butt, then I get pretty crazy. I go off on my own, stomp my feet, and say a lot of bad words. I get my whole body and mind going. It's pretty insane."

Pluto helped send things exactly there early on, taking out a bunch of trespassing scientists. Later on, he's the one beaten to death by the daughter's husband. "You know the saying, 'It's not a party unless someone's crying'?" Smith quips, probably rhetorically. "Well, for filming, I say, 'It's not filmmaking until someone's bleeding.' I seem to do a lot of bleeding in my films. Not that fake blood. The real thing. A gash to my head, a broken nose, cracked ribs, busted-up hands. Ninety percent of the time, no one knows about it. I keep the bleeding to myself. I'm quite a bleeder."

Pluto's brother Mars was switched to Lizard, and Robert Joy slipped away from what he learned from zombies in *Land of the Dead* and outer space critters in *Aliens vs. Predator* to be a not-quite-human earthling, a mutant who carries a tail as he and Pluto visit dirty deeds upon the inadvertently invading Carter family. (So scary as Buffalo Bill in *The Silence of the Lambs,* Ted Levine found himself on the run from the cannibals as the Carter patriarch.)

With a cleft palette full of broken teeth jammed into his mouth, Joy could hardly articulate, not that spoken communication was all that normal for Lizard and his family. "I had a very subtle bump on my jaw, to imply that I had a congenitally misplaced jawbone," he says. "Other than that, Lizard is all sun damage and skin cancer."

Though his character wasn't a dad in the film—or maybe he was actually Ruby's dad, one couldn't be sure of anything with these people—Joy also glanced toward his own parenting experiences to find Lizard's personality. "I found that there was an energy in the character that reminded me of that game we all play with our children, called Monster, when you just chase your children around," says Joy, who coincidentally has a daughter in real life named Ruby. "'I'm gonna get you!' You take them prisoner and their friends have to tag them to get them free. In a funny way, it was the dark side of that energy that I kept.

"There's a thing when we're children that we tap into, where our imagination runs free, when we imagine that we're anything, like animals," he continues. "Kids are always imagining they're wolves or whatever, and it was that kind of imagining that was called for Lizard. Lizard called himself a lizard, not because of the personality, just because of that tail he carries around, using it as a weapon. I didn't use the lizard animal as a guide so much as I tapped into what it must be like to be hungry all the time, rather than being a predator or something. You add the streak of cruelty that he enjoys his prey and however he could dominate. When you're in a horror movie, you employ those kinds of impulses."

Laura Ortiz made the new Ruby lovely in a macabre sort of way. She was just getting started in the acting world, and got into Ruby mode by checking out the first film and a bunch of interviews with those she'd be working with.

"I would never say no to a Wes Craven project," Ortiz says of getting ready. "The character breakdown said that they wanted a really cute, deformed, small girl. There was a vulnerability to the character that I understood and that made me think I could do this."

One such vulnerability came in the lack of vocalization; without a way to learn formal speech, Ruby and her family had a tough time communicating with outsiders like the Carters. "They were looking for an essence," Ortiz says. "She didn't know she was 'deformed' and she certainly wasn't evil. Ruby is a young girl with a good heart; she is a child. By reading about her physicality and seeing that, for example, she had clawed hands, I began to work on her movements. I was very detailed and specific with her physicality."

He'd be a dentist's dream: Robert Joy played the creepy Lizard in 2006's *The Hills Have Eyes*.

Running into Bobby (played by Dan Byrd), Ruby's as far off-balance as he is. Who is he? *What* is this strange-looking creature in her world? "He's different, and he is the only thing around her that's her age," Ortiz says. "I focused on her movements and what she was feeling and what it would be like for any young girl who's been sheltered to see something new and different, her curiosity and how scary and exciting that might be. How conflicted she must have been, as the events around her unfold. There's something deep within her that knows what's good and what's right, and as much as she loved her family, she also wants to help, and that's something she struggled with. It was something I played with: Aside from her physicality, there was so much going on with her internally."

Just as before, Ruby's the only member of the family with some outside compassion,

Ivana Turchetto (left) and Laura Ortiz (right) prepare to represent their family in *The Hills Have Eyes*.

her sacrifices even greater this time; with the Carters' lives in Lizard's disfigured hands, Ruby sacrifices herself to take him out and save them.

In keeping with the overly violent nature of today's movies, *much* more blood was spilled in the remake, to the extent that some new characters were added to have more people to be violently killed. Stumbling into a home in the locals' unfamiliar town, the Carter baby's daddy runs into, almost literally, the aptly named Big Brain, equipped with a huge IQ and unable to move.

For the first time, both the characters and audience learn something about the background of the attacking family. These people, not too far from the Beanes of times and/or imaginations past, were deformed physically and emotionally by the government's nuclear blasts, in the wrong place at the wrong time and forced to pay for it with their exile from society.

"I'd have taken any role because I thought the script really advanced the genre, but Big Brain appealed most because of the nuances of his character," says Desmond Askew, "a person so physically weak and pathetic, but simultaneously so evil and threatening."

After about six hours a day in the makeup chair, Askew wasn't permitted to move anything above the neck. Unlike the rest of the family, all Big Brain's gifts were of the mental kind. "The first stage was the rig for my head, so from the moment that was applied I was unable to move my head for the rest of the day," Askew recalls. "That daily process really helped me get into character. Being 'handicapped' like that, albeit temporarily, made the simplest of tasks like eating or going to the bathroom so much more difficult and it wasn't too much of a stretch to imagine how I'd feel if the situation wasn't self-inflicted and if I weren't being rewarded by doing what I love."

With so many other *Hills* stars having to develop their characters and show emotion with little or no vocabulary, Askew had to show some touchy-feeliness without moving. And maybe more so than anyone else in the family, we had reason to feel extra sympathy for his plight, and through it, that of his family members.

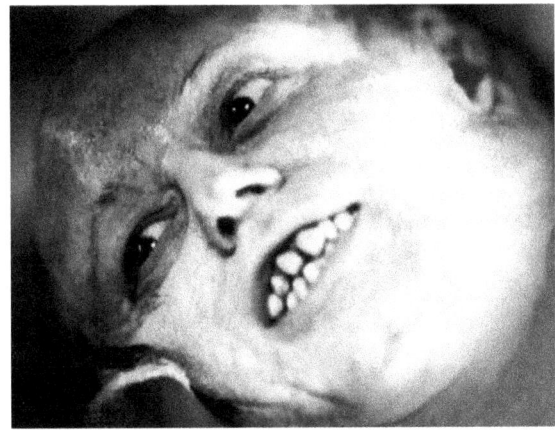

Big Brain (Desmond Askew) was a new face in the 2006 remake of *The Hills Have Eyes*.

"For me, this made some of Big Brain's lines, like 'You destroyed our homes' and 'You made us what we've become' all the more poignant," he says. "I feel like an actor must always find some level of sympathy (or at the very least, understanding) for their character in order to play him or her realistically. One doesn't necessarily have to agree with the character's decisions, but should always understand the circumstances that *led* to those decisions. This is, I think, what separated the mutants from the average horror movie villains: They had been forced into their nauseating lifestyle by the public at large."

So impressed were audiences with the new *Hills* that a sequel remake came along the next year, with Smith in a different role (a different name, at least), leading the mutants against a group of Marines.

Michael Berryman has appeared in films that made audiences laugh. Some that made them cry. Some that scared and probably disgusted them, through gory terror (like *Hills*) or sad ignorance and neglect (like *Cuckoo's Nest*). But just as audiences did with *Cuckoo's Nest*, just as Craven did during his Beane research, and just as all the filmmakers who used *Hills* as their own jumping-off points, Berryman hopes that the film world, will inspire.

"It would behoove [audiences] to get out and about and go to film festivals and enrich your creative experience," he says, "because it will hopefully stick on you and then you can express your own thoughts and feelings. You must have self-worth, self-appreciation and the ability to reflect and make tomorrow a better experience." He's done a lot of work for animal rights, and those for people with disabilities, including an organization for children afflicted with cleft palates that Paul Newman helped begin.

"My biggest passion is the quest for humanity to be honest and create a benevolent future for our children, which includes a planet that will hopefully not be completely devastated," he says. "I'm not an alarmist or some old hippie, to think this is not a finite earth is foolish. I'm very concerned about our future because war for profit has been a staple in human behavior for way too long and we need to wake up and realize that you shouldn't have children if you're not going to preserve their future."

Askew, Desmond. E-mail interview. July 19, 2013.
Berryman, Michael. Phone interview. March 20, 2013.
Joy, Robert. Personal interview. April 3, 2013.
Juvinall, Michael. "More Horror Exclusive: Interview with Michael Berryman." *More Horror*. 2013. Re-

trieved July 25, 2013, from http://www.morehorror.com/More-Horror-Exclusive-Interview-with-Michael-Berryman.

Lanier-Bramlett, Suze. E-mail interview. March 27, 2013.

Locke, Peter. Phone interview. April 9, 2013.

Martin, Todd. "Interview: Michael Berryman (Below Zero)." *HorrorNews*. Aug. 29, 2012. Retrieved July 25, 2013, from http://horrornews.net/55889/interview-michael-berryman-below-zero/#fbJT60cWpkut7idX.99.

"Michael Bailey Smith." *Pit of Horror*. n.d. Retrieved July 25, 2013, from http://www.pitofhorror.com/newdesign/interviews/baileysmith.htm.

Mondozilla. "Michael Berryman." *Horrorpedia*. March 12, 2013. Retrieved July 25, 2013, from http://horrorpedia.com/2013/03/12/michael-berryman-actor-article-and-interview/.

Tibbets, John C., and James M. Welsh. *The Encyclopedia of Novels into Film*. New York: Facts on File, 1998.

∙∙∙∙∙∙∙∙∙∙∙∙∙∙∙∙∙∙∙∙∙∙∙∙∙∙∙∙∙∙∙

Doug Bradley: The *Hellraiser* films

Doug Bradley spent hours in the makeup chair to become the horror world's newest sensation, and now the looks were going to carry the character.

At least Jason Voorhees and Michael Myers were human, or had been. This Frankenstein-esque creation was there to scare in another way.

Bradley had done what he could to interest and terrify his audience of cast and crew, forcing into their minds the hell that he, or his character, was ready to unleash upon the set, and ultimately the film world.

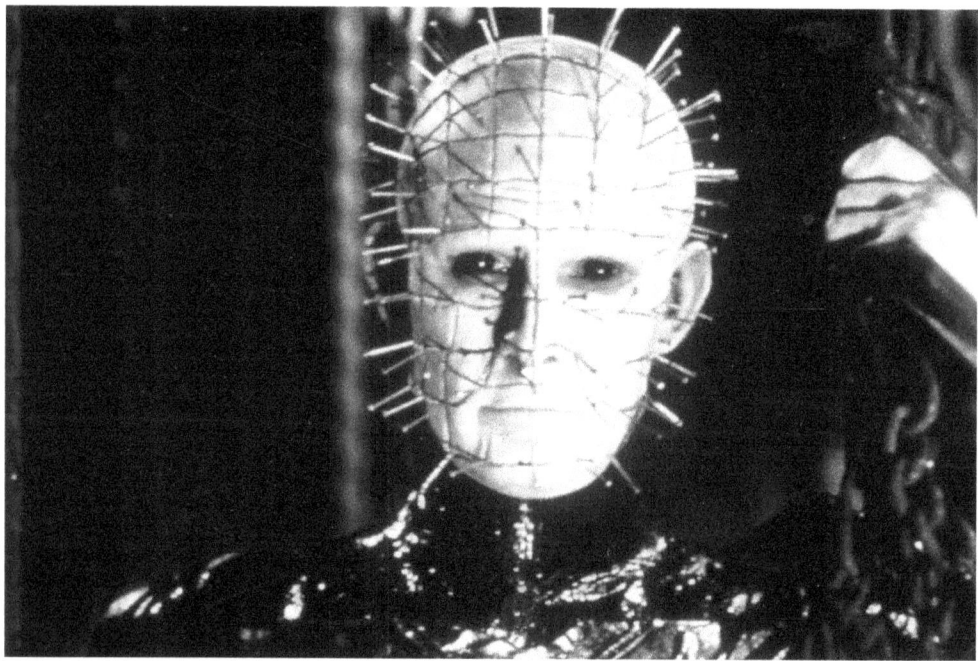

Pins pounded out of his face, Doug Bradley's Pinhead led the Cenobites into horror history through *Hellraiser*.

"From day one, [director Clive Barker, once a high school buddy of Bradley's] told me to do less, to take it down," Bradley recalls. "I was making friends with the makeup. If my face is dead, the makeup is doing it for me. I pinned onto this idea that [the character] had an awareness of once being human, which I link to his interest, his fascination with humans, that he had a sense of mourning for his own lost humanity, no sense of who he was or had been."

Doing less is, "the bit you can't see as an actor, because you act from inside your head outward, whereas the audience watches you from the outside inwards."

As Barker and Bradley had put together the 1978 horror short *The Forbidden*, Barker had put together what he aptly entitled the "nail-board." A thick, rectangular piece of wood had been painted white, with a black grid pattern atop that. Nails were pounded into the board at each intersection. Barker would then wave a light before the board, checking out where the nail shadows went.

Nearly a decade later, Barker decided to take the words of his story *A Hellbound Heart* and move them to full-length horror cinema. The nail-board technique would move to humanity. A person who would then become something different. Much stronger, maybe smarter, and definitely much more evil.

He was the title character in *Hellraiser*. One sequel later, the character would officially be monikered Pinhead ("Lead Cenobite" was his first credit; the new name was actually a nickname given by the crew).

"I approached *Hellraiser* thinking, great, I get to play a monster in a horror film," recalls Bradley, who'd played Satan on English stages beforehand. "I've always been a fan of horror films."

With nothing but their imagination limiting them, the *Hellraiser* makeup crew got to transform into doctors creating a monster. Cakes of makeup were layered around his face. His skull was almost totally covered. Over 130 pseudo-nails were fastened to his head. As hour after hour passed, Bradley watched himself become something out of this world.

After about six hours in the chair, the crew told him the job was done. Bradley asked everyone to leave the room. Staring into the mirror, he felt something new starting to take over inside.

"Where was I?" he asked. "Left behind somewhere, an identity in my head, but according to the mirror not here any more. I moved my head a little, this way, that way: I went close to the mirror, moved back from it. Then I began to tentatively move my mouth and face. A frown. A sneer. Raise an eyebrow. Smile. Laugh. Scream. Then words: 'I'll tear your soul apart … Angels to some, demons to others.' I bathed in the sense of power and majesty that the makeup gave me. I felt a sense of beauty: a dark, mangled, inscrutable beauty."

Physicality aside, he thought of some inner developments for the fellow. He remembered some images from magazines and history books. He considered those who had pierced their bodies for personal pleasure, then to the religious aspects. Bradley recalled the many African and Native American tribes that use the practice to show their devotion, as do many of the Hindu faith.

"The first ingredient to chuck in the melting pot was religion," he says, "some kind of priestly or monastic life, which implied a withdraw from the world, an aesthetic existence, firmly bound by rules, obedience, and a sense of devotion to some deity or higher authority.

"The guy has a whole bunch of nails banged into his skull, and I remember trying to make a list of associations with that. Top of the list, inevitably, was crucifixion … I am making no theological comparisons whatsoever, but the clear and obvious association was nails driven into flesh."

While adrenalin-based rage had driven previous horrors like Jason and Michael, Bradley saw sadness winning out over anger in Pinhead. "The first feeling I got was a deep sense of melancholia in the face, powerful and unsettling. The layout of the nails being symmetrical helps. It was clearly something that was done to him. The melancholy showed me he was human, once. He was, in a way he could not express, mourning the loss of his humanity."

Well, maybe he could, just a bit. Unlike Jason and Michael, Pinhead could speak. Unlike Freddy, he wouldn't fire off one-liners punctuated with evil grins.

With Barker's cousin Grace Kirby as his Cenobite backup (Barker's original tome had a woman leading the dark group), Bradley kept readying his creation. "For the voice, I simply went with how I was hearing the lines in my head, which was low, slow menace," he says. "The dark, bleak irony of treasured lines like 'No tears, please, it's a waste of good suffering,' suggested to me not so much breathy excitement as something rather tired and cynically mocking of human emotion, with a definitely vicious undertow." Barker's instructions of stoicism were starting to pay off. Just as Hannibal Lecter and the title character of *Candyman* would turn their own speech patterns into standout menace during performance, Bradley did the same with Pinhead.

As he geared up to represent the dark side of afterlife, the rest of the crew set about looking for the heroine required of just about every great horror franchise. Looking all over America, they couldn't locate the right Kirsty.

Back in London, Ashley Laurence was taking a drama class. A phone call came to ask her to visit the U.S. for an acting tryout. With just an inkling as to who the character was and what she'd be doing (or fighting), Laurence got a pretty tough tryout instruction: "[The crew] said to me, 'Okay, your Uncle Frank is in your father's skin, and he wants to kill you and have sex with you!'" Laurence remembers. "How do you feel about that?"

How in *hell*—an appropriate term in this case!—could *anyone* even consider such a situation? But that's how things go for Kirsty early on in *Hellraiser*. Her Uncle Frank's diddling around with a box in his house. The puzzle in it allows the box to open (the brain teaser would eventually be called the Lament Configuration, but we didn't know that yet). Then hooks and chains roar from it, and casually rip him to shreds. Pinhead steps forward, retrieves the box, and steps back to hell.

Frank's brother Larry and his wife Julia (Frank's ex-mistress) later move in. Larry cuts himself and blood drips onto the floor where Frank's body secretly rests. Julia happens upon him, and Frank tells her he needs more of this plasmatic stuff to get back to normal. A killing spree later, he's about there. But Kirsty nabs the box, and accidentally brings his captors out to play.

Kirsty begs the Cenobites to take Frank instead of her. Surprisingly, they're okay with it. Unlike many other main monsters of horror, it appears that these guys aren't here to kill and maim for the sake of enjoyment.

Back home, Frank's disguised as Larry, ready to ravage Kirsty. But the Cenobites arrive and take him down. Kirsty reverses the box's puzzles and sends 'em home.

"As the movie went on," Bradley remembers, "I realized that Pinhead is not the monster. The monsters are Julia and Frank. Pinhead is more like an impartial judge. He doesn't have an opinion about what people are doing is good or bad. He just sits there, like a demonic umpire at Wimbledon and keeps score."

The box, Bradley recalls, "had enough echoes of the Faustian Pact (an exchange of one's soul for supernatural power) for me to make another connection to Pinhead: Mephistopheles, the demonic seducer and go-between."

"Pinhead had to be malevolent and threatening," Bradley says, "but he doesn't operate by hiding round corners with a six-inch blade, or leap out at you with a chainsaw. In most of his entries in the movies, he is simply suddenly there: calm, still, and quiet. So the first thing he presents is himself. 'Look at me,' he seems to say. 'Look at what was done to me. Look at what I carry with me. Now think about what I might do to you.'"

Kirsty starts out the first sequel in a mental hospital, only to get dragged down to hell when her friend unknowingly solves the Configuration. Once again, Pinhead would have a lady at his side. But Kirby had decided not to reprise the role, and Barbie Wilde was hired. After checking over *Hellbound Heart* and sharpening the miming skills she'd been working on for a while, Wilde wowed the crew with her Cenobite knowledge.

Contrary to popular film fan belief, the term "Cenobite" wasn't created for the *Hellraiser* films. As horror-film–sounding as the word can be, it actually refers to a member of a communal religious group, usually based around a monk.

"I think that it was the fact that I knew what a Cenobite was that got me the job," Wilde recalls. "The difference between mime and dance is the difference between stillness and movement—another reason why mime artists are often used in roles like these."

Like Bradley, she'd be in the makeup chair for hours a day: several hours to make her up, and then even more time to get fitted for the costume. "Then you have to get into character, which wasn't that difficult: All I had to do was look in the mirror!" Wilde says. "I asked [director Tony Randel] what my motivation was … and he just said, 'You're dead.' Short, sweet, and to the point."

Viewers learned a bit about the man Pinhead had already been. An Englishman fighting in the first World War, a fellow named Elliott Spencer ("some lowly clerk in a corporation," Bradley labels him), had stumbled onto the box, then forcibly morphed into Pinhead. It's this that brings Pinhead's former humanity back out. Back on Earth, the Cenobites trap Kirsty and her friend. But her photo of Spencer reminds them of the people they once were, and they turn against the other Cenobites and save her life.

With Laurence out of *Hellraiser* action for a while, Bradley had a new chance to give Pinhead a realistic side. Just before filming on *Hellraiser III: Hell on Earth* kicked off, Bradley checked out a documentary on the Battle of the Somme, one of the bloodiest of World War I. As Allied forces roared into the German line near the Somme River in northern France in early July 1916, nearly 60,000 were killed or injured. One of the darkest days of the war, it became one of the strongest blows against Germany's army.

Bradley hadn't been around during either World War, but he could imagine what it would be like to feel its pain, an easier task than hell's leader. Spencer, he says, "felt as though he had cheated, that he was in the wrong place, that he shouldn't have lived, that he should be dead and he should have been buried along with his comrades in France." With Spencer's spirit away from his counterpart, Pinhead's back to pure evil, slaughtering innocent people with his hooks and chains. But his former human shows up and fuses the two together (the flick was the first-ever horror tale to use CGI, demonstrated strongly in the merging scene), sending them back to hell again.

Hellrasier: Bloodline (1996) played some serious games with time travel. Things started out at a space station in 2127, its builder solving the Lament Configuration. When he's captured, we learn that this stuff was firing long before Spencer was around, with the story jumping back four centuries.

The Configuration was actually created by Philip Lemarchand for a rich wannabe magician, and used to summon the beautiful (well, as Cenobites go) Angelique. She and another guy kill the "magic" man and the inventor, with Lemarchand's bloodline cursed forever because of the box.

Hundreds of years later, Angelique is back on the attack, killing the man who'd called her and forcing another to figure out the Configuration. This brings Pinhead to diabolical life.

"I had nightmares about Pinhead coming to kill me, so I was very scared when I started the movie," remembers Valentina Vargas, the lady Angelique. "I thought to myself, 'Should I do this or leave it?' because I didn't want to get into those dark places. Finally I said to myself, 'Maybe I should tap into those areas and find out what they're about.'" She found out—and it wasn't always pleasant.

"It really helped me to discover my own dark side," she continues. "I just wanted to experience it, and oh, did I experience it. I felt like when I put on the makeup, I metamorphosed into my character. I started being that other person." Perhaps those other people would be a more precise way of saying it, as she would find out.

"[Angelique] is totally playing and having her power, control, her clowns, and her harlequin version of hell," Vargas says. "She's half human and half demon, which was very interesting to play because she wants to be evil, but at the same time, she has these feelings for LeMarchand. She's always trying to use her power to get LeMarchand to love her so they can build bigger doors to hell."

The plans backfire, and everyone's sent straight to hell. But unlike the previous films, that's not the end. Back in the 2100s, the Cenobites are loose and back on the attack, trying to keep the door between Earth and hell open for good.

The last part is "going to hell with Pinhead and making love with him, mentally," Vargas says. "He turns me into a Cenobite, but with more power trips and mental things. Not with real love—it doesn't exist for them. It's more of a power trip, a mental and calculated love. Afterwards, he made me chief of his troops.... Since I'm female, I play with my victims more to get my pleasure. She's like a serpent where even at the point where she's going to bite you, she's still nice to you." But even her charms can only go so far, as a field of perpetual light is implanted in a huge box. It blows up and sends them to hell.

As the next series entry of *Inferno* gets going, there's a detective roaming the crime scenes of Denver. He long ago lost the ability to say no to drugs or women, his marriage notwithstanding. A puzzle fanatic, he finds an ominous box at a crime scene, and we on the outside know what this schmuck's in for.

It takes over his mind. His friends and colleagues start showing up dead. Creatures with no eyes or legs still find a way to chase him. Then a pair of ladies so lovely we nearly forget their scars and dismembered limbs arrive on the seduction trail so many she-devils tread upon. What are they? Who are they?

Those who checked out *Inferno* probably know the ladies' real name. Now let's get a closer look at how one woman got ready to play part of a twosome.

With modeling and dance already on her résumé, Patricia Kara went to a new spot in the acting world. "Up to that point, I had never seen any of the *Hellraiser* movies before," she admits, "but I had heard enough about them from their reputation in the industry. I have always loved horror movies and murder mysteries ... I was very excited when the opportunity came along and I was able to be a small part of a legendary series of movies." Patience is a true virtue is any aspect of performing, and, with about four hours a day in the chair to be transformed, alongside Lynn Speier, into one of the Wire Twins, she'd need it.

"Once it all came together, I felt different," Kara says. "I did not even feel human any more. It helped while I was embracing that otherworldly feeling that came with the transformation of my appearance and it all made playing the character a lot easier."

She and Speier's main scene would become a dark pleasure favorite for *Hellraiser* fans (mostly of the male persuasion), teaming up on the detective for a massage to which heaven could hardly compare. Later on, Kara got to show, and feel, the effects of another Twin highlight: their snake-on-steroids tongues, killing a fellow by wrapping hers all the way around his neck. (*A Nightmare on Elm Street* fans were probably having flashbacks to the deadly tongue scenes from *Dream Warriors* and *New Nightmare*.)

"Obviously, my tongue is not that long," Kara remarks, "so I had to go through the motions and let the special effects people take over from there. When I saw the final cut, it was really incredible to see how talented those artists are."

The detective goes to a therapist who knows a bit too much. The doc, we finally learn, is Pinhead. All the murders, death, destruction, they're all real ... in the cop's mind. And this practitioner is using his powers for punishment, not help. Pinhead and his crew have been torturing the detective for all the harm he's caused. As Pinhead's trademark hooked chains wrap around the detective, Pinhead joyfully lets him know that this is just the next step in a journey without an end.

Bradley worked just three days on the month-long shoot. But the third one was truly a charm; behind his back, his friends had figured out that it marked his 100th day in Pinhead garb, and a lunch party was thrown.

By now, despite the hours spent in the makeup chair, becoming Pinhead was more and more commonplace for him. "It got easier to find my way to the character. Early on, I used the makeup process as the journey to the character. At the end of the first few applications, I felt completely dislocated, emotionally displaced from everything going on around me, which is a very good place to be to play a character like Pinhead, so I used that to take it on set and use that detachment from the human beings around him.

"They say the devil has all the best tunes, so I think the psych element is that you carry the threat, you carry the danger, but there always has to be something running counter to that, some charm, some humor, or whatever it is, that undercuts the two-dimensionality of playing a villain." Pinhead continued to bring that to him, and to millions more as the saga continued two years later in *Hellseeker*.

With the new film, *Hellraiser* fans got a welcome gift, a re-gift in this case. Laurence brought Kirsty back to action—and her aggression went to a level that would have impressed even the pinheaded one himself. She and her husband Trevor (Dean Winters, later of *Oz* fame and Mayhem car insurance commercials) are in a serious car wreck, and she's apparently dead, with his brain broken almost beyond repair. Eventually it's up to Pinhead to show Trevor his philandering. Then Kirsty shows back up, and the Cenobites are here too.

Of course, Trevor's going to pay dearly, and Kirsty's going to make certain of it, offering Pinhead five souls to let her continue on. The lead Cenobite's gal backup this time is the Stitch Cenobite.

"I like the idea of the morality tale that they present," says Stitch lady Sarah Hayward. "If the character makes a bad choice, all hell breaks loose. The idea that [Hellraiser] is a morality tale is very interesting, because you are always faced with moral issues daily."

As Kirsty starts to fulfill her end of the bargain, the women who grabbed her man begin to pay. Three of them don't turn up alive. A friend of Trevor's, plotting Kirsty's death, becomes number four. All the while, the Cenobites are on Kirsty's side.

"We spent hours deciding how to make the skin look distressed," Hayward says. "One of the most challenging things was when I saw my costume headpiece, I realized I was going to feel claustrophobic. The rubber mask had tiny slits for eyes and small breathing holes for the nose." So she had a quick chat with a representative of the mental health field.

"I went to see a therapist to get an idea of what I should be thinking about, rather than panicking because I couldn't breathe," Hayward says. "He said, 'Just know that you can still breathe, and when you breathe in, imagine the air filling every single cell in your body with this beautiful blue, clear oxygen, to think that every breath was filling every part of me with oxygen.'"

"I think that people can only be courageous if they're afraid," Laurence says, "and in Hellraiser, each person found out what they were made of. I don't think that Kirsty knew how strong she was…. There's a courage to Kirsty, a stand-and-fight aspect to her personality."

Bradley reprised the role twice more, in 2003's *Deader* and 2005's *Hellworld*, alongside longtime horror icon Lance Henriksen. He stepped away from the character in 2011 for *Revelations*, and Stephan Smith Collins played the role.

But Bradley might still become the pinned man; by the time this is in print, he may have donned the blue makeup and pins for the ninth time, which would break his tie with Robert Englund for most times playing the same villain champ.

"I think people like the intimacy, and the danger, and the rawness, and the ugliness," Laurence says of the eternal Cenobite appeal. "It's so grotesque that I think it's really beautiful. It's so human and it's so flawed that I think makes it more easy to relate to, because it's damaged and it's open."

After eight tries, Bradley knows what's in Pinhead's head. And he knows exactly all the right ways to bring it out. "If you're going to be asked to play Adolf Hitler, Pol Pot, or [Cleveland kidnapper-rapist] Ariel Castro, you have to get inside that person's head and understand them," he says. "It's not about being sympathetic, but you try and make sense as to why they did it, to get to a place of understanding. It can be very hard to do. The Ariel Castros, they shit and piss like the rest of us. Pinhead is an extraordinary character. He looks extraordinary. He's an original. He gets their interests, like Freddy and Michael. He's not a monster, but a fairly impartial character, a judge, almost. Also, he's so damn intelligent and witty! He might even string you up with hooks and chains and tear you to bits."

"Ashley Laurence." Monsters from the Basement. n.d. Retrieved Aug. 6, 2013, from http://monsters-fromthebasement.com/interviews/ashley-laurence/.
Barker, Clive, Dir. Hellraiser [DVD]. Cinemarque Entertainment BV.

Beeler, Michael. "Valentina Vargas Raises a Little Hell." Femme Fatales 3.4 (Spring 1995): 24–31, 61.
Bradley, Doug. Behind the Mask of the Horror Actor. London: Titan Books, 2004.
Bradley, Doug. Personal interview. May 10, 11, 2013.
Eichenbaum, Rose. The Actor Within. Middletown, CT: Wesleyan University Press, 2011.
Ferrante, Anthony C. "Hellraiser IV: Bloodline." Fangoria 141 (April 1995): 40–45, 69.
Harris, Will. "Done Raising Hell?" The Virginian Pilot, May 9, 2013, p. 4.
Hayward, Sarah. Phone interview. July 9, 2013.
"Interview: Michael Bailey Smith." Movie Hole. Feb. 24, 2006. Retrieved July 25, 2013 from http://moviehole.net/20068417interview-michael-bailey-smith#JGGYF3StCtrcmt6B.99.
Jones, Stephen. Clive Barker's A-Z of Horror. New York: BBC Books, 1997.
Kane, Paul. The Hellraiser Films and Their Legacy. Jefferson, NC: McFarland, 2006.
Kara, Patricia. E-mail interview. Aug. 4, 2013.
McIntee, David. Beautiful Monsters. Tolworth, Surrey: Telos, 2005.
"Talking With the Dead: 13 Questions with Barbie Wilde." Horror Society. June 4, 2013. Retrieved Aug. 6, 2013, from http://www.horrorsociety.com/2013/06/04/talking-with-the-dead-13-questions-with-barbie-wilde-female-Cenobite-and-the-venus-complex-author/.

Jonathan Breck: *Jeepers Creepers*, *Jeepers Creepers 2*

Over the past few years, Jonathan Breck has helped unleash a brand new terror on film horror fans around the world, turning a film with a cartoonish title into a sensation. Millions have seen him work his grisly magic on the big screen.

Still, if the man himself strolled through the legions of those he's horrified, the fans probably wouldn't know who they were looking at. They might recognize him from *elsewhere*; Breck showed up in the George Bush biopic *W.,* as well as several other films and TV shows. It's just that people might not make the horrifying connection. That's the case for many top horror stars; like the parade of actors who played Jason Voorhees, and those who donned Predator gear, Breck looks quite a bit different out of character.

Breck helped turn *Jeepers Creepers* into one of the unexpected hits of 2001. Two years later, he became the limb-liberating critter once again. "If I was going to be typecast in any particular bunch, I'd go for horror," Breck says. "Horror fans are some of the most loyal, down-to-earth people. I'm lucky to able to entertain that fanbase.

"I wasn't a huge horror fan growing up," he admits. "I approached it just like any other acting role. I just really trusted my instincts. I'd gotten my start in live performances and learned to trust my instincts as an actor. Any actor that wants to start out should start out on stage and develop their craft. It doesn't matter whether they're making horror or comedy; the same principles apply in creating a strong, dynamic character, which is what you need."

For his *Jeepers Creepers* role, strength and vibrancy would be his main keys to success. "I said for them to send me the script," he says. "They said that there wasn't any dialogue. They told me to give my take on a character—he was a couple thousand years old and he ate people." Weirdly, Breck felt he understand the Creeper perfectly.

For his tryout, he says, "I worked a lot on the Creeper's behavior. I shaved my head for the audition, because I felt like the character wouldn't have any hair. They liked it. It

Jonathan Breck underwent quite the makeover to become the Creeper in the *Jeepers Creepers* films.

was all about the Creeper's behavior, how he stalked his prey, that sort of thing. It was a strange audition, believe me."

The Creeper didn't speak, but he could smell and hear prey hundreds of yards away. He could certainly move, flying across cornfields at high speed towards a quarry that would never know what hit it.

"I did a lot of reading on different animals," he says. "I wanted the Creeper to have certain animalistic traits, but I didn't want people to be able to pin him down and say he was a bat, a falcon, or any particular thing. I figured the Creeper was like a super hunter, so I took a bunch of animals' traits and melded them together.

"The first time we did makeup, I walked in front of a mirror and scared the shit out of myself. I caught myself up in that character."

Self-fear would soon be the least of his problems. The oppressive summer heat of swampy central Florida brought on a whole new set of horrors. "I was encased in latex," Breck says. "There wasn't even any place in there to go to the bathroom. After you've spent five to seven hours getting the makeup on and then working for twelve hours, it was crazy." Perhaps, subconsciously, he used the Creeper to take his frustrations out on his victims—or maybe it was just hunger-induced insanity. When one only gets to chow for 23 days every 23 years, as the Creeper Legend went, those pangs have to be hitting like lasers.

On a deserted highway (never a safe place for young teens in a horror film), a brother and sister see a tall, dark, and definitely unhandsome character tossing something down a tunnel. With curiosity getting the better of them, the two decide to investigate. There are piles and piles of mutilated bodies, including a pair of the siblings' pals. It's the midst of the Creeper's dinnertime, and he's not letting it go to waste. Suddenly the siblings are in a race for their lives with something not of this species—or any other.

In the end, the sister makes it out but the brother's not so lucky, as the Creeper snares him and takes off just before the credits roll. The film's gross of $37 million was over three times its budget.

It's always better if the monsters in horror films have a motive. The Creeper, much like those anti–Earthlings that targeted Ellen Ripley, is hunting not for sport, but survival. His motives are horrific, but again, there's some substance behind them.

"It's not just a horror film; it's a good movie," Breck says. "From the cinematography, to the editing, to the sound effects, all the way around, it was a good movie first. There are so many horror movies that creating something fresh and original is not easy to do, and [*Jeepers*] kind of tapped into something people wanted to see. It was a throwback to old monster movies of yesteryear, and I think people were hungry for that, no pun intended."

About two years later, Breck learned that a sequel was in the works. He jumped again—and landed right in a boot camp.

"I went to camp for a couple of months to get myself right," he says. "I got in a lot better shape. It's a really physically demanding role, takes an incredible amount of stamina. If I came back, I wanted to do something different and fresh. I expanded on what I'd done in the first film."

Just as before, he was in character long before the first "Action!" Some cast members, many in their first film, might glance toward the ceiling, only to come face to visage with their non-human co-star. "I had a lot of fun scaring the hell out of them," Breck says. "In the second movie, we just had fun."

Like the first *Halloween* films, in which the second edition starts mere minutes after the first (in movie-time), *Creepers* got going fast as well. This time, he morphs into a scarecrow to make off with the son of a farmer, then terrorizes a busload of basketball players, cheerleaders, and coaches. In the end, the Creeper's caught, and seemingly killed. But in the last scene, we see him being used as a sideshow attraction, with a man nearby wielding a gun, warning passersby that its 23-year diet is about to end.

Breck can only hope that making a strong mark in horror won't necessarily hold him there permanently. "It's been really tough for me to break out of that," he says, "but over the last few years, I've been lucky enough to work outside the makeup and work outside of horror. But you don't really get to choose your career at certain times, it chooses you. You make the most of it. If you've got a hit movie, or two, you have to be thankful for that, and just do your best.

"Has it limited me some? Probably. But the other side of the coin is that I've had a blast and met a lot of great people. I don't think it's slowed me down that much."

Breck, Jonathan. Phone interview. April 3, 2010.

Jamie Brewer and Naomi Grossman: *American Horror Story*

When the issue of the nation's mentally challenged is discussed, the word "special" typically comes straight to the forefront. As in special school, or special education.

It's there for the right reasons; anyone who has spent time working in the Special Olympics can tell you all kinds of details about how doing so makes it impossible to be in a rough mood.

Still, as well-meaning as the term is, others might consider it a bit stigmatizing, a message that those afflicted should get extra treatment, a veiled missive that they're just not on the same level as the "normal."

One way or another, Jamie Brewer's been out for her whole life to prove it and other such stereotypes far off the mark—and succeeded.

Diagnosed early on with Down Syndrome, she spent her educational career right there next to every other student—no special forms of school treatment. She's never gotten any more or less care or concern because of the Down, because she never wanted any.

And not just in the classroom at school. Her first acting steps fell on the stages of junior high and high school. Brewer rocked her local Fort Bend community theater groups, and became a fixture in local classes. Along the way, she spent four years as a member of Texas' Association for Retarded Citizens board, which helped find food, work, and shelter for the challenged community of one of America's largest states. She asked the Texas State Capitol for better treatment for the disabled. She appeared on a national commercial for the food banks.

"I was a theater girl since eighth grade, so I definitely wanted to go into acting," recalls Brewer. A friend told her about a new show called *American Horror Story*. Sort of like a horror film split into episodes, an entire storyline would start and finish in a season, and scare the holy hell out of viewers in the process. "I couldn't *wait* to audition!" she recalls. "I studied the script and became Addie."

In the opening moments of *American Horror Story*, it's late 1970s Los Angeles, and two youngsters try to break into an abandoned house, apparently unaware that the season is called *Murder House*. A little girl playing outside tries to warn them but, in typical young boy form, they sneer and stroll in, only to become victims.

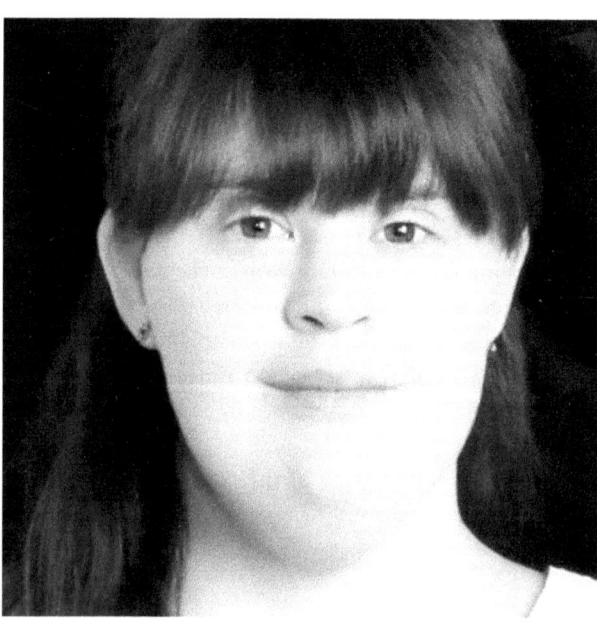

Jamie Brewer stole the show in the first and third seasons of *American Horror Story*.

By the way, the caring child was Addie, but not played by Brewer, not yet. Katelyn Reed played the youth version. "She's a very sweet girl!" Brewer recalls.

Eventually we skip ahead to the present day, and the Harmons, a family nearly destroyed by the philandering daddy Ben (Dylan McDermott), head to the home. Wife Vivien (Connie Britton) and daughter Violet (Taissa Farmiga) aren't sure that they want anything saved just yet, and their new neighbors aren't the most welcoming. It's Constance Langdon (Jessica Lange) and her young one Addie, now quite a bit different than she was before.

"Addie's very mysterious," Brewer says. "She didn't judge other people. She was a sweet girl, even though there's a lot of mystery to her."

Ben, a home-based shrink, starts seeing new patients, and his first is Tate, a young man who connects with Violet. Moira the housekeeper shows up; women see her as a kindly matron, men see a young nymphomaniac ready to give it all away at a glance.

Still, no one's on to anything just yet, except someone who doesn't speak much. Addie seems to feel at home as a stranger in the Harmon place. She reaches out from under a bed to startle Violet, then scares the mom with her laughter.

And us as well; Addie sees the two kids who teased her younger self, and doesn't seem the slightest bit fazed by the undead sight. It's clear she knows something she's not telling.

"It's about being mischievous," Brewer explains. "If you look at me in the first season, you can see it in my eyes. You play it through the eyes; the eyes are the body language."

Over at the Langdon home, Addie dreams of simply being a "pretty girl," but Constance, in full *Carrie* mode, can't wait to knock her dreams dead, shoving her into the "Bad Girl Room," a closet with mirrors everywhere. Addie flips out, and that wasn't all Brewer's acting. "It was crazy!" she says of the scene.

More harsh truths start to come out. Over twenty people have died in the house. Tate, who we learn is Addie's brother, went on a long-ago school shooting spree that left rooms of people dead. Including him. We now know how Addie saw the dead kids, and why Moira changes shape and form: In this house, the ghosts decide who sees them and how.

Constance is aware of this; it's why she's aware of Tate. And it's how she grabs desperately one last time at the daughter who she never got to tell how much she loved.

It's Halloween, and with the help of a mask, Addie's finally her own version of a "pretty girl." But a car strikes her, and Constance can't get her body onto the Harmon property quickly enough to keep her daughter's spirit among the living. "It wasn't something I was used to doing," recalls Brewer, who, through a spiritual medium, helped Addie say a forgiving goodbye to her mom. "I had to lie real still and everything. It was an out-of-body experience with the body changing a little bit."

In the second *Horror Story*, the storyline was different, with new names, characters, motives, and setting. Based in the 1960s—a full decade before *One Flew Over the Cuckoo's Nest* helped America find a new sense of compassion for sanctuary residents—the second season, simply subtitled *Asylum*, put a new spin on the much-utilized tradition of making such a place a scary land. After playing tortured evil as Tate, Evan Peters was now Kit, framed for serial murder and stolen from his true love, a black woman. After showing up as Moira, Frances Conroy was now the Angel of Death, one of the first women to take on such a role. After a shorter showing in the first season, Lily Rabe was Sister Mary Eunice, a young, eager soul that would eventually be stolen by those that can only be exorcised. McDermott showed up as someone new as well.

Lange was again in the lead, playing Sister "Jude" Martin, who ruled the place with an iron fist and the switches she used to beat some discipline into employees and residents.

Brewer wasn't used in the second season; producers may have feared that utilizing an actress with Down Syndrome in the midst of a storyline of an asylum might have reinforced the negative stereotypes far too many mentally challenged faced (and, many would say, still do).

But just as Addie was one of the first we'd meet on the season opener, another relative newcomer got to snare her own shows. From the beginning stages of Naomi Grossman's performing career, she was in musical motion. "Ever since I was a toddler, dancing in the aisles during the film *Fantasia*," recalls the Denver native, "my parents and I knew I was bound for the stage and screen." No one could have known that, decades later, others' first view of the actress would be so strangely similar.

After spending the majority of her childhood on Denver stages and occasionally on the small screen—she showed up on *Father Dowling Mysteries* and *Sabrina the Teenage Witch*—Grossman attempted to cross the gap between child and grownup performer.

"It's like the chicken or the egg," she says. "No one will hire you without a résumé, but how do you get a résumé if no one will hire you? So, you hire yourself. Or at least I did."

Peppering her acting resume with a plethora of self-created shorts and one-woman shows helped Grossman show that she didn't need to be told in advance what to do or how to work. "Ultimately, it reignited my passion for performing, which was waning after years of rejection in Hollywood, instilled in me a certain confidence, which is crucial to getting cast, and provided the powers-that-be that résumé with which they could actually hire me."

It worked: Her agent called to say she had a shot at the second *Story*. Grossman seen the first season and, as the stories change every season, it might not have helped if she had.

"I went to casting without any real information as to what the role was," she says. "As a rule, *American Horror Story* keeps things extremely under wraps. It wasn't until after I was cast that I learned—and was obviously onboard. I have always had an affinity for big characters, which I think lend themselves well to horror. But in this case, I think the genre more picked me."

With Britton and Farmiga also gone, Sarah Paulson stepped into the lead as Lana, a reporter hellbent on exposing the truth about ominous Briarcliff Manor. The first person we see is clearly a princess of her own world, someone who finds normalcy in a lifestyle that many would dislike, perhaps even fear.

As the cautious journalist makes her way toward the Manor, we see the figure joyfully turning circles on the lawn. Far from the cinema aisles of her childhood, Grossman was now grooving for a much larger audience.

Lana's not sure what to make of things, but her new acquaintance knows how to make an impression, charging forward with a flower. "Play with me!" the woman blurts out, clearly used to this manner of making impressions, perhaps with former visitors. And, in a strange way, nostalgic B-movie fans might be having flashbacks.

"I've always modeled myself after chameleon-type actors, like Lon Chaney and Lily Tomlin, who really transform themselves altogether," Grossman says. To become her new persona, her alterations came from the inside and out. She spent a great deal of time in the makeup chair, hiding her original lovely form to become her character.

One of Grossman's inspirations: The 1932 Tod Browning film *Freaks*, the tale of a circus troupe of freaks who band together to take revenge on the trapeze artist who married their midget friend for his money. Still criticized by many, called exploitative for making so many disabled characters its centerpieces, the film nonetheless has garnered quite a cult following. One of the main characters plays himself. Like many afflicted with microcephaly, a disorder that leaves sufferers with undersized skulls and brains, Schlitzie could only speak a few syllables and the occasional phrase. However, he became a huge circus attraction throughout the 1920s and '30s, including time with Ringling Brothers and Barnum and Bailey. He's one of a few microcephaly victims in *Freaks,* and appeared in several more films. His circus career continued, on and off, until the late 1960s, and he lived to age 70. Grossman planted herself before *Freaks,* learning more and more about her muse.

She used it to play the young lady known as Pepper, whose cheerful demeanor covers up the past that landed her in Briarcliff: drowning and mutilating her nephew, or so Mary claims. In her first few episodes, there's not much to Pepper; she occasionally steps into the spotlight to fire off a few monosyllabic phrases and insensitively get labeled "pinhead" by the staff. Lana's a focal point here, soon committed for lesbianism. Mary's body is slowly being taken over by a demon. Jude goes to battle with Dr. Arden (James Cromwell), determined to find the secrets of madness through any means necessary, including torturous experiments he may have learned of during his days as a Nazi guard.

But soon enough, the fantastic surrealism of the storyline grabs hold. A pregnant woman thought dead has somehow survived, and Pepper's mindset and vocabulary have taken a collective 180!

She's now not only well spoken but *out*spoken, determined to take care of her expectant friend.

"Pepper is so rich," Grossman says. "She has so many dichotomies at play: evil vs. good, victim vs. advocate, naive vs. wise, comedic vs. serious. It's like two roles in one, really, which is a gift to *any* actor. But a non-name actor like myself at the time? That level of trust is truly rare in Hollywood, and speaks volumes of the producers and casting.

"While I had ample time to prepare for early Pepper, I only had about a week for the later, smart, evolved Pepper. Being subtle and still has always been more of a challenge for me, so while early Pepper came very naturally, later Pepper required more concentration."

Pepper's mental power keeps evolving, and no one's sure what to make of it. Pepper faces Arden, letting him know she was framed for killing her nephew (his

Naomi Grossman played Pepper from both sides in *American Horror Story.*

dad did it), and that no one, including him, is getting anywhere near the pregnant woman. The lady eventually gives birth, although *that* story doesn't have a happy ending. She gets closer to Jude, whose past is starting to overtake her own mind, culminating in a musical number that flashed back to Jude's past as a singer. With Jude blasting out "Name Game" (the song whose lyrics include "Bananafana!"), Pepper and the rest of the crew are clapping along. Perhaps *Horror* co-creator Ryan Murphy was having flashbacks to his creation of *Glee!*

"The 'Name Game' routine was when I was most in my element," Grossman says. "I was allowed to really go for it, and be bold and playful. I remember a crew member calling out through a megaphone, 'Everyone can go bigger *except Pepper.*'"

Jude's memories, including Pepper, are swept away by the insanity that eventually makes her a patient. Unbeknownst to her, time skips ahead, and we learn that Pepper passed away during the period.

As *Horror* attempted to make the third time a charm with *Coven*, the storyline switched to someplace not entirely unlike Hogwarts, with Farmiga back as Zoe, the new student at Miss Robichaux's Academy for Exceptional Young Ladies, a front for a school that teaches the ways of witchcraft. Paulson was headmistress Cordelia Foxx and Lange was supreme as Fiona, Cordelia's mom and head of all local witches. Conroy and Peters were also around, and Lily Rabe and Denis O'Hare, who'd been in *Murder House*, were there for part three. Kathy Bates played serial slaughterer Delphine LaLaurie in a role that won her an Emmy, while Angela Bassett showed up as Maire Laveau, renowned voodoo queen.

Brewer played Nan, Zoe's classmate. Like Addie, she knew more than she was letting on, but this time, more of it came into play. Clairvoyance is Nan's gift; she uses it to not only embarrass her classmates about their past, but to put together some crime solutions, such as helping find the body of LaLurine, whom everyone only *thought* was dead. Nan acts as a medium for the muted and the passed. With her everpresent small smile that called up memories of the Mona Lisa, Nan knew more than anyone else ever hoped, and time would tell if her powers would be used for good or evil.

Of her two roles, Brewer says, "There's some similarities, but they're very different. I did a lot more studying for this one. I studied about the powers of witchcraft, and witchcraft alone. Nan is a student of witchcraft. Being clairvoyant was one of the fun things. It was really humorous."

As loyalties bounce back and forth in the tradition of the show, Nan forms a bond with new neighbor Luke (Alexander Dreymon), her psychic abilities telling her that some seriously horrible things are going on at his home with his mom Joan (Patti LuPone). But before Nan can save Luke from the abuse, Nan's stalker shows up with a gun and blasts Joan. Before he can shoot Nan, Luke leaps into the way, taking the bullet himself.

"The scene with the shooting was very difficult for all three of us," Brewer says. "I had to deal with a lot of things that brought me to that point. I had to prepare, to utilize certain things that I've gone through in life that lead you to a certain point. You listen to what the direction is, you hold back, and then you give it your all."

As Joan is resurrected, Nan, herself now telekinetic as well, speaks through her son. But, as before, there's no happy endings, as Nan learns that the death of Joan's husband wasn't an accident, and she's driven away while Joan takes out Luke.

Brewer's never wanted to be defined by her disability, to be seen as one in need of or even desirous of "special" treatment. It's why her advice to upcoming performers, of either gender, any race or faith, disabled or otherwise, rings true to all: "Always go to your dreams! Be true to your heart, not just for [people] with Down Syndrome, but for anyone. Always be true to yourself, and be ready for it!"

Brewer, Jamie. Phone interview. Jan. 5, 2014.
Grossman, Naomi. E-mail interview. Jan. 6, 2014.

Stacy Chbosky: *The Poughkeepsie Tapes*

No invisible demons hiding in the closet or under the covers. No witches slipping between the trees. This was going to be a different type of self-filmed film. The cameraman (and woman) would be both narrator and participant in this flick, but the movie itself would put a different spin on horror, and it hadn't looked so real since we saw through Michael Myers' eyes in the legendary opening of John Carpenter's *Halloween*. And this was going to be more horrifyingly real than many of its genre, because it was more true, and yet more possible, than anything *Paranormal* or *Blair*-based.

It's a rite of passage in the ranks of childhood mischief to check out material—printed, electronic, or otherwise—that Mom and Dad don't know we know about, and Stacy Chbosky and her brother Stephen were no exception.

"We gobbled up every horror movie that came on HBO," she recalls jokingly. "We even used my stuffed animals and our giant camcorder to shoot our own version of *Friday the 13th*. My mom taped *Family Ties* over it, otherwise I'm sure it'd be a cult classic today!" Stephen ended up directing his sister in 2012's *The Perks of Being a Wallflower*, though her scenes ended up on the cutting room floor.

Still, even after kicking off her acting career in a preschool talent show, Chbosky (Shuh-BOSS-key) was angling toward the humorous side of the business. It's why, when she and her husband John Erick Dowdle started to put together the flick Dowdle had written with his brother Drew, Chbosky figured she'd stay away from the "Action!"

The Dowdles had decided to put their own spin on the "found footage" genre and make it a bit more real. Inspired by both horror and documentaries like 1988's *The Thin Blue Line*, which helped free a man wrongfully convicted of murder, the two knocked out *The Poughkeepsie Tapes*.

"We didn't have a name for [the films] then," Chbosky recalls. "Shaky cam movies, POV films, mockumentaries, faux documentaries. The genre was too new for me to be a fan of it: there was just *Blair Witch* and the opening scene of *Halloween*." Just after finishing his film, Dowdle sat on a convention panel with some others trying their hand at the genre, young filmmakers just hoping to re-capture the magic that had made *Blair* the then-highest-grossing independent film ever.

One such searcher was a guy who'd set off on the unenviable task of having about three-fourths of his film take place in a bedroom, often during sleeping times, relying on bare-bones special effects and weird noises to terrify his viewers.

A few years and (as of early 2014) four sequels later, Oren Peli and his *Paranormal* pals hadn't just hit the filmmaking jackpot; they'd beaten it into oblivion.

"Now I think Oren is worth forty or fifty gazillion dollars," Chbosky says. "Good for him! Sometimes nice guys finish first. Horror people tend to be wonderful people: nice, nerdy, not too full of themselves ... I have seven or eight friends who have made their own features. To me, that's the most admirable thing you can do in Hollywood. Making your own feature is just the epitome of cool."

Helping people try out for the murderous role of Ed, the never-fully-seen killer and oft-filmer of *The Poughkeepsie Tapes*, Chbosky found herself connected to teenage Cheryl Dempsey, who becomes Ed's abductee. Finding herself brought to tears while watching others act out the scene of the captive begging for her mother, Chbosky started to see a part of herself.

"I wasn't supposed to be Cheryl," she recalls. "I was a 33-year-old comedienne; Cheryl Dempsey was the 19-year-old ingénue. But I got really into it. At first, I just enjoyed being in the zone. It felt good. But pretty soon, I was secretly trying to win the part. And once John and Drew started auditioning young women for the role, I *really* wanted it." She got her wish. Ben Messmer played the murderer.

One of the biggest challenges for performers is putting themselves in a situation they've never been anywhere near and trying to make it real. While Chbosky hadn't shared Cheryl and Ed's lifestyle (the most relative of terms in this case), many others tragically had, and she'd soon get to know some of them, in the literary sense.

The film's title characters show up early, with cops searching the house of a suspect, only to find videos of his deed, his proud declaration of abduction, torture, and murder of both genders and all ages. A little girl is the first to go. A man is decapitated, his severed head sewn inside the stomach of his wife. Now Ed sets his sights on Cheryl, albeit with a different objective in mind.

"Here's what I love about Cheryl: She's ordinary," Chbosky says. "She's a small town, bored-with-her-boyfriend, community college B-student who is sick of living at home with her parents. It felt very daring to embrace Cheryl's ordinariness, and not try to glamorize her by making her, oh, secretly brilliant or secretly artistic or something. It was exciting to play a normal person who is dragged into a nightmarish situation, and destroyed. I prepped for about a month to play Cheryl. I read true-crime books about women who were abducted and kept as sex slaves." Ironically, one of Philadelphia's saddest stories would be one of her biggest assets: Chbosky got a great deal from the tragic tale of Gary Heidnik, who held captive, tortured, and raped several women in late 1986 and early 1987. One of his victims died from the torture and another was electrocuted. Heidnik was executed in 1999.

"I bound myself up and just sat with it for a bit, to imagine how uncomfortable it would be to be kept that way for days," she says. But the chains that keep hold of Cheryl's body aren't nearly as strong as the ones Ed places across her mind; they're the ones that bind him to her forever, forcing her to rely on him. Tied up in pitch-black rooms, she's commanded to gasp out her devotion.

"My most powerful preparation was to repeat the words, 'You are the master and it pleases me to serve you' for an hour or two at a time," she remembers. "Doing that was awful. It hurt my voice; it was miserably depressing. In my imagination, I decided that Ed made Cheryl repeat that phrase every waking moment for two years. Repeating it for an hour or two got me into an appropriately hopeless state." Soon, Ed moves into Jack the Ripper territory, posing as a policeman to prey on prostitutes, and making his "creation" do the dirtiest of his work.

Ed's evil spreads. The film wisely doesn't try to explain it, as nothing would come close to sufficing there. He frames an innocent man, who's executed for Ed's crimes. He even goes to see Cheryl's mom, traumatizing her into shock before gleefully escaping.

"The movie is 'found footage,' so I was constantly trying to make the most realistic, least clichéd choice," remembers Chbosky. "I loved the scene where I'm chained up and begging to see my mom. How often do you get to sob and howl until snot runs down your face? It's awfully good fun to play something so intense."

Even after locating the tapes, even after digging up Ed's victims in the backyard, even after learning of even more crime and horror from hundreds of hours of film, the cops manage to find Cheryl, still (barely) alive.

Hoping to spread the word far enough amongst the public to entice Ed to come forward, perhaps feeding his ego enough to *want* credit for his proud deeds, the filmmakers have Cheryl sit down for a chat. But the pains she's been inflicting upon herself since "freedom" still aren't her deepest wounds.

Stuck in the terrifying grip of Stockholm Syndrome, in which captives develop an unexpected connection to their captors, she can only gasp out a terrified belief that Ed still truly loves her and will return for her. And, more saddening than frightening, she wants him to.

"I played it as quiet as the sound guys would let me," Chbosky says of her favorite scene. "My inspiration was a little girl I used to babysit. We reunited after years apart, and she was so shy to see me that she spoke only in a whisper. I thought, that's what Cheryl should sound like. After eight years in a dark cellar, can you imagine the shell shock of normal life? Of a *television interview,* for God's sake? I love that scene. I love the cruelty of the reveal."

Perhaps Cheryl was right, although she'll never know. She's found dead by her own hand shortly thereafter, her last words a written love letter to Ed. But, now channeling the spirit of his namesake, serial killer–necrophiliac Ed Gein, Ed soon digs up her body.

Along with Ed, it's gone for good. We're left with the message that his deeds will be used for training in criminal psychology, and a warning that law enforcement will be watching closely anyone who dares to show the film: Ed's too full of himself not to want to see others' response to it. Like the *Witch*, the *Paranormal* activists, the *Cloverfield* monster, and so many others from the self-filmed area, he's not caught, not yet.

Chbosky played a car crash victim in her husband's 2010 demonic thriller *Devil*, and cleaned up the mess of new horror face Chromeskull in *Laid to Rest II*. Back in the self-filmed genre, she was trapped inside an apartment building with other folk—like Jennifer Carpenter's protagonist news reporter and Doug Jones' villainous mad scientist—in 2008's *Quarantine*, with Dowdle again behind the camera. As Elise, she's an early victim of the rabies-like virus that Jones's character is secretly pumping through the place from upstairs.

"I watched clips of dogs and even people who have rabies, and I spent a lot of time practicing drooling with these foamy seltzer tablets," Chbosky recalls of getting ready for the role. "To quote Gene Kelly, 'Dignity. Always, dignity.'"

As blood and sanity start to leave everyone's body at alarmingly equal high speed, no one's sure what to do, and soon murder's the only way out, as Elise finds herself brutalized with a TV camera.

"What a great death!" she says. "Getting beat to death with the camera in a found footage movie? That's just fantastic."

As of the end of 2013, a full six years after *Poughkeepsie Tapes*' release was limited to a few festivals, it still wasn't available commercially. Look for the film on YouTube if you haven't seen it, and spread the word to your fellow horror movie fans. If we can get loud enough to get the attention of certain studio higher-ups (the film is owned by MGM), maybe we can get it out to a greater audience.

Chbosky, Stacy. E-mail interview. Dec. 9, 2013.

•••••••••••••••••••••••••••••••••

Noell Coet: *Mischief Night*

Early in their careers, actors will probably spend a lot of time at high speed. That might mean dropping everything at a nanosecond's notice and roaring off to work with people you've never heard of. It's about grabbing what you can get when it's offered as often as possible, because it's not going to be there for long. Directors and producers, particularly those equally new to the business, have to answer to the people that put up some folding green for the film, the company that's going to release the flick, and others.

They're not going to wait for you to decide. Quite literally, it's now or never, because if you don't, they're going to keep calling around, and they *will* find someone to take your place.

"If you don't believe in yourself, why should someone else?" rhetorically ponders Noell Coet, who found herself in said predicament more than once during her teenage years. "If you don't work hard, 100,000 other people will."

Noell Coet portrayed a blind heroine in battle in *Mischief Night*.

Top billing in *Mischief Night* sounded pretty good to the young lady. "I really liked the idea of supporting the film, mostly, on my shoulders," she recalls. "When I read the script, I thought that it would challenge me as an actor and that excited me. I don't like doing roles that aren't challenging. What's the fun in that?"

To be honest, the character was not new to the thriller world. Emily was a young student that found herself alone one night, her lovesick widowed dad out looking for a new lady, and her "sort of" boyfriend not sure what he thought of her. Sounds like the perfect target for a group of sicko home invaders. It's Mischief Night, the evening before Halloween, and it's the time for tricks without treats. Only this time, as they often do in Hollywood, someone's taking the pranks a bit too far.

But that wouldn't be the actress' toughest challenge; she could have learned from years of previous horror flicks for that education. Noell would have to fight the battle that so many impromptu heroines have found themselves in the midst of through decades of horror, but she was facing an extra disadvantage none of them had suffered through: blindness.

Years before, seeing her mom die next to her in a car wreck forced Emily's brain to trick her eyes into not working any more.

"I went to the house we shot in and counted out how many steps I needed to take to get everywhere," she explains. "Ten steps to the bathroom, twelve steps, then turn right and take another seven steps to my bedroom. Emily had just moved into this house, so she was learning it just as I was. It was cool to have that experience with her outside of the scenes that we filmed. I also wore a blindfold at home to capture the way my body reacted to things differently when I couldn't see. I was covered in bruises by the end of the shoot!"

As the attackers closed in, Noell's work got tougher and tougher. She couldn't react to things happening right in front of her, even if it were wannabe killers just toying with her. She had to make Emily hysterically run and hide from them, even if Emily couldn't always know where she was or who was in the room with her. When the father's girlfriend stops by and becomes a victim, Emily couldn't tell she was alone with a corpse. When she yanks up a huge knife in self-defense and waves it, Noell couldn't be careful not to hurt anyone.

When Emily runs down a flight of stairs and then out the door and across a field, the hysterics that anyone would feel in such a situation were multiplied. Running in terror, not knowing what's in front of you, or even which way you're going, what you're going toward, and whether it might be just as deadly. The dirtbag after you might be a step behind. He might be way back at the start, mocking you. Emily couldn't know.

"We shot [the staircase] scene with a cameraman running backwards and me running toward him—*down* the stairs!" Noell says. "I had paced myself to coordinate my speed with the cameraman and to make sure I stayed in focus, not look down at the stairs, and be *running* for my *life*—and not trip! Before shooting *Mischief Night* I don't think I ever walked down a set of stairs *successfully* without looking down."

Noell advises those looking to take a similar journey to acting success, "Don't take yourself too seriously. If you take yourself too seriously, how are you supposed to believe that you're a warrior princess? Umm ... how awesome would *that* be?!?"

Coet, Noell. E-mail interview. Jan. 16, 2014.

∙∙∙∙∙∙∙∙∙∙∙∙∙∙∙∙∙∙∙∙∙∙∙∙∙∙∙∙

Lora Cunningham: *The Book of Eli*

Education is one of the keys to making it in the acting world. Acting classes, coaches, workshops—it's all there for the learning and networking. It's what we do with it that makes all the difference.

Watching her workshop teacher in action, Lora Cunningham suddenly got the message.

Jo Edna Boldin, who helped cast *No Country for Old Men, Office Space,* et al., looked across her students. "You are enough," she said. In the audience, Cunningham felt something new for herself, and her acting career. "From that moment, my life and, as a result, my work changed," she remembers. "'You are enough.' That's what I would tell anyone in any industry. It applies to us all."

When Boldin helped her land a role in 2010's futuristic apocalyptic soothsaying *The Book of Eli,* Cunningham went to put the words to work in the story of a man out to protect the last surviving Big Book on the ravaged planet. Playing a hijacker who tries to lure Denzel Washington's title character into helping her (he realizes it's a trap), Cunningham had a lot to do, with only a few scenes to do it. She straddles the line between good and evil: Her character is forced to do the jobs by several other men. When Eli's impromptu partner Solara (Mila Kunis) arrives, Cunningham's character tries to get her away at high speed. She looked for a way to make a horrific act understandable.

"I wanted her to get the hell out of there because she was younger and prettier," Cunningham says. "If the hijackers had her, they wouldn't need me! It was a choice of survival, not pity. Of course, I didn't want to see her brutalized, but I had to save myself by saving her. I enjoyed the fact that it would appear I was being compassionate when, in fact, I was being selfish.

"The desperation of this woman is what got me," she says. "How bad did things have to be in order to do what she did? What horrors did she endure from these brutal men day in and day out? How far will/would she go just to survive? What joy did she have in life? Did she come to like the hunt and the trickery? Did the taste of the flesh become a delicacy, at some point? All of these questions intrigued and excited me!"

Armed with a script and two small but important facts, Cunningham headed for her audition. All she knew was that her character (a) shook during her conversations with Eli, and (b) ate people.

"Thus, I delved into researching cannibalism and the shakes," she explains. "I found there is a degenerative neurological disorder called Kuru that cannibals can develop if they eat less than fresh dead flesh, especially the brain matter. It's also known as 'the shiver' because those infected are ailed by loss of control of limbs, headaches and ultimately the inability to swallow, causing them to ironically die of starvation!" Many people who get the disorder don't survive over a year.

"I had decided that, since my character was written to have the shakes, she was pretty far along in the stages of the disease," Cunningham says. "Thus, she'd be shaking, losing use of her legs and … well … a bit crazy, by the time Eli crossed her path."

Throughout his film career, legendary film producer Samuel Goldwyn used the English language as his personal punching bag ("Include me out," "A verbal contract isn't worth the paper it's written on," and "Listen to me slowly" are just a few gems). But once in a while he came up with words to live by, not only to laugh at. One of his beliefs was, "The harder I work, the luckier I get." It's become another of Cunningham's mantras.

"The big break can come at any time," she says, "so be prepared by studying and developing your talent and yourself. I believe you are in work as you are in life. Come from your truth. Be authentic. Believe that you are enough!"

Cunningham, Lora. E-mail interview. Oct. 1, 2010.

....

Fiona Dourif: *Curse of Chucky*

Englund. Langenkamp. Craven. Hodder. Hitchcock.

These are last names we horror fans can automatically tie to our favorite genre. It may not be the only thing these performers or directors have ever done (or even the best, particularly in Hitchcock's case), but there's a groundwork laid for their names and the series they proudly represent.

For fans of a certain series, the name by Dourif. But an extension on that moniker arrived in 2013.

For the first five *Child's Play* flicks, the only regular was Brad Dourif, who undoubtedly had one of the quicker jobs in horror cinema history. As the series began in 1988, he actually had to step in front of a camera and play Charles Lee Ray, a serial killer. A voodoo guru

After her dad Brad voiced Chucky (right) through the first few *Child's Play* films, Fiona Dourif (left) carried on the family tradition in 2013's *Curse of Chucky*.

transplants his evil soul into an ironically entitled "Good Guy" doll, soon to carry on his work and name as the former plaything known as … Chucky.

Through that film and most of the next four sequels, animation and robots took over for the doll. Searching for a new human to re-enter Ray's eternal soul—preferably a youngster, which would provide more life time to do his bloody work—Dourif voiced Chucky as he killed and died over and over.

With *Bride of Chucky* (1998), things started to get a bit farfetched, even for a horror series about a killer doll. Impressing and depressing male fans across the world, Chucky managed to land Ray's gorgeous ex Tiffany (Jennifer Tilly), only to have her transfer into a doll. Not only that, but the two dolls would have an offspring who got his own film six years later in *Seed of Chucky*.

The *Child's Play* people brought their man-doll back in 2013, reverting to the same ideas that had made Chucky so scary to begin with. Dourif was back, and we'd again both see and hear him this time. But there would be a new reason to remember the name after *Curse of Chucky*.

His daughter Fiona had taken her first acting career steps with a small role in HBO's series *Deadwood* in 2005. She'd played in other small shows and films, such as a horseback rider paralyzed in a fall in the 2010 TV flick *After the Fall*. On HBO the next year, Fiona helped them find out, as she broke into horror of a different kind in *True Blood*, playing a Wicca woman who helps her coven fight the series' regulars, the fanged ones.

"I'm not sure even the writers knew what the small characters were going to turn into when I auditioned," she recalls. "There was very little on the page. There was only one scene written but it was clear that the character was going to reoccur in several episodes. The casting process was a whirlwind: I was probably in the room for three or four minutes and got the call that I got it a couple hours later." Her Casey helped resurrect coven leader Marnie, who'd end up killing Casey a few episodes later.

"My mother, when I was a kid, was into magic, and kind of considered herself a 'white witch.' The mindset of believing in magic was something I had been brought up with and understood, so when I was preparing, I was just thinking about that, and how fun it would be if I were that person. I just prepared the fantasy.

"Acting and auditioning for television is a little different than working in film. In television, you tend to have to be more precise with language and actions. It's a moving machine and it needs to move quickly. In a film, particularly if you're the lead, there is usually a little more room to collaborate and change a scene on the spot. Things can kind of happen a little more organically."

One day, she opened up a new script. A new *Chucky* chapter was being made, and she was getting a chance to be a part of it. "It said I could audition for any part in the movie," Fiona recalls. "When you are not a name, like I'm not, you just audition for stuff, and you give your version of it. I found something in Nica I thought I could do."

In *Curse,* Chucky is mailed to the home of a lady named Sarah and her daughter Nica, who's unaware that her mom was responsible for Ray getting caught a quarter-century ago. The next day, Nica's sister Barb and her husband arrive, along with their daughter and nanny Alice. As usual for horror films, Alice is quite gifted in the looks department. Originally, Fiona had tried out for the part of Barb.

"The casting director liked my audition but thought I would be better for Nica," she remembers, "I auditioned three times. I really, really wanted it. I felt like I could do it with my eyes closed, because I sort of instinctually got the family dynamic stuff. Plus my personal family connection to the franchise was too cool to even think about."

Nica was an ordinary, bright young beauty except for one thing: She was a paraplegic. Fortunately, Fiona had been there before, and could look back to *After the Fall*.

"When I first prepared *After the Fall*, I went to a hospital and wheeled around," she says. "I spent a day with people who were paraplegic; I went to a mall in a wheelchair. I'm kind of great in a wheelchair now, I can do tricks and stuff. But the fact that Nica was a paraplegic was intentionally treated as an afterthought. It was another thing she had to overcome but it didn't define her. She was just someone trying to navigate her complicated family, and who can't relate to that?"

Chucky exacts Ray's vengeance early on: After disposing of Sarah, he poisons a visiting priest. Then Chucky goes for the most vulnerable, looking for Nica's niece's favor. But by now, Nica's getting suspicious, perusing the web for what exactly this weird-looking thing is.

As she finds the link between the doll and his master, Chucky fries the nanny (the *sister's* secret lover, quite deviant from the norm with this), then uses a knife to make Nica an only child. With her built-in elevator busted, Nica's forced to battle him without her legs.

"For much of the emotional work, I was lucky," Fiona recalls. "Sometimes you get cast in roles that you just *get*, and I *got* this one. I've always fancied myself as something of a caretaker for my family, whether or not that is actually true, and that's kind of what Nica was too."

Even pretending to be in a life-or-gory-death situation sent her pedal to the floor, she says.

"Some of the climactic stuff was tough to do, because the adrenaline had to be so high for so long. It got hard to sustain for two weeks. but it was still fun and I like the way it turned out."

With her brother-in-law also dead, it's down to Nica and the doll—and the lines between the film and reality get a bit blurry, for those in the know. Flashbacks tell us that Nica's mom was Ray's love, until her "betrayal" caused an attack that left her unborn baby half-paralyzed. Now he's left just to kill the daughter he wishes he might have fathered.

The two Dourifs were never on the screen together. "We've never done a scene," Fiona says. "I acted opposite his voice."

Though she'd grown up around the real Ray, Dourif got even more assistance on set from one of the franchise's main men. "I had long conversations with Don Mancini," she says of the creator of the series; Mancini wrote all the films and directed both *Seed* and *Curse*. "He's a really good director and fantastic writer. Every actress says that about their director, but in this case, I swear it's totally true."

Before Fiona can dispatch Chucky, a cop arrives. Surrounded by bodies and holding a knife, Nica's going to get the blame before the doll does. She's convicted and sent off to an asylum. But Chucky might have one more surprise waiting for him … as those who sat through the credits know.

"I was really scared the first time I saw a finished cut," Fiona recalls. "I was terrified that I would be bad in something so connected to my family, but I was proud. The coolest thing that can happen when you're making a movie is that you really connect with the director and love the script. Whether it's a fun horror movie or an art-house thing, it's awesome when you get to make something you really really like.

"If you look at the scripts for *Child's Play*, even when you go to the less well-received comedic ones, they are all just pretty smart and well done," she says. "The movies seem to be constantly reinventing themselves and that's pretty cool. [Mancini] originally wrote them as a response to advertising for children, and how malicious it can be. Something about that—or maybe how creepy and almost human Chucky looks—must have struck a chord because Chucky is in the zeitgeist and I don't think he's going anywhere. Plus, he's just such a fun asshole!"

Dourif, Fiona. Phone interview. Dec. 1, 2013.

•••••••••••••••••••••••••••••

They Came from *Elm Street*!

Heather Langenkamp might have ended up being the female face of the *A Nightmare on Elm Street* franchise, but hers wasn't the first one we series fans saw: Early on, Freddy's on someone else's trail until she ... wait for it ... *has sex!* That stuff always gets you killed in a horror movie...

With the help of some then-innovative special effects and an actress who wasn't looking to take any prisoners, Freddy made one of the most legendary debuting murders in horror history.

The frightful side of acting was nothing new to Amanda Wyss; one of her first roles was a stage adaptation of *The Bad Seed*, the terrifying tale of a young girl who takes down all those in her way (it's been adapted and copied to high heaven, like in 2009's *Orphan*), and starred in the 1981 TV movie *The House Possessed*, a pretty self-explanatory title.

For *Nightmare*, she became Tina, a young woman searching for love, between getting chased through her nightmares by Freddy (actually, he was labeled just "Fred" until the first sequel). Rather than Langenkamp's Nancy, Tina's the female focal point for the first chunk of the film.

Hey—a gorgeous blonde who suddenly gets bloodily slashed to death by a nutcase, and sets the film on its ear?! Haven't seen it since ... *Psycho!* Like Janet Leigh's Marion Crane, Wyss's death would become a landmark moment in fear.

Alone with a caring guy for one of the first times, Tina's search might have come to an end.

That is, if something else hadn't found her.

Suddenly whipped toward the ceiling by an invisible force, she's thrown from wall to wall like a human ping-pong ball. Her nightgown rips open, and slashes appear on her chest. By the time it's over, the audience had a taste of just what the new guy in Horrorland can do. It transforms Freddy's evil from realistic malice to supernaturally terrifying.

"Tina is a full and complex character and she was very challenging to play," Wyss says. "I prepared for my role by really sinking into every detail about her in the script and just letting her come alive within me."

The room, constructed "on a device like a rotisserie," she says, was formed in a huge sound stage, with everything bolted, glued, or otherwise fastened to the floor, construction

The death of Tina (Amanda Wyss) put Freddy Krueger and *A Nightmare on Elm Street* at the center of the horror genre.

taking up a full month. With the cameraman belted into a nearby chair, Wyss was hurled around the floor.

"I knew once we got to a certain point, once there was blood happening, I felt a lot of pressure to really bring it, to really bring the truth of somebody's death rattle, their last-ditch effort, that fight for survival with everything in you."

The spinning room, turned by crew members by hand, gave her vertigo to the extreme. "I think sometimes I would get myself so into that space that I was jacked up with the adrenalin rush that it would take a long time to calm down. I got the shakes. It took a long time to come back down into my body."

Back in school the day after her girlfriend is murdered, Nancy tries to get her mind back to academia. This footage was filmed at Los Angeles' John Marshall High School, where the kids of *Grease* and *Pretty in Pink* acted out their stories, and Leonardo Di Caprio snared his diploma.

Noticing Tina's body next to her in class, she stumbles out into the hallway. Following the trail of blood around the corner, Nancy barrels into a hall monitor, clad in an ominously colored sweater.

"Where's your pass?" the woman snidely snipes.

"Screw your pass!" Nancy fires back (yeah, fight the establishment, girlfriend!).

She steps away, but a new voice interrupts her.

"No running in the hallways!" gloats the woman, her voice (and Vincent Price-esque giggle) suddenly twenty feet deeper—an unfortunately familiar glove on her hand. Leslie Hoffman gave us the first glance at Freddy's shape- and sex-shifting powers.

"I have been told by fans that this one scene really un-nerves them to see me 'talking,' yet Freddy Krueger's voice is coming out of my mouth," Hoffman says. "I actually said that line and then later, in post-production, Robert Englund dubbed in his voice. It was so much fun to wear the glove."

She'd go on into stunt work for the next few decades, stepping in for physical work in *Christmas Vacation*, *Naked Gun*, and *Scream 2*. "It has always been exciting for me to see me on film," she says. "My heart starts racing. It makes me smile. Who would have thought that a girl from Saranac Lake, New York, a town of 5,000, would become a stuntwoman in Hollywood?"

Things went another way as Freddy got *Revenge* in the second film, mainly because a male became his target. Here Freddy focused on his own gender in the form of an introverted nerd named Jesse, whose gender-neutral name would come to mean a great deal.

One week after snaring the role Jesse (beating out Brad Pitt and Matt Damon in the process), Mark Patton had to step into a new world of dreams. With little time to get ready, he and a friend sat alone in a theater, watching Freddy do his bloody work.

"I went, 'My God, this is gonna be me in just a little bit of time,'" Patton says. "I started shooting the next week." Like many horror leads, Jesse's friendly but quiet, not saying much around others unless asked, particularly by bombshell babes like his girl Lisa (Kim Myers). Patton based part of the character on Ally Sheedy's deviant *Breakfast Club* character. And, like Englund, Patton had to endure the trauma of a body cast. "When they build your body cast, they bury you," Patton recalls. "They put the straw in your nostrils and you're covered completely in plastic, and they make that mold ... you're covered in fake blood, which smells horrible, and then you gotta get cleaned up and do it again."

The film suggested an undertone of homosexuality, starting with the protagonist's gender-neutral name. Jesse's rarely fully clothed. He and a tormentor have a sweaty wrestling match. His coach, clad in leather, basically hits on him in a gay bar, then gets killed by Freddy, including a bare-ass spanking. Freddy emerges from Jesse's stomach in the same forced-birth technique that made the *Alien* films legendary.

For most sex criminals (like Freddy was in life), the sex isn't about the sex, but about the power over others, which is what Freddy displays over Jesse until Lisa knocks him off his self-created mental pedestal with a kiss. "Lisa's been trying to help Jessie, not sure if this is fantasy or reality, and getting to the point at the end where she's terrified," Myers says, "but she kicks ass, and she does so by facing Freddy and not backing down."

How many people can say they went one on one with Freddy Krueger—twice even!—and lived to tell about it? At least one woman (well, aside from Langenkamp!) can.

Her name: Alice.

The setting: A church.

The place: the last scene of *A Nightmare on Elm Street 4: The Dream Master*.

The actress behind the character: Lisa Wilcox.

"Truly, the part of Alice really, really spoke to me," said Wilcox, who became Lisa Wilcox Sherman in real life shortly after starting her horror hellcat career. "Some roles just speak to actresses—it's like it's you. Alice was me in fourth, fifth, sixth grade. I was very shy. I had very few friends. I lived in my books and daydreams." Fortunately, Freddy had the common courtesy not to torment her dreams until she stepped into his world over a decade later!

Throughout Freddy's first few years, Wilcox watched him step from fantasy to reality

Freddy (Robert Englund) lost to Alice (Lisa Wilcox) in two *A Nightmare on Elm Street* films.

in the first three *Nightmare* films. "I always liked to be scared," Wilcox said. "I think Freddy's character stands out because he's considered something horrifying in real life—a child molester. There's a background for him. The films are fairly intellectual. They're clever. It's not just him going around killing people; he kills people that have certain fears, and gets them on those fears." Perhaps never more so (at least, to that point) than in 1988's *Dream Master*.

Early in 1988, Wilcox had just procured a degree in theater from UCLA and was looking to make a move from the local stage to the big screen. One day, her manager told her that the *Nightmare* creators wanted to add another chapter to the Krueger story (she'd been a fan of the first few films). Alice Johnson would be the innocent, virginal vixen who, driven by fear and the need to survive, eventually evolves into a supreme fighting machine that not even the undead can stop.

There were just a few things standing in her way. The first was a group of over six hundred other actresses who wanted to be the next Alice. The second was, she was just too easy on the eyes.

"My manager said, 'They won't see you,'" she recalled. "I asked why, and [I was told], 'Because you look like a cheerleader, and Alice is definitely not the cheerleader type.'"

About a month later, the moviemakers were again looking for an Alice, checking back over the people they'd cold-shouldered before.

This time, Wilcox was ready to look her worst. "I went in with no makeup and dirty hair, wearing yellow, my worst color," she said of the audition.

One callback later—on Friday the 13th of April—she sat down with soon-to-be-director Renny Harlin and discussed Alice. But there was just one tiny little problem: Wilcox had already scheduled something else that would be tough to postpone—her wedding.

After taking on the Sherman surname that weekend, Wilcox and her husband went honeymooning in Hawaii. Then her manager called to say she'd gotten the part. The bad news was, the cameras needed to get rolling—and her honeymoon got second priority. Back on the mainland on April 27, Wilcox celebrated her 24th birthday by transforming into a 16-year-old character.

"Playing the part of Alice, I had to go back to the early part in my life. Alice had many, many elements of who I am … I was totally a wallflower in high school, so there was a lot of myself in the character of Alice. There's a lot of Lisa on that screen.

"Alice just needed to get out of her daydreams and live life. Alice daydreamed, she stayed behind the cash register, hid behind her brother, hid behind her best friend. She was shy, even though she had all these capabilities within her. Many of us have times in our lives when we don't believe we possess any kind of power, but with the encouragement of her friends, Alice got her game on."

As she plied her trade at a nearby diner (the Crave Inn, a wink-wink, nudge-nudge to a certain series creator), Alice stood helplessly by while her friends lost their fight to live. Alice's martial artist brother Rick was killed in an explosion. The class brain suffered a fatal mid-class asthma attack. All Freddy's doing, of course.

But not necessarily all in his form. As one of Alice's friends relaxes across his waterbed, he feels something pounding up from beneath. Yanking back the cover, he sees something that rarely happens even in the movies: It's a beautiful lady who decided to go skinny-dipping at this exact location and moment. Bearing a strange resemblance to a pinup on his wall, the seductress baits him towards her.

"I am a Pisces, so the water is where I'm most comfortable," says waterbed beauty

Hope Marie Carlton's waterbed beauty put a temporarily gorgeous face on evil in *A Nightmare on Elm Street: Dream Master*.

Hope Marie Carlton. "I also have always been my own stuntwoman! And the other requirement was you had to be a pinup girl to boot, so that's how I got the part." She's not only a licensed scuba diver, but a former Hollywood Stuntmen's Association member. She was also *Playboy*'s Miss July 1985.

"The preparation was fairly simple," Carlton recalls. "I just went to a pool and practiced holding my breath while floating upward, so that once we were shooting in the tank I was able to do lengthy takes. There was an air tube and a diver in the tank with me if I needed it or him for emergency, but didn't end up utilizing either."

Of course it's too good to be true for the kid: the saber-fingered fiend, through with his alter ego, comes up from under the bed and drags the kid down with him for the last time.

"Talk about a wet dream!" he snarls, just one more of a novel's worth of Krueger one-liners.

"I thought it was awesome to be turned into Freddy Kruger!" Carlton says. "Although I'm not a fright film kind of girl, I do like being in the scary movies. There is something fun about being a villainess!" She'd find herself on the other side of fear a few years later, dying with her husband and son in a getaway car escape in the opening moments of the marathon TV adaptation of Stephen King's *The Stand*.

During her far-beyond-reluctant journey, strange things started to happen within for Alice. She picked up a cigarette, only to remember that she didn't smoke. Awkwardly holding a pair of nunchucks, she suddenly started whipping them around like a 20th-degree black belt. Her attitude became tougher, more assertive—enough, even, to land resident school hottie Dan, who'd get closer to her as the series went on.

Freddy may have stolen her friends' souls, but their talents had taken up residence in Alice's wonderland—all gifted from Kristin, who suffered her own painful demise courtesy of Freddy.

During filming, Wilcox said, "I marked scenes—at this point, she's died, he's died. I needed to know each scene, what powers I needed to be showing. Taking on the personalities of everybody required studying the actors, and them doing their parts, because I really wanted to absorb them, as my character does, and be true to what they'd given me."

As her friends continue to fall, Alice can see more of herself; where her bedroom mirror was once decorated with them, photo after photo is removed as they pass away.

"My character is starting to reveal itself in that mirror," Wilcox says, "and looking in that mirror, taking the pictures down, something is changing. I'm getting stronger, and looking into that mirror is very symbolic. It conveys the story of Alice finding her power."

That power's handed out by her friend Kristin—Tuesday Knight, an automatic contender in the "Best Name in Hollywood" sweepstakes—just before she loses a fight with Freddy, and it's time for the final showdown. (Nostalgic *Nightmare* fans would get a special gift when Knight cameoed with Langenkamp in a funeral scene in 1994's *New Nightmare*.)

"What made Alice remarkable," Wilcox says, "is that audiences watch Alice become stronger and stronger as the movie plays along, and you can't help but be a part of her journey because she's so relatable."

It was just Alice and Freddy in a place of worship. Spinning into action, Alice back-flipped her way to the front as her nemesis strolled forward in the ever-confident way that made him so horrifying.

"They'd sent me off to martial arts school for a day so I'd be able to handle the nunchucks," Wilcox said. "I'd had some gymnastics experience to at least start some of the moves. I did the cartwheels, and we had some stunt girls who did the flipping." Some had been Olympic gymnasts.

The same thing applied to Alice's machine-gun punch-kick routine that left Freddy cracking up (after all, as he so ominously put it, "I ... am ... eternal!"). "I'd be on the set," Wilcox said, "and there would be four people dressed like me, with the shirts, the jeans, the hair, with a wig."

But when she flashed a mirror in Freddy's face, invoking the old line about evil dying after seeing itself, Freddy's stolen cargo ripped its way out of his body, and he went down.

After watching it on film, Wilcox said, "I was like 'Wow!' There was blue-screen stuff. It took a lot of imagination to picture what's on the blue screen and what I'm looking at, and wanting to believe what I'm looking at. It's important to keep that childhood imagination alive." *Dream Master* was the most popular of the first seven *Nightmare* films, grossing $49 million, higher than all but three other horror films in the entire 1980s.

A year after *Master*, Wilcox (who finished her honeymoon after the film wrapped) was back in the ring to take another swing, at Freddy in *The Dream Child*. He couldn't get to Alice or her friends, so he'd get to her through her newfound passenger.

"Once a character has developed for myself, it's always there," Wilcox said. "It's like a memory, but it's stronger than that. When you manifest a character, it gets into your skin and your blood, and you're able to bring it back. The part of Alice was very innate to my own life, so it was a graduation for Alice. She had her strength now, standing up for herself and her baby, against [Dan's] parents." After Dan becomes Freddy's next victim—dressed up in the disguise of a car accident—Alice is off to war once again (his parents try to take the baby away).

"I had not had a child at this time in my life," said Wilcox, who'd eventually have a few, "so I definitely had to do some exploration within myself. I had to imagine what it would be like to have a life growing inside me and make that feeling a reality."

It probably didn't help to go through so many dream sequences of being waited on by psycho doctors and a nurse who had an Adam's apple, showing that she was Freddy in drag.

"Being on a gurney and scooting through the hallways, in an abandoned veteran's hospital near UCLA, and seeing the texture of the halls and the lights was funky," Wilcox remembers. "In [*Dream Master*], there were many scenes that were brightly lit, such as a scene at the beach and other scenes outside. [*Dream Child*] was a much, much darker film, dealing with topics that were popular socially, like abortion and single motherhood. [*Child*] took on some pretty serious topics for teens."

It told the story of Amanda Krueger, Freddy's mother, who was raped after being locked in a mental ward. For one scene, Alice becomes Amanda, experiencing for herself the horror of society's worst crime. "I was playing a nun in a room full of crazy maniacs, a person surrounded by a hundred men who are all sweating and wearing no clothes and looking at you like an animal," she said. "That was pretty wild. To imagine being in that room in real life was pretty terrifying."

One particular inmate got an unusual amount of screen time—and sharp-eyed viewers noticed that he was none other than Robert Englund himself. In other words, Freddy without makeup, and presumably Freddy's pappy in story talk.

As more and more of her friends perish, Alice starts to realize that Freddy's reaching through the dreams of her unborn young one. Eventually, she meets a young boy named Jacob, who's more into this than anyone realizes. Finally, back in the asylum basement, she and Jacob realize the true meaning of the relationship between Alice, Jacob, and Freddy. It's at this moment that Alice truly reaches heroine mode, more so than ever before in the films. She's forced to fight an enemy on the inside and the outside.

"All right, Kruger," she declares. "This time it's for keeps!"

Alice tries to rip Freddy's power from herself, in every sense of the word. He takes over her face, and eventually her entire body, before Jacob saves her.

"I wore Freddy makeup for one whole day," Wilcox says, (Puppets were used for part of the scene, the same tools that would reappear in *New Nightmare*.) "That was pretty freaky. You don't want to be looking in the mirror too much! Eating was bizarre that day."

It was her farewell to Freddy; Lisa Zane was the heroine in 1991's *Freddy's Dead*.

"They completely changed course and went on a new storyline and everything, which I understand, because they gave Alice two full movies," Wilcox said. "I had no idea when I started the project, that it would be part of history in a way. The series has done so well. We all like to root for the underdog, and Alice was really an underdog that we could relate to. The script, the movie, and hopefully the performance, touched a lot of people." Eventually, Alice learned that Jacob was the son she so desperately wanted to save, and Jacob realized that Freddy wasn't his friend after all.

After starring in Englund's *976-Evil* and on an episode of *Freddy's Nightmares*, Lezlie Dean (Englund called her work in *Evil* "evocative of Jodie Foster") finally got a chance to go one on one with the king of bad dreams in *Freddy's Dead*, playing Tracy, a shelter escapee who gets caught up in the black magic with her friends. (Johnny Depp, never shy about self-deprecation, has a hilarious cameo as a guy kayoed by Freddy doing a "This is your brain on drugs" commercial parody.)

"I was determined to work with Robert again!" exclaims Dean, who'd tried out for roles in *Dream Warriors* and *Dream Master*. "He must have thought I was a stalker. Tracy is a survivor in so many ways, and I wanted to play that."

Tracy's friends relied on the tough lady to get and keep them out of trouble throughout, as she coldcocks a few fellows and beats up Krueger himself near the end. It was something she'd shown from the moment she'd gone for the role. "I went in and had to do a fight sequence with the guy named Roger," she recalls of her tryout, "and I really fought him. I think it really freaked him out, and [director Rachel Talalay] liked that.

"I was privileged to be given martial arts lessons by the studio," she says. "That was a blast, and also the hardest scenes to do as well [she learned how to use chains in battle]. I had a 13-hour day of just kickboxing: very grueling, but very fun!

"I was about ninety-eight percent of [Tracy]," she says. "I'm always the badass with a heart of gold."

Of course, in one scene, things got a bit too close to reality when Englund accidentally backhanded her. "I drove to the hospital, got stitches, and got a tetanus shot," Dean says. "I have a scar, and I get to look at it every day and be reminded of Robert Englund."

Midway through the film, we see the source of the fear and anger that ruled and almost ruined Tracy's life: Her father, whom she meets (and whomps) in a dream sequence, did things to her that many feel should warrant a trip to the electric chair. Dean couldn't help but wonder why the scene seemed so simple.

Lezlie Deane turned Tracy into one of Freddy's toughest opponents in *Freddy's Dead*.

"Thought to myself, 'God, this scene's coming really easy to me,'" she says. "I didn't even have to go prepare for it." Soon after, however, something strange started to happen. "Months later," Dean says, "I started getting flashbacks of being molested. It was weird having to pull that scarf back. It took me on a journey of dealing with my life and my own fears." As it turned out, she actually had been violated in her younger years, by a caregiver.

"I can really connect with being a survivor," she says. "Horror appeals to me because it makes you face your fears."

Carlton, Hope Marie. E-mail interview. May 17, 2011.
Dean, Lezlie. E-mail interview. April 25, 2010.
Farrands, Daniel, & Andrew Kasch. *Never Sleep Again: The Elm Street Legacy* [DVD]. 1428 Films, 2010.
Hoffman, Leslie. E-mail interview. May 9, 2013.
Jar385. "Horror on the Boulevard 2012: Tim Interviews Kim Myers and Mark Patton." *Youtube*. March 1, 2013. Retrieved July 25, 2013, from http://www.youtube.com/watch?v=d1blzro4R-0.
Wilcox, Lisa. Phone interview. March 7, 2009.
Wooley, John. *Wes Craven: The Man and His Nightmares*. Hoboken, NJ: John Wiley & Sons, 2011.
Wyss, Amanda. E-mail interviews. April 8, 11, 2010.

•••••••••••••••••••••••••••

Katie Featherston: *Paranormal Activity*

Perusing the Internet, a few hundred young actors noticed an ad that looked as ominous as the premise of the film it was promoting.

There was no script, just a few directions. Filming would only take a week or so, but it was a non-stop, all-hours-of-the-day-and-night workathon. Two people alone would have to fill up nearly two hours' worth of screen time; a third of the $11,000 production budget went to editing so there wouldn't be much for special effects, or anything else. It would all be up to the actors, themselves paid about $500 each.

But the end product would be the equivalent of winning the film lottery.

One 2006 day, video game programmer Oren Peli announced he was putting together his first feature film *Paranormal Activity* would be a self-created "documentary," the story of a young couple stalked by a demonic presence in their home. Like the *Blair Witch Project* title character, the entity would never be seen by the audience.

Like many budding actors, Katie Featherston and Micah Sloat were hard at work, trying to find that big break that would push them into stardom. Between auditions, she was waiting tables, and he was programming computers.

At the *Activity* audition, surrounded by hundreds of others looking for a shot at prominence, the pair was asked to improvise in a fantastic situation. How could someone even imagine the situation of being terrorized by an evil with no name, no face, no motive, nothing?

"I went in, sat down, and Oren said, 'Why do you think your house is haunted?'" says Featherston. "There was no 'Hey, how are you? Can I have your head shot?' So I just started talking. I went with it. And that's kind of how the whole process was."

Featherston and Sloat made the impossible plausible, and won their parts. After meeting at the callback, the two wowed Peli with an impromptu tale of the beginning of their characters' relationship.

"There were no scripts," recalls Sloat. "We shot at all hours of the night, without sleeping, not even knowing really what was going to happen next.... We had to do a lot of quick thinking on our feet." In October 2006, at Peli's San Diego home, they got to work.

"It was seven days, around the clock," Featherston says, "not only because we had a lot to do in a short amount of time, but because we were all focused and determined to get

Katie Featherston became a demon's transporter in five *Paranormal Activity* films, her first victim being her on-screen husband Micah.

the best quality and the best product that we could while we were there.... We had to create this buildup of dread that would speak to people. It was the best environment you can ask for as an actor."

Without much direction, it was up to the two performers to develop their characters and characteristics alone. The film starts out innocently enough: A man and lady have been experiencing weird phenomena throughout their home, with pictures falling off walls, strange night noises, etc.—and try to find the truth by creating their own surveillance system (Sloat filmed a good part of the film himself). It becomes clear that this is no mischievous poltergeist.

"The truth is, it wasn't hard to get into that frightening zone because that's all there was," says Featherston. "There were no outside influences, no trailers to go to, no craft services. There were no crew members or people on the phone, just the three of us in this house [she, Sloat, and Peli], filming this movie. So the atmosphere and the tension were kept up for the majority of the week, mostly because we were just continually filming."

As the flick progresses, Katie's character recalls that things like this have happened to her before, and that she's the prey of a hunter not of this dimension. Katie's being taken over, physically and mentally by this thing, and Micah can't figure out what to do. Perhaps he's in denial, or too scared to do anything. Either way, things are heading toward a tragic conclusion.

What that finale would be, however, was a mystery even to the cast. Micah wasn't getting out no matter what—every climax had him meeting a violent end. It was Katie's fate that was in doubt. One ending had the possessed woman killing Micah, then regaining her facilities but being shot dead by police officers. Another conclusion was her kneeling before the camera, then committing suicide.

"We scared ourselves because that was where we needed to be, but it was an exhilarating kind of fear," says Featherston, who found herself repeatedly yanked from the bed, using a harness, rope, and some editing. "We knew the structure after a while. We knew what would happen, and we all got pretty good at figuring out what to say.... There were specific things we needed to hit in each scene. The movie suggests things; it's your mind and your imagination that take it to the next level.

"At the end of the shoot, I was definitely getting a little bit loopy from the lack of sleep," Sloat recalls. "But it fed into the performances.... I've always been fascinated by the occult and the paranormal, by ghosts and demons and UFOs—anything that all the hardcore horror fans are into as well. As far as this movie goes, I think it unconsciously intensified all of my experiences. For example, we were playing around with a Ouija board..., and normally, when I did that as a child, it was always fun. But this time it was a little scary. I have to attribute that to the experience of making the movie."

Even after filming, the performers, cast, and crew had to wait for years, hoping that someone could be talked into backing and distributing the film. The film was acclaimed at festivals over the next two years, but no one made an offer. Eventually DreamWorks (then part of Paramount) reached an agreement with Peli, but it appeared that the film would be remade by others, not released.

Then one of the most recognizable names in film history got behind it: Steven Spielberg. The legendary director got his hands on a copy of the film and checked it out. Unfortunately, even the director of *Jaws* couldn't get through it in a single night.

"It just killed my marrow—it was too real to watch in the dark," Spielberg recalls. "The next morning, in broad daylight, I watched the whole picture and it still scared me beyond measure."

There was one thing he didn't like—the ending. Paramount handed Peli a few extra grand, and he put together the final piece, which Spielberg helped create.

DreamWorks and Paramount ended their relationship in September 2008. Fortunately, those at Paramount decided to release the film in its original form—but not widely. No one was convinced that a first-time director and a pair of unknowns were guarantees for box-office success. The flick was released in just thirteen theaters, mostly near colleges, with the promise that a million visits to the film's Internet site would get it out across the country.

In less than a week, the seven-figure mark was well in the past. In its opening run alone, the film brought in over $77,000, already ensuring that someone was going to make some serious green. A month later, it was the nation's top box-office hit. Before it was through, *Paranormal* had rushed past the $100 million mark.

Featherston and Sloat were on the cover on *Entertainment Weekly* and on talk shows across the country. The film's poster of the pair lying in bed together (but not alone!) became one of the most recognized in the country.

"There are a lot of scary movies out there that throw it all out at you," Featherston says, "and they definitely have a lot of blood and gore, and there's definitely a place for those. But [the *Paranormal Activity* films] really get under your skin and the scares stick with you and tap into your imagination, and I think people really respond to that. I think the idea of something happening in your own home is really relatable. Everybody has to go home when the movie's over, so it adds an extra level of fear."

People came up to them in public, shocked that the two were still alive—alive enough to do some sequels a few years later! Part two showed Katie prequelly inheriting the demonic genetics from her sister, whom she and the demon would eventually kill; part three went farther back in time, telling the story of Katie and her sister's childhood, raised by a family with an affinity for "outside forces."

The fourth film came back to the present, told from the perspective of Katie's new next-door neighbors and, not surprisingly, future victims. After doing little more than step in and out for the second and third films, Featherston had a larger role in part four, playing the "mother" to her kidnapped nephew as their new neighbors taped their terrifiers. She ends up leading an army of afflicted against the trespassers—and as usual, the good guys and girls all end up dead.

"I think as the sequels progress," Featherston says, "the worlds have gotten bigger and the story becomes more specific in some way so the story has to be a bit more structured, but it's still really improvisational. It's like if somebody has a thought or concern on set, everyone's always very good with saying, 'Oh, this is good, let's try it.' It's how we started and I think it serves the story to continue with that."

With just about every box-office smash, someone eventually goes for a one-off. That's a small, usually less expensive, oftentimes nearly identical film that shows up on video store shelves about a year later. Films such as *Transformers, Independence Day,* and others have inspired them.

Ever since *Blair Witch Project* revolutionized the horror film industry with the "filmed by the performers" aspect, other such flicks have been popping up regularly.

And when someone put such a story in a house, spent a week and chump change to film it, and ended up making over $100 million at the box office … well, it wouldn't be long before someone else tried to get a piece of that action.

Enter *Paranormal Entity*.

On the coattails of the smash *Paranormal Activity,* filmmakers made a few alterations to the story, called out a few actors, and got rolling at high speed.

Erin Marie Hogan got the call to play Samantha. Along with her mother Ellen (Fia Perera) and brother Thomas (Shane Van Dyke—Dick's grandson—who also wrote and directed the film), she is tormented by an unseen evil. Is it the spirit of the family's recently passed father? Who is it after? How did it leave footprints on the ceiling?

"I've always been a horror movie fan," says the native of St. Louis. "I'm too ADD for romantic comedies! Something needs to be happening all the time. I'm on a mission to see all [horror movies]." The original *Halloween* and the Stephen King TV adaptation of *It* are two of her favorites from the genre.

After seeing *It,* she says, "I was scared of drains my whole life. [In one scene, a young boy is terrorized by a clown who makes its—or *It*'s—way up through a shower floor.] I was traumatized. When I was draining a bathtub, I'd get out fast! But I wanted to do that—I wanted to make people horrified."

Hogan found herself quite bewitched with the revolutionary *Blair Witch Project. Cloverfield, Quarantine,* and other such flicks started coming out, and the technique's newness started to go away. Then millions of people saw a married couple get terrorized by an unseen force in their new home, one that eventually overtakes the wife, making her do its murderous dirty work.

"It was a horror movie about demons, which is kind of a favorite genre of mine," Hogan says. "I like the idea that there's something that we don't necessarily know about. I liked that it could go in so many different directions. There's so many ideas and theories about the paranormal. People are scared of things that they don't understand."

Hogan soon got a call to step inside her own haunted house. She'd become Samantha Finley, whose brother Thomas was allegedly arrested for her murder, as well as that of a visiting paranormal expert. (Like *Blair Witch, Entity* was passed off as a "true story," and had no opening credits.) Ellen, in a mental hospital at the time of the "killings," committed suicide, as did Thomas. Checking out the film, however, viewers realized that there was much more to the murders that met the eye.

"I liked Samantha because she was around my age," Hogan says. "Almost all of the script was improvised. They pulled a lot of actual experiences into it." Her audition consisted of her wowing film officials with her own ghost story, one of being in a bedroom alone with something evil.

"Since it was improvised, Samantha was whoever I wanted her to be," she says. "[The moviemakers] wanted her brooding, not talking too much, but it was open as to how I wanted her to be. It was cool that I could do whatever I wanted, to make her myself.

"I actually had a fairly benign ghost in my last house. It may sound kooky, but I kind of believe in that stuff. It freaked me out at first but then I made light of it, and called him 'Alfred.' Whenever he was lurking around, I would feel this cold draft of air and have to yell at him to stop his lurking."

Faced with a relatively small budget, not to mention the notoriously short memories of American filmgoers, no one messed around getting the film filmed.

"I didn't have a whole lot of time [to prepare]," Hogan says. "But sometimes, right before we shot, I took a few minutes out to think about what was going on, and if I didn't know what was going on, I tried to relate it to something in my life that would make me upset, make me happy, or something like that, to pull it into the story. It took a minute and a half or two minutes to internalize what was going on."

Entity starts out much like its predecessor, with TVs turning themselves on and things falling off walls. But eventually, much sooner than in *Activity,* the unwelcome visitor starts to work its dark magic on the residents. Thomas, in the midst of a lengthy conversation with his mom, suddenly hears Samantha screaming, and finds her in the tub, vulnerable and terrified of something she can't understand.

"When I was in the bathtub, there was a big long dialogue scene before it," recalls Hogan. "So I just started at the ceiling and pretended I saw something creepy up there ... I kind of internalized that there was something up there looking at me, until it was time for me to start screaming."

But things get worse. Thomas, the cameraman for most of the flick, finds his mother, inconsolable in her bedroom.

"What I liked about [the film] was the intensity," Perera says. "I always love to challenge myself and make something personal to me. I trusted that I, as an actress, had the feelings of Ellen. I tried to put myself in her circumstances. In the film, my husband dies in a terrible car accident and now there's this thing that's trying to tear my family apart, trying to kill my daughter. I allowed myself to react to the pure insanity of it."

Thomas is in search of night noises (apparently not having seen enough horror flicks to know that it's never a good idea to investigate those things alone). Inside, outside, and up to the attic he goes, only to find his sister nonchalantly staring off into space. She's not being physically hurt, but her mind is heading away at high speed.

"The attic scene was kind of scary," Hogan recalls. "I often find myself doing things in movies that I normally wouldn't do in real life. I probably wouldn't be comatose in an attic. It was pretty easy to be in the attic, because I literally stood up there for about eight minutes in the dark, staring at the dark and not seeing anything at all. By the time he came up, I think I was actually in a trance."

Finally, Samantha and Ellen have had enough, escaping to a motel. But demons like to tag along, and soon Thomas gets a phone call that the visitor followed them to the new residence.

Preparing for the scene when Samantha breaks down upon her return, Hogan says, "I shut myself in the dark and cried a lot, so I'd be truly upset. I always think of the first things related to the story. If I was actually pulled out of my bed, I was probably thinking about how I was going to be leaving my dog. It really made me upset; my dog is my best friend in the world. I thought about losing my dog and how she'd be all by herself with no one to take care of her. It helped me make these little connections from the story into real life."

Ellen is over the edge as Thomas finds her with her wrists slashed. Apparently, unlike its *Activity* colleague, this creature doesn't want to steal anyone's spirit, but to destroy them, or have them destroy themselves.

"Any person that is driven to suicide is truly horrific," Perera asserts. "I have known people that have taken their own lives and my heart goes out to them. In this film, Ellen is driven to the brink and ends her own life. Although this is something I would never do, I can certainly relate to the feelings of despair, having dealt with periods of depression in my own life. We all have things that trigger us and being able to relate to Ellen was about staying present. It doesn't take me an hour to prepare for a scene, you just do it. You have to be able to be very agile, flexible and not judge the process."

In desperation, Samantha and Thomas turn back to the expert they met earlier in the film. But the camera suddenly fades out, and when it's back on, he's lying dead on the floor, and Samantha is nowhere to be found.

Thomas hears more and more screaming, and charges into the bedroom. Samantha, naked and bleeding from everywhere, is crying out in terrifying pain. It's as if the monster is committing every single horror upon the innocent girl.

She's also hovering a few feet in the air.

Then, just as with *Blair Witch,* the camera drops from sight. No one is seen alive again.

"We shot that scene twice," Hogan says. "Once when I was levitating, and once when I wasn't. There were a lot of intricate things (makeup, bloodpacks) all over my body, that ended up getting ripped off while I was thrashing around. But I felt that the levitating came off better because I was covered in blood. It was scary and icky, a lot of elements that made me uncomfortable, so I felt that it came across better."

Though both films relied more on creating an atmosphere of horrifying tension than actual special effects, *Entity* was quite a bit more graphic and violent than *Activity*. "A lot of people think it's scary, and it's kind of disturbing," Hogan says of Samantha's death scene. "Is she being raped? It's a whole new level of creepy, like it's a perverted ghost all of a sudden."

Ever since she finished playing Samantha, Hogan's not really been bothered by many ghosts, demons, or other types of activity or entities. But she, like many in the acting profession, still feels a connection with the lady she once (sort of) was.

"You're physically that character for a long period of time, so it becomes a part of your life," she says. "In this genre, you bring a lot of yourself to it, and you bring a lot of things from your actual life. If (up-and-coming actors) think they want to do horror, thrillers, things like that, they can't have inhibitions about nudity and all this other stuff. But you don't have to give up on your morals. Don't throw everything away, but you have to be willing to compromise some things. Just go for it, no matter how you feel."

For Eva Mauro, a phone call showed the power of networking. Some friends who had helped Mauro make her film debut in the thriller *Mirror Image* were putting their own spin on *Paranormal Activity*. Even better, they wanted her to star in it.

It all sounded great. Then Mauro heard the starting date: less than 50 *hours* away.

No auditions, no tryouts, no time. Just a quick shot to step in, step up, and scare someone shitless. Five minutes before, she'd had no idea that **616: Paranormal Incident** was even in the planning stages. Two days from now, she had to start filming.

In the same near-panicked mode she'd found herself in while checking out so many horror films before, Mauro rapid-fire-glanced over what she had to work with.

Experience? Not too much time in front of the camera, but a tad—she'd spent some time with horror icon Tony Todd during the making of *Penance*. Plus, she was a horror movie fan.

"Watching scary movies, you get this rush, this feeling like all this blood is rolling

The devil showed he had fine taste in women when he possessed Eve Mauro's Emma in *616: Paranormal Incident*.

through your body," explains Mauro, who cites the *Hellraiser* and *Poltergeist* films as favorites. "These movies are like a drug. They scare you. You're excited. It's funny, because the rush of energy is all these different emotions passing through you. Watching these movies, I'd close the windows and lock all the doors. I liked that feeling so much, and I always thought I could do it, make movies like that." After getting all of one day to read over and memorize her dialogue, Mauro went for it.

In *616*, a young mother grabs an envelope off her front porch and finds a DVD inside. She sits down to check it out. Her little daughter has more on her mind: an upcoming visit from her new friend, who she's artistically introducing to Mommy right now. We ever so briefly see the daughter's scribbling of a young woman, her flowing brunette-ness standing far out. Perhaps it's the youngster's classmate, or someone who just moved in down the street. Maybe she, as so many of us once did, has a best pal that only she can see, hear, and communicate with.

On the DVD, Mom's own father, near to hysterics, gasps out a tale of death and murder, almost begging her to help him spread the word about the story she's about to see, as he won't be around to tell it.

Now the performer-cameraman rolls kick in, and she and we see a team of apprentice paranormal investigators heading towards an old mental hospital to learn more about their field with the father as the instructor. (*Incident* was filmed in an old prison, using some of the same rooms seen in *A Nightmare on Elm Street: Dream Master*.) A psychologist shows up, seemingly overqualified for the job.

The squad starts searching, and one member stumbles, almost literally, across a near-comatose, apparently assaulted woman in one of the rooms. The lady can only fearfully gasp that her name is Emma, and that there's a young boy she needs to go home and care for. But the doctor's not fooled, even if she's not telling why just yet.

"What are you?" she suddenly snarls. Not who, but what. Looks like this was all a setup, the team used as bait to pull out something, or someone, that the doc and her higher-ups knew was there all along.

Meanwhile, still on the hunt for whatever, the crew members start to step out of natural darkness and into the inner type. One woman happens upon some photos of herself. Then her whole view suddenly changes to a part of her past she'd never wanted to acknowledge. She and we suddenly see the inside of a bright room, a woman on a bed, riding a much older man.

It's her father and his mistress. It's what caused her mother to take her own life. The woman glances over and sees her mom on the couch, the bullet wound fresh in her face. She tries to escape, but it's too late; the father's upon her, cackling, his eyes pupil-less circles, strangling her. By the time anyone reaches her, he's disappeared, and she's been stolen from the world.

The shrink's still trying to stay on the interrogative offensive. But something appears to be happening inside Emma. Her body starts to twist in *Exorcist*-type knots. Her voice changes. She alternates between cries of pain and grins of dark pleasure.

"I did a little research on possession," says Mauro, who called this her toughest scene. "I watched videos online. I was watching people being possessed. They were almost trying to get out of their skin, and you could see the pain in their face that something was trying to push its way out, so I worked with that."

One crewman finds himself lynched by zombies. Another, suddenly surrounded by lustful, gorgeous women light years out of his league, sees his dream become a nightmare, as they steal the air from his lungs and life from his body.

Back in the cell, Emma's countenance is found on a "Missing" poster on the doctor's database, but this is clearly someone, some*thing* else entirely. The shrink quickly recounts a list of past tragedies in the area. This thing has been here before. Emma the woman may not be evil, but she's a new puppet of something that is.

The innocent act is gone. Emma, or whatever is pulling her strings, now becomes the taunting temptress who's slowly taking over. Nearly oblivious to her tormentors, she throws out demonic nursery rhymes. Suddenly all-knowing about the downfalls of the crew, she unconvincingly claims that she never actually hurt anyone, only helps them hurt themselves. She omnisciently reminds the doctor of some lives that only used to be inside the shrink—the woman has been through a certain medical procedure more than once, something Emma (the person, at least) could never have known.

Here's where the true difficulty of Mauro's preparation had to come to play. Finding the worst of evil in history or legend, and a way to both implant it within herself and bring it back out again. Hiding the fact that she was *always* running things until it was time to unleash her power like a hurricane.

"When I think of the devil, I think he has a lot of resentment," Mauro says. (According to the Bible, Satan was originally an angel, banished to lead the underworld after attempting an uprising against his Master.) "He was an angel of God. He was this beautiful creature and God cast him away. He had all this built-up anger and resentment. He loved God, but now he hates all mankind. Any emotion like that comes from fear, and I used that and amplified it a little more."

The doctor's composure is now gone. Her bosses arrive, and she and the DVD recipient's dad—one of the few still unafflicted—are removed from the scene. But when one of the new team members (Louis Mandylor, whose brother Costas played a bad guy in a few *Saw* movies) steps too close to Emma, it's too late for everyone.

One man after another attacks her. No one has a chance. Some are quickly beaten to death, another gets telekinetically tossed away with a casual flick of her hand. She steps into another's mind, forcing him to turn a gun on himself.

Nothing could have possibly prepared Mauro for this. Bringing people, some of them men twice her size, to their knees and backs and then gleefully and coldly denying them the mercy they plead for ... that was all new, and it wouldn't be easy if she'd had more time to get ready.

As Emma methodically stalks down the hall, like this stuff is normalcy for her, she's got one more mind game to play: The doctor's suddenly trapped in a dark room with body parts everywhere. The two still fully intact are a pair of demonic young boys, slowly advancing. She didn't give them a chance to live, and now they'll have dark revenge.

The she-devil's dirty work is about finished. With the doctor already dead, another pleading man is taken out. The last one standing, the first woman's father, desperately tries to detonate the bomb he planted, ready to sacrifice himself to take out the enemy. As Emma kneels over him, her face suddenly gives way to the devil's pitch-black mien, much as Featherston's had in the closing moments of the first *Activity*, and gets too close to the screen.

Maybe that's why these self-filmed flicks are so appealing to so many. Maybe we feel like the people on the screen are speaking to us and reacting to us. Trying to scare us as individuals, rather than as the audience as a whole. They're trying to get us, to sneak up on us as people and grab us. Self-filmed films make us feel a certain interaction with the characters in a way that regular flicks can't.

Suddenly, the self-filming ends. We're back at the first house, and the woman tries to convince her mind that her dad may have made it out. Trying to keep control for the child, she calls for the little girl.

But there's a special introduction to be made. That friend that the daughter discussed and drew at the opening? She's real, and she's here, in deadly living color.

She's Emma. A devil's work is never truly done.

So how did she do it? How did Mauro manage to not only locate, but unleash such pain, such fury, such destruction? How did she go from everyday life to terrified to evil's epitome in mere hours, and stay there all the way through filming?

"It was very intense," she says. "You go to a darker place, and you find a trigger for something, either created or from your past. For the action, you go to that, and it helps you get there quick. It's not natural to be evil, but you find something from work you've done, and it takes you right back there."

BackStageCasting. "'Paranormal Activity' Cast Interview." Nov. 6, 2009. Retrieved May 19, 2010, from http://www.youtube.com/watch?v=kHK-RjW_lpM.
BillyBushShow. "Paranormal Activity—Katie Featherston and Micah Sloat—Part 1." Nov. 2, 2009. Retrieved May 20, 2010, from http://www.youtube.com/watch?v=lX5uU1Q-Z9k&feature=related.
Hogan, Erin Marie. Phone interview. Feb. 19, 2010.
Mauro, Eve. Phone interview. Feb. 19, 2013.
Morton, Eugene. "Paranormal Activity Interview with Katie Featherston & Micah Sloat." *Attack of the Show*. Oct. 28, 2009. Retrieved May 19, 2010, from http://g4tv.com/attackoftheshow/moviesandtv/

68884/paranormal-activity-interview-with-katie-featherson—micah-sloat.html#ixzz0oRGRHE00.

Perera, Fia. Phone interview. March 2, 2010.

Reynolds, Simon. "Katie Featherston interview: 'I still find 'Paranormal Activity' scary.'" *Digital Spy.* Oct. 18, 2012. Retrieved March 14, 2013, from http://www.digitalspy.com/movies/interviews/a431704/katie-featherston-interview-i-still-find-paranormal-activity-scary.html.

Schwartz, Missy. "A Shocking Hit." EWwww. Oct. 30, 2009. Retrieved May 24, 2010, from http://www.ew.com/ew/article/0,,20316189,00.html.

SmithAcitivity. "Paranormal Activity Actors Interview—Stars of Paranormal Activity—Katie and Micah." *YouTube.* Oct. 27, 2009. Retrieved May 19, 2010, from http://www.youtube.com/watch?v=dcpQAKbAeLg.

Tribute Movies. "Katie Featherston—'Paranormal Activity 4' Interview with Tribute." *Youtube.* Nov. 2, 2012. Retrieved March 14, 2013, from http://www.youtube.com/watch?v=cNoQbs7XeoQ.

·············

Hannah Fierman: *V/H/S*

A new spin on the first-person horror films we've seen many times over the past decade, *V/H/S* starts out with a group of young morons taping themselves assaulting a young couple, then breaking into a haunted house to steal a very special videotape.

Finding its elderly owner dead in a chair, the men just can't resist settling in to see what he was seeing on the VCR. Then we see what they see, and the fear transforms from realistic to supernaturally unnatural.

Our first episode (they, like the raid, are all self-filmed) deals with a new group of halfwits, spurred on by the troublesome combo of hormones and booze. There's a rented hotel room, a bar downstairs full of willing beauties, and a small camera hidden in one of the guy's eyeglasses to record everything for later bragging rights.

With lottery-esque luck, the men manage to quickly finagle a pair of the establishment's finest and head back upstairs for a private party. One of them is named Lily, and she seems a bit distant. Maybe it's the drink, maybe the uncertainty of making a new acquaintance … or maybe something else entirely.

"I've been an actor since I can remember," says Hannah Fierman. "It is more of a calling for me and less of a decision to become an actor. It's who I am … I think what I like most about [horror and science fiction] is how flexible the artists can be. There are very few limitations, so the writers, actors, makeup artists, wardrobe, directors, everyone can be as free as they like and it can still be believable."

Back in the room, the other woman has succumbed to the drink and passed out. But Lily's into it, getting aggressive with one of the guys. He's having second thoughts(!), but another of his friends is all too eager to take his place. Lily's upset at the first turnaway, and it's starting to show—not only through her emotions, but physically.

Before we can fully enjoy the majestic sight of her unclothed body, something else reaches out and grabs our attention: the scales spreading across her feet and legs. Yeah, this is going to end badly for someone.

Another of the men tries to take advantage, but Lily's heading down the animalistic path quickly, and not in the way so many men secretly welcome in the bedroom; she turns a chunk of his hand into an after-dinner snack.

Hannah Fierman straddled the line between evil and beauty in *V/H/S*.

"I was inspired by the role of Lily because I could incorporate animal and human behaviors," Fierman says. "Emotions, carnal needs, and fears. The role allowed me to be as outrageous as I wanted as long as the character still held a human and sympathetic element. This is what makes acting both a challenge and fun for me."

As the men try to recover in the bathroom, Lily's non-human side is getting too strong for her (or them) to stop. Two guys are killed. The other desperately tries to escape.

Lily's stunning natural features having given way to a demonic countenance, she pursues the last man left, the one she first tried to be with, down the stairs, nearly pleading with him to care for her. Like too many other naïve young women, Lily seems to have fallen for the fallacy that promiscuity leads to popularity, that it's possible to sex one's way right into a man's heart. Unlike many of them, however, she has a Ms. Hyde side that comes out when her heart gets broken—and the men will pay.

"The more uncomfortable Lily became, the more she was not able to hide her true form as the monster," Fierman says. "She was trying to fit in because she fell in love. The more they invaded her space, the more irritated she became."

The man makes it outside and appears to be on the way to freedom. But it's too late: Lily, now in giant bat-like succubus form, swoops down and carries him away to parts we'll never see.

So how can we finally classify exactly what Lily became? With her super strength, we saw remnants of a She-Hulk; her flying fashions and taste for blood indicate a relation of Dracula.

"I see Lily as the classic 'misunderstood monster,'" says Fierman, who spent five hours a day in a makeup chair during filming. "[The director] and I were both collaborating to define what the Lily monster was. I looked to different animal behaviors and emotions. I was most inspired by bats, birds of prey, and cat-like qualities."

Meanwhile, back at the original burglarized house, the corpse vanishes, then reappears. The men start to disappear themselves. But the tapes continue, and we see a story of an invisible force stalking a group through the woods, and another of a young scientist victimizing several young woman. We see another group of fellows try to save a lady in peril, only to fall victim to her demonic powers.

Again we return to the men who broke into the house to kick off this merry-go-round of horror. The leader finds (most of) one of his men, the guy's cranium in a separate location. Carrying on the self-filmed films' tradition that no one ever gets away, the "dead" man suddenly comes back around and takes care of the last of those that broke into his house.

It wouldn't be Fierman's only foray into the bloodsucking world; also in 2012, she showed up in an episode of TV's *The Vampire Diaries*, about a young woman torn between a few debonair plasma drinkers. "TV moves more quickly than film and is generally less forgiving. There is not as much time for multiple takes, rehearsal, and general preparation," she says. "You just need to show up on set with all your choices made, on your own…. *Vampire Diaries* was working with pros. The wardrobe was the best part because it was set in 1912."

Like many in her profession, the young woman has adapted a dictum that just about every performer demonstrates in one capacity or another: "Bold choices are rewarded," she proclaims. "I believe this is true for much of life as well as in this career. As for actors who wish to make horror movies, you will probably be cast and do well. Horror is the bubble that never pops, so go for it and get crazy."

Fierman, Hannah. E-mail interview. Dec. 18–19, 2012.

•••••••••••••••••••••••••••••••

Friday the 13th: Their Names Was Jason (Voorhees)

For budding horror stars, the *Friday the 13th* series was a gold mine. Unlike the *A Nightmare on Elm Street* films, where one fellow played the main bad guy for over a decade, the role of Jason Voorhees gave several performers a chance to terrify one audience after another.

It all started with a fellow who got to kick off the series for the sole reason that he had the ability to freestyle through the waters of Crystal Lake.

"It was kind of a combination of pure luck, nerve, and bravery," says Ari Lehman, who became the boy who'd become one of the horror cinema's favorite slaughterers. "I heard there was an audition at the YMCA. I went down there and brought a clipboard to look official."

The tryout was for *Manny's Orphans*, about a group of inner-city kids who find solace in soccer. The director was a fellow named Sean Cunningham. Shortly after filming, Cunningham gave his Lehman a call. "He said, 'Can you swim?' I said, 'Yes!'" That was enough. He had a role in Cunningham's upcoming horror feature.

"When I saw that Jason had no lines," Lehman says, "I became determined to create a detailed background story in my mind, so that his actions would reflect a true inner motivation through body language and facial gestures."

He visited horror special effects legend Tom Savini to help create Jason's face. "Being at Tom's studio was like walking into Merlin's workshop," he says. "Everywhere you looked, there were realistic replicas of decapitated heads, severed limbs, disemboweled torsos, as well as busts of all the great horror actors, including Bela Lugosi, Lon Chaney, Boris Karloff, and Christopher Lee."

For weeks they worked on the mask Lehman would wear as Jason.

"One time, when my entire head was completely covered in plaster," Lehman says, "Tom put on Jim Morrison and The Doors' 'Strange Days.' It was the first time I heard music like that, and I was impressed."

They filmed Jason's first appearance, his heartbreaking drowning scene, and everything seemed done,

Kane Hodder shows the author that he'll always be the scarier Jason.

as the film was to end with Alice in the hospital. Then Cunningham saw *Carrie*'s legendary twist ending, and decided to add one of his own.

"They wanted Jason to be both repelling and pitiable at the same time," Lehman says, "so Tom fashioned a new version which I wore in the final scene. Of course we also covered the mask and myself in muck and vegetation that Tom asked us to scrape from the bottom of Sand Pond the night before. Tom also applied additional latex, which he allowed to dry, and then peeled back to look like decaying flesh.

"I wanted to get way into character, so before filming, while in makeup, I would stare into the waters of Sand Pond, trying to imagine what I would feel like if I went through what Jason went through."

One day, Kevin Bacon strolled up and asked Lehman what in the Sam Hill he was up to.

"'Getting into character,' I told him, as seriously as I could," Lehman says. Bacon walked away howling with laughter. But no one was cracking up during the film's final sequence, which set the tone for the remainder of the series.

"The best part was [actress Adrienne King's] reaction," Lehman says. "Tom had instructed me to stay away from Adrienne while in makeup, so she did not know what the mask really looked like right up until the shoot. When I jumped out of the water, she was truly frightened. She practically jumped right out of the boat!"

Lehman didn't do much acting after becoming Jason; music became his game and he keyboarded for bands across the world. Soon his punk-metal band FIRSTJASON, turning out the tunes "Jason Never Dies," and "Machete Is My Friend," became a fixture on the convention circuit and in clubs across the nation.

"I think the first [*Friday the 13th* movie] is the best," Lehman asserts. "It's about acting and characters; the whole kind of splatter, gore thing hadn't really created its own clichés yet. *Friday the 13th* doesn't really have those. It has some really interesting characters and clever things, not a ton of blood."

When the first sequel came around in 1981, Jason went on the offensive; apparently the revenge mindset runs through the Voorhees family tree. His legendary hockey mask wasn't yet in place but there was plenty of death and destruction to go around.

The story behind the film is just as interesting as what went down in front of the camera.

Who was the masked (this time, in a burlap sack) man? The credits will tell you that it was Warrington Gillette.

"I imagined that Jason was a survivalist in the woods," says Gillette, who originally auditioned to play one of the counselors. Following in Mommy's footsteps, Jason hacks his way through the Lake people, impaling and slashing. The killer doesn't show much until near the end.

"I was only in makeup for the final scene in the movie, which took a few days, for the ending sequences," says Gillette, who spent seven hours in the makeup chair, preparing to hurl himself through a window to attack Ginny. "The most annoying element was closing off one of my eyes for about 20 hours at a time. You lose all depth perception with only one eye functioning. The dental implants were annoying as hell. When the final scene took place, I was absolutely in the frame of mind to kill my final victim."

As shooting kicked off, though, a fellow named Steve Dash (Daskawisz was actually his moniker back then; the name change didn't come about for a few years) got a phone call, saying his stunting skills were needed. He hopped in the car, drove to Connecticut, ready to be the next titan of terror.

Director Steve Minor and stunt coordinator Cliff Cudney brought him into a secret office and informed him that they were looking for an action backup for Gillette.

Then they discussed Jason's attire. "I got a bag on for the whole film?!" Dash recalls thinking. "I'm the lead, and no one can see my face?!" With no facial work, no lines, not even a script, he set about becoming Jason.

"The first thing I did was to go to a drugstore and buy an eyepatch," he says. "I went out in the woods. I put on tight shoes and ran in the woods to get used to the eyepatch. I developed a lope. I started to get into character." And according to him, he did a hell of a lot more starring than the fellow who got credit for the role.

"Warrington went through the window at the end of the film," Dash asserts. "That's all he did. I did everything else in the movie. Every scene in that movie is me with the exception of the last scene where he went through the window. And actually he didn't even dive through the window; they had to build a rig to swing him through the window because he was afraid to go through it." The film outgrossed *E.T.* on its opening weekend. Much like *Saw* would do a few decades later, *Friday the 13th* kept putting out sequels just about every year, as Jason, now with his iconic hockey mask, headed back to Crystal Lake for a kick at the 3D can in 1983. This time, former trapeze artist Richard Brooker stepped into the character. It was the Englishman's first American acting job.

"I answered an ad in a magazine," said the 6'4" Brooker, who died in April 2013. "I showed up … and there was a bunch of guys twice my size, and I walked past them."

Miner saw him, and said to give Brooker the role.

"Starring as a totally mindless killing machine seemed the perfect opportunity to prove that you don't have to talk to act," he said. "The director … agreed that Jason should be played in a largely improvisational manner." But he a hardship that no other Jason performer had faced: the 3D settings.

"The kills were probably the hardest things we had to shoot, because the 3-D process we used necessitated multiple takes on everything," Brooker recalled. "It was not uncommon to do 14 or 15 takes of a simple stabbing sequence; we spent hours and hours on the eyeball squeeze."

In real time, it took another year for *The Final Chapter* (perhaps *The "Final" Chapter* would be more appropriate in hindsight) to be written; continuity-wise, it's less than twenty-four hours after part II.

Holed up in a morgue, never-quite-dead Jason performs his own idea of surgery upon a nurse and doctor before heading back to Crystal Lake where he finds a group that includes young Tommy Jarvis and his family.

Playing Jason wouldn't be the first time Ted White worked without getting much credit; he had stunt-doubled for John Wayne, Clark Gable, Rock Hudson, and others during his half-century career (with everyone from John Ford to Howard Hawks on the other side of the camera). Still, acting out mass murder wasn't the former Marine's idea of fun.

"When I got a call from the studio, I went in and read for a part—not Jason," White recalls. "There were twelve or thirteen other guys there, and I went on and read for the role. After all the other guys had gone, they called me back, and said, 'Ted, we'd like to go with you.'

"I said, 'That's nice. For what part?' They said, 'Jason!'

"I said 'Jason? Jason doesn't say anything. He wears a mask and kills all these people' That's not the kind of thing I'd been doing for the last fifty-something years. It's not the kind of thing I would be proud to do, to have my kids or their kids see it."

He headed home, ready for a few TV jobs heading his way. Then a crew member called.

"He said they had to make a body cast of me," White says. "That was a three-week deal." In layman's terms, once the contract was signed and the cast made, he'd get to do anything else he wanted for the three weeks, until production began, and get paid for it. "When you're on hold in the motion picture business, you get paid full salary," White says, "so I called them back and said I'd take the part." A few days later, the cast was done. While getting paid for a film that couldn't get rolling yet, he got to spend time in Hawaii doing an episode of *Magnum, P.I.*!

It was eventually time to step into one of the few acting worlds he had yet to explore.

"I thought, 'How am I going to scare these kids?' I thought I'd isolate myself from them completely. I don't want to talk to them. I don't want to meet them."

On the first day of filming, he emerged from hours in the makeup chair to get rolling. As everyone engaged in a pre-shoot meal, White went elsewhere. "I took my chair and moved about thirty-five yards away from everybody," he says. "[Director] Joe Zito asked if I wanted to come meet everyone. I said no. I said, 'When it comes time for me to work with them, that'll be all the time I need to meet them.'"

The cast and crew, many of whom were making their film world debut, wondered and worried about their mysterious co-star. White could feel their fear, and fed off it as much as the meal he was consuming. When it came time to shoot, he took his first victim aside for a quick pep talk. "I told him; If you get tight, you're going to get hurt. If you relax completely and let me work with you, you will not get hurt, and it will look very, very good. Don't think of me as Jason, just think of me as a guy doing a day's work.' It came off better than it would if he'd been scared."

In the movie, Jason impales three women, and tosses another from a high window. He bashes in one guy's face and plants a cleaver through that of another. Along the way, White kept Jason's ominous aura running through the set, staying far from those he'd soon pretend to terrorize.

"If people came on the set for a visit," he recalls, "I got up and went into my dressing room and stayed there until they left." He made Jason into a runner.

Tommy dresses himself up like Jason looked back in the first film, distracting the madman long enough for Tommy and his sister to stab him to death. But nothing's ever final in the horror film world…

In the next installment, Jason left the supernatural behind and stepped a bit closer to Michael Myers.

Tommy's older, with John Shepherd now in the role, hallucinating both awake and asleep about the masked man. He's in a halfway house for youths, but rehab's not working for everyone: Resident maniac Vic (Mark Venturini, who tragically died at 35 from leukemia on Valentine's Day of 1996) does Jason's work, fatally planting an axe into housemate Joey.

"I had heard of the series, but I didn't know much about it," recalls Dick Wieand. "You go for everything your agent sends you, and my agent set me up for this. I went on the audition, and I read." He got a callback, and met some of the crew. Then he found out he had the role.

Wieand checked out some of the first Jasons. But as is usually the case with those playing horror villains, his biggest preparation came from within.

"I was asked to visualize my dying son on the table," he says. (Wieand's not a parent, making the mental image even tougher to create.) "It was about reaction. There were no lines there. I had to imagine how sad and angry I would have been, which is the same thing I did during the actual shooting, when I go through that transition in the film. As an actor, you have to use your imagination, to put yourself in that sort of situation." Indeed, Joey was the son of Roy, a paramedic in the story, and about his last link to sanity, as Roy, like Ms. Voorhees had done in the original, is using mass murder for revenge.

"I thought that Roy had actually gone nuts to make him want to do this," Wieand says. "The real Jason was evil, and Roy is taking on the character. I had a psychological idea of how to do that. With something like that, you can't expect someone to have the answers for you. You have to come up with that yourself."

The bodies start dropping fast. Meat cleavers, axes, even a road flare are brought into battle. Eventually Tommy gives Jason a taste of his own medicine, planting a machete into him and sending him down onto a bed of spikes.

To this point, no one, not even much of the cast and crew, knew Jason's secret. Cast members, including Wieand, didn't get the script until it was almost time to shoot, and many had to sign releases promising not to reveal anything. But with Jason dead, his mask finally comes off, and it's Roy.

"When people ask me my favorite death, I say it's my own," Wieand recalls. "You see me lying there in the rain, and they're not sure who the guy under the mask is. It was wet and nasty, but it was okay."

One 1985 evening, a hypnotist and his crew visited the Excess nightclub in Glendale, California, and asked the manager if they could perform these once a week.

The crew, which had done makeup on a previous *Friday the 13th*, decided to incorporate Jason into the show's finale. As participants and audiences watched Jason's latest performances on a screen, he'd get closer and closer before bursting onto the nightclub's stage set, live and in killing color.

They knew just the guy to ask.

"I'd been out of the military for five or six years," nightclub manager C.J. Graham recalls. "I was still about 240 pounds, and I could take care of business." Wardrobed in the same mask used in previous films, he'd be the first one to put Jason on the stage.

The crew was impressed. "They said, 'If we do [another *Friday the 13th*], we're going to call you,'" says Graham, who now manages a resort-casino in Southern California. "I kind of laughed, said okay, whatever."

However, two months later, Paramount Studios called him to try out for *Jason Lives!*. Most of the crew thought he'd be perfect, but without experience on the screen, Graham was passed over—temporarily.

As filming kicked off in Georgia, someone else had the mask. It didn't work out for the fellow. "Anybody can act and scream and yell and show expressions with their face," Graham says, "but Jason is a character where you have to turn your head or tilt your body a quarter-inch to give off that intimidating factor." Confident that he could do so, the crew called him the next Friday. Three days later, he was down south and ready to scare.

Like Ted White, Graham stayed away from those he'd be pretending to kill, all the while checking out the work of the previous *Friday*s. "I never went on set with anybody because I didn't want anybody to know who I was," he says. "I didn't want to talk to anybody because I was supposed to be the monster on the set. In character was the first time they'd seen me, so for them it was a bit of a shock."

Now in the guise of Thom Matthews, Tommy's out of an institution and looking to get rid of Jason once and for all. Burial didn't stop him before; it's time for cremation.

As Tommy and his pal Hawes (Ron Palillo of Arnold Horshack fame) finally unearth the not-so-dead man, Tommy flips once again, stabbing his tormentor with a metal pole. Lightning blasts from the sky, through the pole and into Voorhees, making him go beyond the supernaturally powerful creature he'd been before. Hawes is the first to find out, becoming an unwilling heart donor by way of Jason's fist.

Graham knew that keeping Jason stronger than ever would be just as tough as anything he'd gone through in the service.

"I still worked out every day," he says. "We'd shoot all night, and when the sun came out, I'd always go to the gym, because I still managed to maintain that physical ability. When I came out of that mobile home, the door was off the hinges, because that was me hitting that door full force and blowing it five or six feet in the air. Once you come out of a scene and you're ripped and cut and powerful, you've got eight to twelve weeks of shooting, and you've got to maintain that physical fitness all the way through."

Jason kills his way towards Tommy all across the newly monikered Forest Green, renamed to camouflage its evil past. He does show a shred of humanity, passing over a cabin of youths before going hardcore brutal on a group of cops. Eventually, Tommy lures him back to the lake where it all began. He puts a chain around Jason's neck and anchors it to a huge boulder at the bottom of the lake.

By now, Graham could feel Jason's power becoming his new lifeforce. Near the bottom of an Olympic-sized pool, its top covered over with tarp, he struggled with a real chain, with divers nearly to place a regulator in his mouth if things got too hairy.

During filming, a crew member came to Graham and asked for a break, as the divers were feeling the watery chills. The star hadn't noticed. "When the adrenalin is there," he explains, "the water temperature doesn't really bother you any more."

As Freddy Krueger met his longtime frightening rival in *Freddy vs. Jason*, the Jason role was taken over by Ken Kirzinger. "I never read the script," Kirzinger recalls. "It was more fun to work on that way. I knew the story outline, had [director Ronny Yu's] notes and had no lines. Ronny and I discussed Jason's movements and motivations closely and he was fastidious about these. Once I wasn't in character behind the mask, and Ronny could tell. He called me on it right away in front of everyone. That was the last time I wasn't in character behind the mask!"

For one of the first times, he got to show a new side of Jason, a non-evil one. Jason's mother fixation and fear of water became strong plot points, as Jason mostly comes across as the good guy in the war with He Who Wears the Clawed Glove, to the extent that a woman gives him mouth-to-mouth to send him back into battle. "I believe if you are going to do something someone else did before you, you have to try and add something of your own to it, something you think makes it better," says Kirzinger. "That's what I tried to do with Jason. The script was written to show Jason's inner child and that allowed me the opportunity no other actor who has played Jason before me had ever had, and that was to give Jason more emotional depth."

To play the young Jason, Spencer Stump spent six hours a day in the makeup chair, all for about five minutes of screen time and a bit of voiceover work.

"When I got in the room," Stump recalls of his tryout (he was thirteen at the time), "they looked at me for a minute, and said 'Too tall.' Well, being a little cheeky bugger like I was (or still am), I said, 'Isn't Jason like eight feet tall? Wouldn't he have been a tall kid?' The people in the room nodded their heads and agreed with me. The next day I got the part!

"It was tough because my dentures kept falling out, and my contacts kept slipping," he recalls of the scene where Freddy mockingly dunks young Jason in the infamous lake. "The worst part was because water got stuck in the pocket between my real eye and my 'dead eye.' So the makeup artist had to keep popping out the glass eye and draining it. The only part of my experience that was really hard was getting my head cast for the makeup. I was so afraid of my nose getting covered when they were casting my head. It was really scary."

A new version of Jason showed up in 2009—and it was up to Derek Mears to continue the tradition as a character he'd been terrified of. Like many other Voorhees fans, he still found a reason to root for his favorite horror oddity. "It was completely surreal being the character," says Mears, who, like many of his predecessors, had a stunt background, working in the first two *Pirates of the Caribbean* films, *World Trade Center,* and others. "Growing up, I had so many nightmares about being Jason, and now I got to give nightmares to somebody else, a whole new generation."

He read up on surviving in the wilderness and being set apart from society for an entire lifetime. He learned about the effects on a small child of losing a parent, particularly in the violent, horrific way that Pamela met her end.

"He had been abandoned by society," Mears explains. "He was a loner who wants to be left alone. What sparked my brain, was that he was very similar to John Rambo. A little bit of Tarzan, a mixture of the Abominable Snowman and Lenny from *Of Mice and Men*."

To him, the hockey mask became more than just a simple prop. "It's almost like protection from society," he says of the camouflage. "It almost makes him normal. He knows he's been rejected, but it almost makes him human. When he finds the hockey mask … it has that symbol of protection from the outside world, but it makes him more normal. It gives him a facial feature."

A big fan of mixed martial arts, Mears turned Jason into a quick, agile killer, rather than the plodding, methodical monster others had portrayed. "I knew what the guys who previously played Jason had done," he says, "so I had to put that aside and try to forget about it and build the character off the new script. So it's all my own thing, but there are times, being a fan, I would do a tip of the hat, little homages to some of the guys out of respect." His small tribute to White in the form of a head tilt didn't make the final cut. He posed next to a window like Brooker had, and subtly impersonated Graham as well.

"Before, he was more of an entity," Mears says. "This time, he was more of a character. He's more of an anti-hero."

And now for Kane Hodder…

There's an urban legend that, in the midst of the first of his four tours as Mr. Voorhees, the 6'3" Hodder finished up a tough night of shooting in Alabama. To get to his dressing room he took a short cut through the woods, still in costume—and, as a bystander would find out, in character.

"Sometimes when I'm playing the character, I like to be by myself and I keep the mask on," he explains. "That's a little method."

At about 2 a.m., he came upon a fellow night walker.

"Excuse me," the man asked. "Are you with the movie?"

"When someone asks sort of a stupid question like that, I'm gonna make sure they pay for it," he asserts. "So I just stood there and once again did the head-tilt."

The fellow glanced around nervously, and repeated his question.

"That was my cue," Hodder says, "to make a little lunge for him and a little grunt."

The man bolted backwards, sprawled over a tree stump, and ran away, with Hodder trying desperately to keep from howling with laughter.

Hodder was offered the Jason role when he was fresh off playing an undead character in *Prison*. Hodder heard from the producers of *Friday the 13th VII: New Blood*. John Buechler, who'd done his makeup in *Prison*, was helming *Beginning*, and he felt that Hodder could make the seventh one lucky.

"I had watched all the Jason films, never thinking I had any chance to do it myself," says Hodder, whose thick build made him one of the more physically intimidating Jasons. "I watched all the movies again, to see how [Jason] moved, but I went into it without any real plan. I wanted to do what felt natural."

A gang assault by some neighborhood bullies burned through Hodder's nightmares for years. "When I play a killer, the rage and anger come naturally to me," he explains. (Hodder would later portray both Ed Gein and BTK killer Dennis Rader, and appear alongside Charlize Theron in her Oscar-winning portrayal of serial killer Aileen Wuornos in *Monster*.) "The director says 'Action' and I snap into this bloodthirsty monster ready to destroy whoever and whatever is in front of him ... I was so angry, hurt, and scarred by [the attack], that I always wanted to get revenge—hurtful, angry, violent revenge that I never got. Thankfully, I am allowed to act out that revenge frequently and get paid for it."

Arriving at his audition, Hodder quickly dressed in makeshift Voorhees regalia. Then he stood outside the tryout room, yelling and smacking the walls. His pal Alan Marcus, a fellow longtime stuntman, walked in, and made it to the center of the room. It was time for Hodder to become Jason. "I walked in ... took two quick steps and grabbed him, lifted him off the ground, and threw him aside," he says. "From there I dragged him around the room by his hair, tossed him a few more times."

Then he strode over to the table where the representatives sat, and flipped it over.

"It was hilarious," he says. "They jumped back, clenched their papers to their chests, and genuinely looked frightened." Hodder smacked his friend around a few more times before one of them said to stop.

Later that week, he got the part. Then he grabbed a machete, and noticed how good, how *right* it felt in his hand.

Out of the lake for the first time in a decade and up against a young beauty with telekinesis (Jason meets Carrie's twin!), Jason went back to work, slicing, dicing, and (Hodder's personal favorite) grabbing a young woman in a sleeping bag and bashing her against a tree. Like some earlier Jasons, Hodder avoided his castmates before filming.

Filming his first kill, in which he stabs a guy with a tent stake, he felt Jason's emotions running wild. "I felt and thought what he would at that moment," Hodder says. "There was this sort of satisfaction that washed over me, a feeling I could imagine Jason feeling. Sort of like a junkie taking a hit of his favorite drug. It felt amazing, but the feeling quickly fades and you want more." Hodder learned that killing was an addiction to Jason—something to be done quickly, albeit not carefully, to satisfy an urge. Unlike Freddy, Jason didn't torture his victims—too much!—only stepping in for the kill and then back out again.

"In scenes that involved violent stuff," Hodder explains, "I went into it, doing what I felt was right. When I saw footage of what I had done, I thought it was pretty neat. My biggest goal was to not look like I was acting. Some of the things I had to do were not hard to get to; to get to those violent points didn't take long. Maybe I'm a violent guy inside."

Jason was back in the lake as the flick ended, but that had never stopped him before—and a year later, he stowed away on a ship straight to Manhattan for the eighth installment. Hodder had a blast; for the first time, he did his thing in front of a live audience.

"We were there all night, one night, right in the middle of Times Square in the traffic island," he says, "and I'm used to shooting most of my scenes out in some desolate lake [where] there aren't too many onlookers or bystanders. When we were in the city there were hundreds of people lined on both sides of the streets. They had police barriers and everything else and I'm out in the traffic island, in full makeup with my mask on. Because I was so out in the open, I decided never to take the mask off while I was out in Times Square just because I would like to keep a little of the mystique there. I honestly felt like I was one of the Beatles or something, being on that traffic island looking, and seeing hundreds of people cheering and stuff. If I did any kind of Jason move like the patented head-tilt, or just stared at them, they went nuts. I had the best time." After filming wrapped, he appeared on Arsenio Hall's talk show without a voice. Then he played another legendary horror villain, stunting for the title character in *Leatherface*, the 1990 update to *The Texas Chainsaw Massacre* series.

The *13th* series again seemed to end in 1993's *Jason Goes to Hell: The Final Friday*, but once again, the *Final* became a "final," as he returned and headed north in 2001 with *Jason X*, which followed him to outer space.

During *Final Friday* filming, Hodder says, he and a pal pulled a prank on set visitors.

"You can't see one part of my real body because of the latex," he says. "If I sit motionless with the mask on and close my eyes so you can't see through the netting in the eyes, you can't really tell if it is a person or not." Hodder would sit in a corner, and his friend would bring people in and introduce them to the "replica."

"He would say, 'Hey, look. There's the Jason dummy we're gonna use for the explosion scene later. Oh yeah, just touch it. It feels really real.' And they'll be touching me, and poking me, and I don't move at all. And when I think it's the right time I'll jerk to life and make a big roar or something. It just scares the piss out of them."

In *Final Friday*, Hodder got to play both Jason and a doomed security guard, and in *Jason X* (produced by Cunningham's son Noel) he racked up 28 killings, more than any other Voorhees venture. One victim was cult director David Cronenberg.

As the long-awaited confrontation between Krueger and Voorhees came to reality, everyone thought that Hodder and Englund would finally go head to head. Everyone was disappointed. Hodder, and millions of others, were devastated.

Englund and Hodder *were* seen together in *Wishmaster* and the *Hatchet* movies.

Now, nearly a decade after donning the hockey mask for the final time, Hodder's the man whom film fans most closely associate with Jason. At conventions across the country, lines still form for the actor.

"I've always worked steadily doing stunts and I guess I always will," Hodder says. "But [playing Jason] has opened a lot of doors with more acting roles. Even though there was no dialogue in that part, people are more interested to say, 'Let's bring in that guy that played Jason and see if he can act.' I've done a lot of acting parts because of the association with Jason.

"I know other people who have played horror characters [and then] try to forget about it," Hodder recalls, "and I'll never understand that. Because it was horror that put them on the map."

Aloisi, Michael & Kane Hodder. *Unmasked*. U.S.A.:Dark Ink, 2011.
BarryAce. "Kane Hodder Interview." Youtubewww. Nov. 27, 2008. Retrieved Dec. 12, 2010, from http://www.youtube.com/watch?v=8o9Z0gOSRD4.
Bogdanovich, Peter. *Who The Hell's In It*. New York: Alfred A. Knopf, 2004.

Brooker, Richard. *Richard J. Brooker.* 2007. Retrieved Dec. 12, 2010, from http://www.richardjbrooker.com/index.html.
Clark, Sean. "Dash, Steve ('Friday the 13th Part 2')." *Dread Central.* 2006. Retrieved May 29, 2010, from http://www.dreadcentral.com/interviews/dash-steve-friday-13th-part-2.
Dash, Steve. E-mail interview. Nov. 30, 2013.
"DEADPIT Interviews: Ari Lehman aka First Jason!" Youtubewww. March 28, 2008. Retrieved April 4, 2010, from http://www.youtube.com/watch?v=nkfQGHfza6I.
Faraci, Dennis. "Exclusive! The New Jason Speaks." *Chud.* Feb. 12, 2009. Retrieved Dec. 12. 2010, from http://www.chud.com/articles/articles/18143/1/EXCLUSIVE-THE-NEW-JASON-SPEAKS-DEREK-MEARS-INTERVIEW/Page1.html.
Farrands, Daniel. *His Name Was Jason: 30 Years of Friday the 13th* [DVD]. Masimedia, 2009.
Freeman, Royce. "Kane Hodder. *Pit of Horror.*" n.d. Retrieved Dec. 12, 2010, from http://www.pitofhorror.com/main/hodder.html.
Graham, C.J. Phone interview. Jan. 6, 2014.
Hodder, Kane. Personal interview. Nov. 11, 2012.
Hutchinson, Stefan. *Halloween: 25 Years of Terror.* [DVD]. Paramount Pictures, 2007.
"Interview with Warrington Gillette." Fright Exclusive Interview. *Icons of Fright.* June 2004. Retrieved May 29, 2010, from http://www.iconsoffright.com/IV_Jason2.htm.
"JASONS (FRIDAY THE 13th) CINEMA WASTELAND." *Youtube.* Dec. 3, 2008. Retrieved April 4, 2010, from http://www.youtube.com/watch?v=DPQdtGcMVjc.
Keehnen, Owen. *Racks and Razors.* n.d. Retrieved April 4, 2010, from http://www.racksandrazors.com/arilehman.html.
Kerswell, J.A. *The Slasher Movie Book.* Chicago: Chicago Review Press, 2012.
Mears, Derek. Personal interview. May 10, 11, 2013.
"Q&A Ari Lehman webisode 9: favorite Jason." Youtubewww. July 12, 2008. Retrieved April 4, 2010, from http://www.youtube.com/watch?v=r4vQtK613DU&feature=related.
"Q&A Ari Lehman webisode 8: Jason and influences." Youtubewww. July 12, 2008. Retrieved April 4, 2010, from http://www.youtube.com/watch?v=3zHD_b-X7JI&feature=related.
"Q&A Ari Lehman webisode 1: Friday the 13th content and surprise." Youtubewww. July 12, 2008. Retrieved April 4, 2010, from http://www.youtube.com/watch?v=k66KUJxPUv0&feature=related.
"Q&A with Ari Lehman webisode 5: How he got the part." Youtubewww. July 12, 2008. Retrieved April 4, 2010, from http://www.youtube.com/watch?v=EoR9SRZW5yc&feature=related.
"Q&A with Ari Lehman webisode 7: Compares New Jason and old Jason." Youtubewww. July 12, 2008. Retrieved April 4, 2010, from http://www.youtube.com/watch?v=gtXLEpD6jeg&feature=related.
Shapiro, Marc. "Hodder Than Ever." *Fangoria* (Jan. 2007): 31.
White, Ted. Phone interview. Dec. 14, 2013.
Wieand, Dick. Phone interview. Dec. 20, 2013.

The *Friday the 13th* Family

If Betsy Palmer hadn't had auto trouble, the horror film world may never have gotten one of its most famous franchises.

One night in the late 1970s, the acting veteran left a theater in New York and started heading home in Connecticut. That's when her car decided to call it quits. "I spent five hours on the highway, trying to get somebody to fix the car so I could go home," she recalls. Eventually, someone helped her get on a train.

Perusing the car ads, Palmer spied a Volkswagen Sheraco, which ran just a few greenbacks short of $10,000. She remembered a recent call from her agent. "By that time, I was doing a show on Broadway called *Same Time Next Year* and my agent called and said, 'They want you to do a horror film!' I said 'No! My God, no!' I thought it was a stupid thing."

In nearly three decades of acting, on stages and screens big and small, horror was something Palmer had rarely even considered. She'd done a decade of the early game show *I've Got A Secret*, in which panelists—she was one—tried to guess a secret from their guests' backgrounds. She'd acted alongside James Cagney and Jack Lemmon in John Ford's 1955 World War II dramedy *Mister Roberts*, and did *The Long Gray Line* with Ford that same year. She'd been seen as a reporter on *The Today Show*, and appeared in dozens of other productions (as well as on James Dean's arm!) though the years.

But being the villain in a horror flick was something new—and not only that, but how many would take a 55-year-old lady seriously as a psycho killer?

"I said, 'You've got to be kidding!' Then I thought about needing a new car, so I told them to send me a script." Originally titled *Long Night at Camp Blood*, it was the story of a lovely lady named Pamela Voorhees, and her habit of prematurely ending the lives of unfortunate souls who happened to venture onto Camp Crystal Lake—the place where Pamela's beloved son Jason lost his life a few years ago.

"I read it, and I said, 'What a piece of shit! Nobody will ever see this stupid thing!' But I needed to buy a car, and they were going to pay me $10,000" (for just ten days of work).

"I thought, 'What the hell? I'm an actress, and it's a role to be played! It's not me as a human being; I'm an instrument, and I'm doing it,' so I did it. At the time, I didn't think anyone would see the dumb thing. I approached it the way I approached every role that I played since I studied to be an actress back in Chicago, and made [Pamela] as real as possible."

Almost every great villain needs a reason for his or her aggression. Jaws was just hungry. Freddy Krueger was ticked at the kids whose parents had killed him. Michael Myers was simply and naturally five feet off his rocker. Palmer decided to ground Pamela just a bit more in reality.

"My [acting] teacher from way, way back used to tell us that our characters had a life before they walked out on stage or in front of the camera," she said. "We found that life for ourselves, and we decided how we wanted to recreate the lives of our characters. It had to do with how we wanted to recreate the lives of the people we were portraying."

Starting with the minutest of details about Pamela's ring, Palmer concocted some novel-esque fiction. "Pamela had a boyfriend in high school, and she wore his class ring," she said. "That's who I was at this time. Back in those days, you didn't make love with one another. You necked, you petted, but you didn't go to the act of fornicating. I figured that she and he were so much in love, and going steady, and one day she told him she was pregnant, and he said, 'Don't tell me that! I don't want to know!'

"Her pregnancy went on at home, and one day, she began to show. That's when her father, fit to be tied, threw her out of the house and said, 'Never knock on our door again! You're out of here, you're a tramp, you're nothing!'"

Around the time filming began, Palmer was working with the Salvation Army, helping out those in need of food or clothing. "I thought Pamela would go to the Salvation Army and have the baby there," she said. "So there she was, this young mother with a little boy that was growing up."

A few summers later, Pamela decided to take a job cooking for the camp so her introverted son could finally get the chance to be with others his age. But one day, he was paddling through the lagoon, and the counselors took their eyes off him and put them on each

Her son Jason would take over from then on, but Pamela Voorhees (Betsy Palmer) was the original face of the *Friday the 13th* franchise.

other. "Because they went off to make love, the little boy drowns," Palmer said. "As a result, she goes back every year to do something so that other children won't come and die out of neglect. I decided to make that my justification of why she did what she did."

So while trying to save the lives of more innocent children, Pamela decided to take those of their protectors. Considering some horror villains' motives, that's one of the most sensible.

Unlike horror films from only a few years later, the first *Friday the 13th* didn't rely on massive spurts of blood and gore to make its point; it was more about creating an atmosphere of fear. A character turns around just in time for us to see a knife plunge into her, but it's not that bad. Most of the bodies don't show up until they're at room temperature.

And it wasn't too hard for Palmer, either; a male did most of her stunt double work, and she only shows up in the last twenty minutes—just long enough to tell the story of a boy who wasn't being watched.

"What monster could have done this?" Pamela says to impromptu heroine Alice (Adrienne King). Then her eyes and smile grow wide in an evil way, and Alice and the audience know that they've found the villain.

"Kill her, mommy! Don't let her get away! Don't let her live!" the lost soul says through his mother in one of the most chilling scenes in horror flick history. "I won't, Jason!" Pamela says, farther from reality with each passing moment. "I won't!"

"Everything you hear is my own voice!" Palmer said. "They had me come in and do some voiceover work, and I did all these little words that they wanted. It works, doesn't it, in its own crazy way?"

Jason Voorhees' ominous hockey mask has become a landmark in the film world, not just the horror genre.

Palmer finished up, got her new car, and didn't expect to ever hear the name of Voorhees again. But three decades, eleven sequels (counting *Freddy vs. Jason*), and one remake later, Pamela Voorhees still lives in the dark hearts of horror movie fans.

"It became a cult film, and I became a cult killer!" she said with a laugh. "I still think that's a joke! I've only seen the first one three or four times, and none of the sequels."

Despite a slew of offers, Palmer never reprised her role in the sequels. Nana Visitor played the part in the opening moments of the 2009 remake, while Paula Shaw appeared as Ms. Voorhees in the opening credits of 2003's *Freddy vs. Jason*. Stock footage of Palmer was used in *Friday the 13th: Part 2*.

"I've gotten fan mail from Russia, South America, all over the world," she says, "and it amazes me when I get those letters and pictures.

"I'm delighted about the whole thing. At autograph signings, when the people come, they love Ms. Voorhees so much. When I do autograph signings, people stand there and I talk to them and take pictures, and I hold their babies, and I think, 'Why do you love this movie? What makes it so attractive to you?' They say, 'We know why you did it!' Whatever quality that I brought to it, and my reason for playing it the way I did, I don't think they'll ever forget the first Ms. Voorhees."

Many good horror films have a vixen heroine. The one who didn't go out and get drunk with her friends. The one with sense enough not to sleep around. The one who never went off by herself into the woods, a perfect place for a killer to hide. The one who appeared to be something of an introvert, perhaps even a coward, until she was forced to summon the strength necessary (perhaps from unreleased affection tension) to take out the evil creature who'd heartlessly stolen some of her friends, by any and all gory means necessary.

Adrienne King got her start in the scariest genre. But she couldn't know that, in the not-so-distant future, her career, and her life, would be temporarily halted by a different kind of horror—the kind that stepped off the screen and into the real world.

"I did my first commercial when I was six months old," King says. "When I got to about age eight or nine, I landed the featured role of Melinda in the Hallmark Hall of Fame production of *Inherit the Wind*. It was during this incredible experience I realized that acting *had* to be a part of my life and I realized that I was desperate for the camera again." Many plays and commercials followed.

"From ninth grade, I was in and out of [New York City], auditioning," she says. "As long as I kept my grades up, everybody was cool with it. I did extra work and danced in *Hair* and all the disco scenes in *Saturday Night Fever*, but if you blink, you'll never see me. But I was on the set, learning everything I could."

The change from child to grownup actress, however, was a bit difficult. "When you're in your teens or early twenties, you're out there just trying to get an audition, trying to get an agent," she says. "At the time of *Friday the 13th*, I didn't have a theatrical agent."

In the midst of doing a Burger King commercial, King learned of the new horror franchise.

"I had a dear friend whose best friend was a friend of Barry Moss," she remembers. (Moss helped cast the film.) "[Producer-director] Sean Cunningham told me I had the qualities that he was looking for."

At the audition, even up against hundreds of others (Sally Field had been the crew's first choice), King proved him right in a big way. "Every actor hopes for the opportunity to prove himself or herself, and after weeks of callbacks, they brought me in for the final screen test. I knocked the ball out of the park. I'm pretty sure my scream is what nailed it!" she proclaims. "Sean felt that I could handle Alice and give her the dimensional qualities that she needed." After a summer of casting, she headed to the shores of Crystal Lake (actually New Jersey's Camp Nobebosco).

Adrienne King's stepped out of wonderland and into one of terror in the first *Friday the 13th*.

All in all, it was as far from Wonderland as an Alice could get. "I looked deep within myself, but there was very little on the written page," she said of getting ready for the character. "Originally, they didn't have a script; they had sold the title [Cunningham and Victor

Miller were still finishing the screenplay]. The characters and their back stories, we all filled in ourselves. We got a lot of ideas to fill out the characters." Just like King herself, Alice is an artist: King's artistic skills won her a fine arts scholarship to New York City's Fashion Institute of Technology, and her work, some of which was based on Alice's exploits, has been published and bought by fans.

"That's how I got into Alice, just using what I had to work with, on the set," she recalls. "I remember sketching up in the lifeguard's chair, enjoying the scene of Kevin and Harry [Crosby] doing pushups to buff up for the next scene."

Originally, the film didn't include the scene where young Jason attacks Alice in the lake. However, inspired by the legendary shocking ending to *Carrie,* in which the title character reaches out of the ground and grabs one of her tormentors—in a dream—Cunningham decided to give his viewers a similar stunner.

"I will always consider the lake scene to be one of the biggest moments in horror," King said. "It was also one of the more difficult ones, but everyone had a 'get it done' mentality on set so we just pushed forward. The lake was 38 degrees when we shot that scene. There were only two sets of clothes for me, which meant we had two takes to get it right. There were no wet suits or stunt people available, so we did everything we could do to nail it, and we definitely did."

At age fourteen, swimming in the cold November weather, Ari Lehman got to become the latest entry on the "child terror" list.

"When I jumped up out of the water on the first take," says the first Jason, "Adrienne King jumped clear out of the boat and into the lake with a yell! She was then dried off and her hair blow-dried so that we could resume shooting. We got it right the second take, and

Young Ari Lehman became the first Jason Voorhees in *Friday the 13th*.

to her credit, Adrienne looks totally oblivious to the fact that a deranged child covered in pond scum is about to grab her and drag her under."

The production shut down several times because money kept running out. "This is how independent films truly work," King explains. But by the time it came time to shoot the final confrontation between Alice and Pamela—known on set as "The Ballet of the Machete"—neither money trouble nor her previous uncertainty was going to stop King from making Alice into the fearless heroine. When the film was screened a few months later, King got to see her final work. "When I saw it, I was able to remove myself from it and say, 'That's intense!'" recalls King, who did all her own stunts for the film.

With her mom Anita sitting beside her and distributors behind them, King watched herself on screen. When Anita saw the shocking final scene, she "totally jumped at least three feet out of her chair and screamed," King says. "Behind me, I saw handshakes going on. I think my mom was instrumental in the quick sell of *Friday the 13th*." According to King, the film finished atop the box office charts its opening weekend, even beating out Best Picture–winning *Ordinary People.*

"That amazed everyone," she says. "I'm pretty sure that that was the weekend they decided there was going to be a sequel. If you had told us while we were filming that the film would ever, one, be finished; two, be a hit; three, have a sequel; four, be a billion-dollar franchise; five, still be here in 30 years, talking about it, never in a trillion years would we have believed it."

But now, decades after its inception, fans who weren't even alive when the series kicked off still identify with the story of Crystal Lake and the only one lucky enough to survive the opening round.

"I ask anyone who wants an autograph why they like the film," King says, "and a nine-year-old girl said, 'Because it's a classic!' It's real, because everyone in it is real, and that's what Sean wanted from the beginning. It still packs a punch. It still rings true. All these people over the course of time really identified with Alice as a survivor. When everything looks like she's going to die, she survives.

"My fans have become my friends," she says. "They are the reason that I'm back after all this time after my nasty stalking incident."

That's one dark side to stardom. The unluckiest of the famous inspire just a little too much enthusiasm in their fans, and the line between fantasy and reality becomes blurred.

People have been sentenced to time in jail and/or psychiatric confinement for stalking John Lennon, Rebecca Schaeffer, Mel Gibson, David Letterman, Gwyneth Paltrow, Catherine Zeta-Jones, and too many others. Theresa Saldana, who played Joe Pesci's wife Lenore in *Raging Bull,* was attacked and stabbed by a crazed fan in 1982; she recovered, continued her acting career, and formed an organization to help women who have had similar experiences.

Shortly after *Friday the 13th* wrapped, King had another terrifying experience, but this time there would be no director to yell, "Cut!" "He was a very talented wacko, which is a horrible combination," she says of the man who disrupted her acting career. "People think of stalkers as mentally ill people who just live in the shadows. This was a mentally ill person that had a lot of connections. Right out of the gate, unfortunately for me, I was dealing with some very bizarre behavior, and it escalated."

The stalker managed to learn King's address, where she ate lunch, exercised, nearly everything. King found Polaroids slipped under her apartment door, sometimes of herself the day before.

The person snuck into her apartment and defaced her artwork. Then he found her and put a gun to her head.

"The problem was that back in the 1980s, stalking wasn't taken seriously, and unfortunately, unless something happened to us physically, the authorities dismissed it very casually. It wasn't until there was a physical altercation that the person was slapped on their wrist, and then the game was done, because it was a power play, a control play. All stalkers want to do is be close, be in control, and have a part of your life. Luckily, it ended quietly without physical harm, but still there was a great deal of emotional harm. It's a story that resonates inside of me."

The person spent time behind bars (though not nearly enough, according to the actress). But while she was physically fine, King, and her acting career were almost irrevocably damaged. Aside from showing up long enough for Jason to take her out in the opening moments of *Friday the 13th II* (1983), she dropped off the Hollywood radar for almost a decade.

"It took me a while to get out of it," she says, "but that's when I started my dark-artist phase." A visit to a London college helped kick-start her career in art. She got back to movies in the 1993 Mel Gibson flick *The Man Without a Face*, but this time she wasn't in front of the camera. Her new job was looping voices (actors and actresses create background dialogue, usually for films with crowded group scenes). In 1993 alone, King worked behind the scenes of *Philadelphia, The Pelican Brief,* and *What's Eating Gilbert Grape,* then showed her talents in the box-office smashes *Jerry Maguire* and *Titanic.*

"Voiceover work saved me," she says. "There's no question that it all came around full circle, and I'm a better, more compassionate and stronger actor and artist. There's such a wonderful camaraderie between me and my fans.

Ginny Fields (Amy Steel) is determined to make it through *Friday the 13th II* alive.

"It took a long time to get whole again. The fans were responsible for that last piece that was missing when I found out how much they cared. When I was made aware of the incredible fanbase of loyal and devoted fans that Alice had, and how much they cared about why I had disappeared from the series, it helped me fill in the missing piece and realize that it had all been for a reason.

"I think it was a really brilliant move to make the villain the son in the [*Friday the 13th*] sequels. It was a new direction, and you can get more out of the movies that way. The only thing fans always ask me about (and I still have no idea) is how Jason exists. They want to know if it really was a dream, and if so, how Jason would have become an adult in just a few months. Thirty years later, I still don't have those answers."

The first *Friday the 13th* sequel was again set at the Camp, with a new batch of counselors getting ready to reopen the place. "I think I got lucky with the role of Ginny, on a couple of fronts," remembers Amy Steel, making her film debut as the new heroine of horror. "She's pretty much who I am. It wasn't really a stretch. We have the same energy, so you could say I was typecast. But the hard part is really owning who we are as women, all the strength, faith, and calm … at the same time."

Viewers got the feeling that Ginny might have been a class president back in school, on the way to a good college, heading into the medical field. Maybe not much in the fun-loving sense like her co-workers, certainly not the boy-crazy sort who really thought much about love just yet, but someone you could sit down and have a long, deep conversation with about some serious subjects.

"I liked my character Ginny because she wasn't a total bimbo," Steel remembers. "She was smart and confident and you knew she had something driving her. When I played Ginny, I was really young and different from a lot of the people working at the time so that came out in my character. I was naturally suspicious of cocky guys at that age, and you see a lot of that when I'm on screen with Paul. I tried to put so much behind the actual words in the script just so she felt almost unreachable, to Paul and to audiences. I wanted her to have some power."

It's Jason (Steve Dash at first, Warrington Gillette during the last scenes) with the power at the start. His head is still draped in a pillowcase—the hockey mask would debut in the next film—and counselors keep winding up at the business end of his machete. "Working for two months at night on a film eventually gave me the heebie-jeebies," Steel admits. "Constantly having dirt and water thrown at you, and watching these actors you're working with killed and blood pouring out of them—you know it's not real, but at a certain point, it all becomes a very tense experience. I even had nightmares about Steve Dash chasing me. I definitely would get caught up in the anxiety when I was shooting scenes. Working in some of the environments I did for *Friday the 13th* really gets you into a vulnerable mindset."

Ginny's chased into a cabin, only to find Pamela's head on a table, and the carcass of the Alice that removed it laying nearby. Clad in Pamela's sweater, Ginny tries to turn the frightful tables on her tormentor. Paul arrives as the two go blade to blade (his ax, her knife), and Ginny goes metal (not mental!) on Jason, pounding the machete through his arm.

"Being scared is a relatively easy emotion to reach for," Steel says. "It's not that hard to imagine somebody coming after you with a knife." But just as he always did, Jason finds his way back one last time. With Ginny and Paul seemingly safe inside their cabin, he blasts through the window. The sack over his head gone and, *man*, do we wish he'd put it back on. The two manage to fight him off, at least for this cinematic round. "The first time I saw the movie, all I heard was this group of woman saying, 'Why didn't she run? Why did she go back in that place?'" Steel remarks. "Like I had a choice!"

Decades later, Steel (who, like Ginny, became a therapist in real life), can still feel the character's effects. "It's a hindsight 20/20 kind of thing. Now I look to her for inspiration when I am afraid, just in facing challenges—not lie there as some monster chases me!"

When Jason decided to disregard his own *Final Chapter* and go looking for a little *New Blood* in 1988, he found some prey that could fight back with more than fists and knives. Long before Jason and Freddy went boot to boot over a decade later, the *New Blood* group made some minor modifications to a trendsetting lady of horror, and gave Jason an opponent that even he had reason to fear.

"I didn't even know it was *Friday the 13th*," Lar Park Lincoln recalls of getting ready for the seventh installment in 1987. "It was called *Birthday Bash*." She played the lovely innocent Tina, traumatized by her abusive father's death (he drowned in Crystal Lake). Things start to happen around her, such as things flying off the wall and structures collapsing when she gets upset. On a break from institutionalization, Tina's back at the Lake, with a group of teenagers next door living it up. The typical scared introvert that horror heroines usually begin as, Tina soon finds some acceptance, even if her telekinesis scared them into liking her. "I had to cry very quickly," she says. "I got a *lot* of migraines."

Still, becoming Tina, and learning to control the techniques that torture her at first, took Park Lincoln farther than high-speed facial tremors (watching Tina's countenance jump around). She studied people who did visualization, and met with psychics.

"The psychics were trying to teach me not to make her psychic ability what you've seen in movies," Park Lincoln says. "A thought will come into your head and you'll react to it, and it's not necessarily the big psychic-looking stuff we'd seen in movies. That's what I wanted to come across."

Unlike Carrie White, Tina maintained a sense of stability when using her powers, at least once she could control them. Also unlike Carrie, Tina had but one target on her mind, and her vigilantism was a bit more justified. Jason kills one friend after another, soon slaughtering Tina's doctor and her mother.

She drops a porch on

Lar Park Lincoln's Tina used her gorgeous looks and telekinetic mind to battle Jason in *Friday the 13th Part VII*!

him, then drenches him with gas and blasts him and the house. But the masked man keeps coming, until Tina's mental strength resurrects her dad to save her.

That same year, Park Lincoln took on another icon in an episode of *Freddy's Nightmares*.

"Freddy was tougher, because he was on TV," she laughs. "On TV, you have to work *fast!*"

King, Adrienne. Phone interview. April 22, 2009.
King, Adrienne. Personal interview. Nov. 11, 2012.
King, Adrienne. E-mail interview. Oct. 11, 2013.
Nutman, Philip. "King Talks." *Fangoria* (Dec. 1990): 22–26, 59.
Palmer, Betsy. Phone interview. Jan. 23, 2009.
Park Lincoln, Lar. Personal interview. May 11, 2013.
Shapiro, Marc. "The Women of Crystal Lake." *Fangoria* 83 (June 1989): 18–21.
Steel, Amy. Personal interview. Nov. 11, 2012.
Wixson, Heather. "Interview with Adrienne King." *Dread Central*. 2006. Retrieved May 31, 2010, from http://www.dreadcentral.com/interviews/king-adrienne-final-girls.
Worland, Rick. *The Horror Film*. Malden, MA: Blackwell Publishing, 2007.

•••••••••••••••••••••••••••

Sid Haig

From the moment we first met a man named Captain Spaulding, we were scared, but also sort of awed.

Moments into our first introduction to him in *House of 1000 Corpses*, Spaulding has a robber's gun between his eyes. But even then, there's no fear, no backing down—Spaulding's gesture of "surrender" is punctuated by a double-bird hand gesture and a bunch of F-word-riddled one-liners. Moments later, the offenders have gotten deadly tastes of their own medicine, and Spaulding's going on about his business—and his business is his Museum of Monsters and Madmen, a shrine to lovers of fried chicken and serial murder.

Maybe you're one of those people that has a deep-seated phobia about clowns, the fear caused or at least grotesquely exacerbated from watching *It* or *Poltergeist*. Perhaps Spaulding just pounded that right back into your psyche, but there might be a bit more to Spaulding's terrifying appeal that made him frightening but still fun. Charismatic. Cool.

"The best part about playing a 'good' villain is that you can help to propel the story further," Haig says. "You keep it moving. The heavies in a film are like the drummers in a band; they set the tempo."

Spaulding was quite a bit different from the bad guy Haig played against James Bond in *Diamonds Are Forever*. Actually, he was quite a bit different from just about anybody in horror film history. It's tough to find much on Haig's résumé that would help him get ready for this role.

He didn't research the scare factor of clowns. As a certified hypnotherapist in real life, he didn't examine the history of patients who'd had run-ins like this in the past. He just became. That's not a sentence fragment.

"It's who I am!" Haig asserts, perhaps not entirely seriously. "I'm crazy. It's organic while you're doing it, and clinical after you've done it. You just go for it. Within every

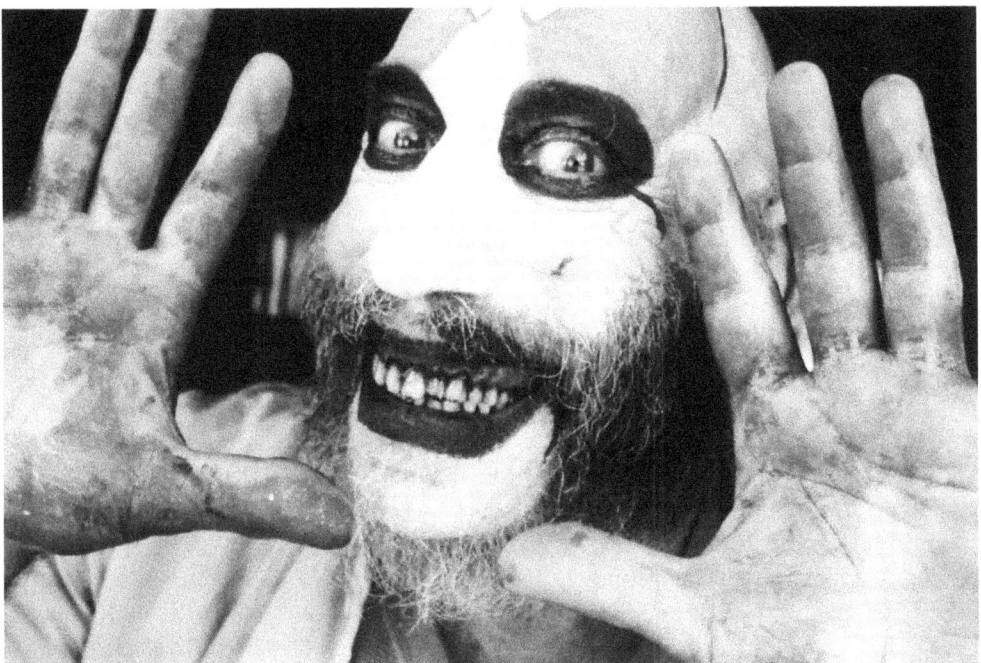
America's clown phobia kicked into overdrive with Sid Haig's work as Captain Spaulding.

person is every personality type, so you just have to find that personality type inside you and let them out. You just have to remember to put them back at the end of the day."

Through our first meeting with Spaulding, we weren't quite sure what to make of him. In *House of 1000 Corpses,* we don't know what's up with this. We get the feeling that he knows more than he's telling anyone on either side of the screen. We see Spaulding on TV advertising his company, but we're not really sure if that's who he is; you spend a big part of the first half of *1000 Corpses* waiting for him to wash his face and take that tiny hat off and return to (what we call) normalcy.

Eventually, however, we accept that the man on the TV is the man away from it as well. Spaulding's who he is, no matter who's looking or speaking. But we're still not sure what's driving him, only that he's acquainted with the royally screwed up Firefly family, unofficially led by beautiful young daughter Baby (Sheri Moon Zombie, whose husband Rob directed it), a group delighting in killing and torturing everyone they draw into their crowd. Not until the very end do we really see Spaulding's direct link to the family, as he leaves his heavenly amusement park to deliver their final victim.

It's the nature of film audiences to start to care, if not always consciously, about the people they see on screen, the more time we spend with them. That's why, even after watching the Fireflys work their dark magic in *1000 Corpses,* we wanted to see more and know more.

Fortunately, two years later, Haig and the Zombies, who'd also worked together in the *Halloween* remake, teamed to bring the family back to life, becoming *The Devil's Rejects.*

In the *Rejects* opening, copied in 2013's *Texas Chainsaw 3D* update, we saw the Fireflys exchanging sad goodbyes as vengeful police opened fire upon then, asking us the audience to sympathize with them. Some die and others head to the clink, but a couple get away, including Baby. One quick phone call later, we find out the true relationship between her and Spaulding: He's her daddy. And, as Baby and her brothers nab a few hostages in a motel, he's coming to help her out.

"I know it sounds weird," Haig recalls, "but [becoming Spaulding] wasn't that difficult, 'cause all I really had to do was hook into my own insanity and just go from there. You know, there's a little craziness in everybody, so I just plugged mine in."

As his family joyfully tortures and slaughters a few victims, Spaulding arrives (there's a special *Texas* tribute when one of the Fireflys wears a mask made of a victim's face). The group escapes, but a former friend betrays them, and an officer whose brother they iced in *1000 Corpses* starts putting them through as much suffering as any of their victims. Keeping with the short memories of film audiences, it's easy to forget their past actions. And that respect we had for Spaulding goes in a different and stronger direction.

Is he crazy? Is he evil? Both? Whether he's laughing, crying, or even getting his ass kicked, Spaulding never surrenders. When you kill him, if you ever could, you might be able to get over on him. Maybe not even then. Maybe never. Maybe he'll be up or down, wherever he's going, in the afterlife, still laughing at you.

"As a hypnotherapist and someone who works in the area of the mind," Haig says. "I kind of know how it works, and in order to keep order in your own head, your fantasies have to be a little more extreme than your reality. And since we're living in a reality which is extremely extreme, with bombings every day and people doing weird stuff right and left, then the fantasy level's gotta kick up even more. So the idea of runnin' around and shootin' people and gettin' it on is never really that big a deal."

Haig turned Spaulding into the type of guy you'd want to drink beer with if he went on a killing spree—it's why, even after watching he and his family torture and slaughter a multitude of innocents throughout *The Devil's Rejects*, we still wanted them to escape at the end.

You can't *dislike* Spaulding. It's his personality. We probably enjoyed watching Freddy Krueger, rooted for him, laughed at his one-liners. But he still wasn't really someone we *liked* as a person. Spaulding's the type of guy you admire for fighting, even if he's fighting for something evil (in your eyes, of course, probably not in his).

Spaulding and what's left of his family manage to get away, but the cops have the upper hand again, forming a blockade across the highway. As so many film villains do, the group goes out in a blazing bullet barrage of glory. Rather than live apart, they all go down together.

But still, we never see Spaulding dead.

"The guy is an absolute maniac," Haig says. "Totally fearless. He doesn't care about anything. 'I am the epiphany of the American spirit. I'm what this country used to be all about, and that means if you're going to fuck with me, you better bring all your shit, 'cause I don't know nothing about no Berlin Walls, no 38th Parallels, no DMZ, no drawing lines in the goddamn sand. You piss me off, I'm gonna come over there and put my boot all up in your ass.'"

Carle, Chris. "Comic-Con 2005: IGN Interviews Sid Haig." *IGN*. July 15, 2005. Retrieved June 5, 2012, from http://www.ign.com/articles/2005/07/17/comic-con-2005-ign-interviews-sid-haig.

Garentano, Christopher P. "An Interview with Sid Haig." *Icons of Fright*. 2006. Retrieved June 4, 2012, from http://www.iconsoffright.com/IV_SidAYG.htm.

Haig, Sid. Personal interview. Nov. 11, 2012.

"Interview with Sid Haig." *Badmouth*. 2012. Retrieved June 10, 2012, from http://badmouth.net/interview-sid-haig/.
Juvinall, Michael. "More Horror Exclusive: Interview with Captain Spaulding Himself: Sid Haig." *More Horror*. 2013. Retrieved June 5, 2012, from http://www.morehorror.com/More-Horror-Exclusive-Interview-with-Captain-Spaulding-Himself-Sid-Haig

Celebrating *Halloween*!

As a means to measure the fear factor of a horror film, this one might be tough to beat: are *its own stars* afraid to watch it?

Yes, yes, so elementary school students shouldn't be watching gory horror films, even if they happen to be perpetrating the violence. But even the smallest star of *Halloween* couldn't bring himself to watch himself become cinema's newest pint-size murderer.

"I had no idea who Michael Myers was before I got this," admits Daeg Faerch, the fourth-grade star of the 2007 Rob Zombie remake, the ninth installment in the series. "I submitted and I got an audition and I surprisingly didn't get a callback. I just got it.... They just told me to give them a scary look and read the lines."

The newer version spends quite a bit of time showing Michael as more than just a slashing psychopath. Here we meet the first Myers family, and see the son slowly being driven out of his wits. The original portrayed the youth as just naturally evil, probably from the point of conception; here, he gets shoved down the wrong path.

"I think, as a kid Michael Myers was a completely normal, lovable kid," Faerch opines. "And then his family started going downhill, like [his mom's] boyfriend being mean to him, his sister being mean to him and everything. He went downhill with them and kept on going and going."

He not only got to cuss out a school principal but beat the snot out of a bully and cut down (literally) four other kids.

"There was only one part where I kind of got chills," Faerch recalls. "The house that we were filming in, the Michael Myers house, it was really close to the original. There's a scene that I did and I was in there all by myself. Between takes, I got so scared. I have a knife in my hand, it's bloody, I'm bloody, it's like, 'This is creepy.'

"I only read my stuff and then I couldn't read the rest," he remembers, following Mother's Orders. "I have not seen the movie and I will not see the movie. Only the first 10 or 15 minutes."

He was following in the shady footsteps of original young Michael Will Sandin, who'd had quite a different part to play back in John Carpenter's original 1978 film, which put Haddonfield, Illinois, on the map for all the scariest reasons. In one of the most ominous openings in film history, the original *Halloween* begins from the first-person perspective of the clown-masked youngster stalking his family members throughout his house (producer Debra Hill's hands became the youngster's). Without so much as a word, he slaughters his sister, then terrifies other siblings until that shot at the end when the clown mask is torn off and his dazed-looking face stares off into the night.

Sandin stayed away from the cameras after that, but the welcoming arms of the horror movie community kept reaching out, and brought him into the world of conventions decades later.

"I prepared for the role by just trying to look as scared as I could as a seven-year-old kid. That day, I was just going over it, practicing with my mom. Once we started filming, I wasn't supposed to look scared, just to have a regular blank look on my face. Preparing for the role was different than what I was shooting that night."

But as the film neared its end, another's countenance would appear.

"I was a struggling actor who was at the time sleeping on a friend's couch," remembers Tony Moran, the first adult Michael. "My agent called and started to apologize for the lack of job opportunities."

But she might just have had some good news: There was going to be a new terrorizer called *Halloween,* starring a young starlet named Jamie Lee Curtis as Laurie Strode, sister and prey of the man named Michael.

"I went on to tell her that I didn't have a clue who Jamie Lee Curtis was and I really wasn't into doing a horror movie," Moran says. "I was still also unaware of the fact that the role called for a mask to be worn. What ended up really getting my interest in the role was that my agent had mentioned Donald Pleasence was also going to be in the film. I was a very big fan of his." Pleasence was Dr. Sam Loomis, who would chase Myers through five *Halloween* flicks before his 1995 passing.

Now psyched about the break, Moran didn't sleep, bathe, or shave for days before the audition. Clad in unwashed clothes and steel-toed hiking boots, he strolled into a dirty office to meet with producer Irwin Yablans and director John Carpenter, just beginning his ascent to horror fame.

Moran sat down, raised his boots into the air, slammed them onto the desk, and demanded coffee. Jumping straight up in shock, the officials knew he was their man. Before sunset, Moran was Michael.

"The first day on set, I find out I have to wear a mask!" Moran says. "I had longer, thick hair at the time. So the crew tells me I should think about putting Vaseline in my hair so when the mask is being ripped off my head, the hair doesn't stick to the mask and get pulled out. I was thinking, 'Oh, great!'" We only get a fleeting glance at Moran's face when Curtis yanks off his mask (which has morphed from a clown to Bill Shatner) in the closing moments. In its day, *Halloween* was the most profitable independent film ever.

Nick Castle played Michael in costume. According to Castle, the moviemakers "wanted a certain look for the person that was going to be Michael Myers when the mask came off. They didn't want someone handsome like me! They said they wanted someone who looked angelic, more against type, but I'll let the audience decide whether they made a good casting decision."

When the sequel showed up in 1981, Dick Warlock was behind the mask. Having everything but an atomic bomb used on him, Myers appeared to be finished, apparently polished off by his sister's jamming of a coat hanger through his eye. But it took much more to stop Jason Voorhees and Freddy Krueger, and Myers wasn't going down after being "killed" just once.

"I was interviewed for the job as stunt coordinator on the film," says Warlock, who'd stunted for Richard Dreyfuss in *Jaws*. "At the time, I hadn't even seen the original *Halloween*. It wasn't until I talked with [director] Rick Rosenthal that I was aware of the original film and viewed it for some hints as to how to play him. I chose the scene where Michael rises up from the bedroom floor after Laurie has stuck in … the coat hanger as the idea to play him in a mechanical manner. I went down the hall to meet [Rosenthal]," Warlock recalls, "and the mask was laying there, so I put it on, walked to his doorway, and just stood there and looked at him. He said, 'Who are you?' and I didn't answer, just stood there and looked at him."

He'd taken quite the chance, and it paid off, as Warlock nailed the part.

Now stalking his sister through a hospital—why he's so angry at her individually still isn't clear, and never really was throughout the series—Myers stabs with scalpels, puts a sledgehammer through a guard's head, and drowns a hot nurse in a hot tub. Finally Laurie and Loomis trap him in an operating room and set him on fire, until he finally collapses.

"First off, you need a good special effects team and a group of dependable safety people," Warlock explains of the final scene. "In my case, the safety team was all stuntguys…. The effects team sets up the fire portion of the gag: When, where and how it will work. We do a walk-through rehearsal with them, the safety guys and the camera and lighting departments so that everyone knows what will happen. Next, I determine that all departments are ready. I then put on the fire suit that protects me from the flames and heat. I don't do this too soon as if I do I will begin to sweat and that means steam. Steam is the enemy of the stunt guy when doing a fire gag. It causes severe damage to the skin tissues, etc.… After the suit is on, the mixture that will actually catch fire is applied by the effects guys." Through two takes of the scene, his arm was burned.

This profile will not be discussing 1982's *Halloween III: Season of the Witch* (in which Warlock had a small role) because it deviated from the Michael Myers formula, instead telling the story of an evil toy company planting explosives into its masks to kill children. Myers came back in 1988 for the aptly titled *The Return of Michael Myers.* This time, George Wilbur would be playing the masked madman, now stalking Laurie's young daughter Jamie (Danielle Harris); his sister had been killed in a car accident, but that would be tossed out the window a decade later.

"A friend of mine … was the stunt coordinator for *Halloween 4*," recalls Wilbur, "and he told me to come in for an interview since I fit the producers' ideal body type for Michael Myers." Seven years later, he'd become the first performer to don the Myers mask twice, getting back into character for *The Curse of Michael Myers.*

"I absolutely would have been excited to have taken the role in *Halloween 4* had I known what I was stepping into," he says. "Of course, after part 4 came out, I knew how big of a role it was. When I was called back to do *Halloween 6,* I packed my bags right away."

As part four ended, we thought Jamie would be the bad girl (see Danielle Harris' profile for more on *that*). But things wouldn't continue that way in 1989's *Halloween 5;* Jamie's having *Shining*-esque communications with her uncle early on, but she's frightened back to normalcy after he makes another attempt at her life. Don Shanks became the new Myers, and to make Mike his own, Shanks decided not to watch the previous movies.

"What you have to do, especially when you don't verbalize anything, you have to internalize the part," he explains. "You get the script. You read what's supposed to be happening and you try to imagine what you're supposed to be doing. And when you think about that, it changes your walk, it changes your attitude. It puts you into that character without saying anything.

Halloween has been an unlucky night for generations of Michael Myers men.

"There was that one scene where [Dr. Loomis is] talking out into the woods because he knows that Michael's out there," Shanks recalls, "and I had wrapped for the night, but [Pleasence] came to my dressing room and politely asked me if I'd stay. I said, 'Sure.' He was having trouble really getting into that scene, so he asked me to stand in the woods. He said, 'I just need to know that you're out there. I don't need to see you. But by knowing you're out there, it'd help.' Because he'd tried it in rehearsal and he wasn't able to focus unless he felt Michael was out there."

In 1998, Curtis returned as the elder Strode sibling to take on her brother in *Halloween: H20*. Dozens of potential "Myerses" tried out for the role. "They had interviewed 50 or 60 people, and were completely unhappy," recalls Chris Durand. With some experience in both stunts and horror—the year before, he'd stunted as the killer in the second *Scream*—he made it to the top five, then to the top two. "What it basically came down to was, who did they want to hang out with for the next three months?" he remembers. "I must have made a good impression!" As for playing Myers, "I wasn't really worried about trying to match what everyone else had done," he says. "I was a clean slate."

With several of her friends and students dead and her son's life in danger, Laurie, now a college professor, braces for a one-on-one with Myers. The scene where the two meet and stare through a door window became one of the most memorable in the entire series, and trailers used it to bring viewers both new and experienced into the theaters.

"There's a lot said without saying anything, on both sides," Durand explains. "I made him essentially the boogeyman, the guy who chases you in your dreams. He keeps coming."

When Laurie chopped off her brother's head at the end of *H20*, everyone thought that the series was over. But four years later, Myers came back once again in *Resurrection*, proving that two in the family could play the death-fabrication game: Laurie had removed the wrong guy's noggin. With her now in a mental institution, Michael finally gets his prey, stabbing her and launching her off a building.

On the other side of the mask this time was Brad Loree. One of the moviemakers called him and asked how tall he was. "I said, 'Well, I'm six foot and a half,' and she said, 'Oh, that's perfect! Can you come in tomorrow to meet the executives about doubling for Michael Myers?' So, I said 'Yeah.'" And I thought, "'It's kind of strange that Mike Myers is doing this horror film.'"

The next day, Loree sat down with Rosenthal, who was getting his second shot at directing a *Halloween*. "Rick had me stand against this wall and walk towards him, imitating 'the walk.' We did it like four or five times. And then he turned to the producers and said 'Yeah, this guy'll be fine.'"

Loree went over the first few films, but kept coming back to the original. "I remember being on the edge of my seat," he says. "I watched the first one over and over and over again and just tried to copy Nick Castle because to me, he *is* Michael Myers."

For years, Rob Zombie had been the one doing the entertaining. He and the rest of White Zombie and his various other shock-rock bands had been making audiences scream, sing, and mosh for years. But to put together his own version of something that had been told over and over again, Zombie decided to be the puppeteer himself. He chose to step behind the cameras and into the audience, and allow others to tell the story he created (or re-re-re-re-created).

Just as Zombie was never shy about pushing the envelope on stage with his bands, his screen story went much deeper and detailed than any of the previous films. For the first time, audiences would get to see and meet Michael up close and personal, and learn not just about who he was and what he did, but *why* and how he ended up with such a taste for death and destruction. For the first time, Michael would play a role as big or bigger than those desperately trying to elude and destroy him.

Zombie had put his directing boots on the ground with 2005's *The Devil's Rejects*, and figured that one of the fellows he'd filmed there would be perfect for the role. "It's a fan favorite," Tyler Mane says of the *Halloween* franchise, "and there's a little bit of pressure there, but I think everybody was really happy with the way it turned out. I just hoped that they saw Michael as more than a one-dimensional character."

Though he'd roared into action in *X-Men, The Scorpion King,* and other such films, some of Mane's main experience at acting out violence came from pro wrestling. At nearly seven feet tall, he was used to being one of the biggest around. He also knew the basics of making things look quite a bit more painful than they actually were. "Any time you're doing any violent scenes," he says, "you have to make sure you take care of [your co-star], and still make it as real as possible."

Though Myers' face would be hidden by his long hair and slumped posture through much of the film, Mane would get to spend more time without the mask than many of his predecessors.

In the early days of filming, he also oversaw his younger self—or Michael's, in the form of Faerch. (Zombie's wife Shari, who'd be a cornerstone in all his films, played Michael's mother Deborah, and Malcolm McDowell became the new Dr. Loomis, with Scout Taylor-Compton snaring Laurie's role. Harris came back, playing her friend Annie.)

Mane also spent a bit of time thinking about his own past, including some battles with dyslexia.

"Everybody has their awkward moments growing up, whether they admit to them or not," he says.

Mane had to step inside the mind of someone who was not necessarily a madman (that's too easy a label to place on people), but someone who took psychosis to a new level, a person who was perfectly at home in his own little world, but could never have survived following the rules of another. He read up on those who had committed such acts in real life. "They interact with society, and most people don't even know who they are," he says. "[Michael is] like a hobo, and he interacts with society, going back to where he came from."

It took Faerch's work in Zombie's prologue to develop such a mindset, and not only for the audience's benefit. Mane watched his character's younger self, then brought it to a much more violent level.

"You hand someone a mask and a butcher's blade," Mane says, "and 99.9 percent of the people will just put it down and walk away, but there is that odd person out there who will put it on and do something like that. Even if you are a sick psycho killer, everybody has a soul and a thought process to take them to that point in their life with their situation. I hate saying his name, but look at someone like a [Ted] Bundy ... and there is a thought process even though it's not normal. It would make no sense to a normal human being, but to that person it does, and it's the same with Michael Myers."

After young Michael [Faerch] sets the film's bloody tone in the early part, he's sent to a sanitarium where he kills a nurse, driving his mother to suicide. The two deliver a knockout punch to Myers' psyche, and he doesn't speak for over a decade. Then he becomes Mane's large, muscular form, well equipped to kill the guards and a trucker on his way to escaping. Back in his old house, he kills three of Laurie's friends and terrorizes Annie.

Laurie comes home and Michael grabs her. An attacking Loomis shoots Michael and begs him to release the little girl. Just as the long-hidden human side of Michael comes out, just as he lets Laurie go, the police—led by Annie's sheriff father—show up and shoot him dead.

Mane and Zombie knocked out a sequel two years later. Like the first part two, this one started just after the first one, as Loomis, Laurie, Annie, and Michael's dead (?) body are taken away in ambulances. Myers' transporter gets into an accident, awakening him. He makes the drivers his first new victims.

After some time healing in a wooded cabin, he decides to go back to lowering the Haddonfield population, one by one. Laurie, now living with Annie's family, has seen her own mentality affected, to the point where she's envisioning recreating her brother's murders.

Of getting back behind the mask, Mane explains, "It was just picking up the intensity level, and making him more aggressive. I didn't want to do the same thing for a second picture." Back hard at work, Michael's killing his way to Laurie. Annie becomes one of his unlucky finds. Then he finally nabs Laurie and takes her back to his cabin.

With the cops backing him up, Loomis steps into the shed, and Laurie pleads for his help. But something's wrong; as far as he and the audience can see, there's nothing holding her. Instead, it's just a vision of her mother and brother. Then big brother steps in and stabs Loomis to death. Outside, Annie's father fells him with a shot, and Laurie appears to be freed, physically and mentally. Crouching over her brother, Laurie gasps out her love. Then she sees him lift his machete one last time.

It falls without hurting her, but no chances are being taken; Laurie goes animalistic and gives Michael as harsh a slaughter as he, or anyone else who played him, ever handed another victim.

She steps outside, but she'll never be the same. Laurie's now wearing Michael's mask. It's *déjà vu*, or *Halloween IV*, all over again. Seconds later, she's locked in the same sort of facility where her brother spent his early years, and the evil Norman Bates–type grin across her face shows that it's the safest place for her … and everyone else.

"Everything fucked up that you can possibly imagine is going through her head," Taylor-Compton explains. "Just imagine the whole world you knew was gone. It only took a night to take everything that you knew and she's just become this very vulnerable, angry, bipolar person. That's the only way that she knows how to deal with it. She can't vent to Annie. She went through the same thing. She can't vent to Sherriff Brackett. She feels like she's on her way. I think everything is going through her head and she can't control it."

"Behind the Mask With George P. Wilbur." *Horror Bid.* n.d. Retrieved July 11, 2011, from http://www.horrorbid.com/forum/viewtopic.php?f=210&t=3028.
Carpenter, John, Dir. *Halloween* [DVD]. U.S.: Compass International Pictures, 1978.
Elmstreetgirl22. "Original Halloween Q&A Panel at Monster Mania 13." *YouTube.* Aug. 24, 2009. Retrieved on Jan. 16, 2014, from http://www.youtube.com/watch?v=ju1T7ccawiw.
George Wilbur. *Bloody Good Horror.* Sept. 4, 2007. Retrieved July 11, 2011, from http://www.bloodygoodhorror.com/bgh/interviews/09/04/2007/george-wilbur.
Farinella, Tony. Danielle Harris of Halloween 4 and 5 Interview. *Matchflick.* 2013. Retrieved Sept. 10, 2012, from http://www.matchflick.com/column/1498.
"Halloween: Daeg Faerch and Tyler Mane Interview" Cinemawww. 2011. Retrieved July 11, 2011, from http://www.cinema.com/articles/5193/halloween-daeg-faerch-and-tyler-mane-interview.phtml.
"Halloween II Retrospective." *Halloween Movies.* Oct. 31, 2006. Retrieved July 11, 2011, from http://www.halloweenmovies.com/h2retro/dickwarlock_lobby.html.
iamFunnyBones. "Chris Durand." *Youtube.* Feb. 19, 2009. Retrieved July 11, 2011, from http://www.youtube.com/watch?v=7weSXp2lEts.
Kirzinger, Ken. E-mail interview. Jan. 15, 2014.
Lawton, Adam. "Interview with Tony Moran." *Movie Mikes.* Jan. 6, 2011. Retrieved July 11, 2011, from http://moviemikes.com/2011/01/interview-with-tony-moran/.
Mane, Tyler. Phone interview. Jan. 13, 2014.
Michael Myers. *Chasing the Frog.* Retrieved Jan. 16, 2014, from http://www.chasingthefrog.com/unmasked/michaelmyers.php.
Newgen, Heather. "Interview: Halloween II's Scout Taylor-Compton." *Shock Till You Drop.* Aug. 26, 2009. Retrieved July 11, 2011, from http://www.shocktillyoudrop.com/news/topnews.php?id=11532.
Otherin-Girard, Dominique, Dir. *Halloween 5* [DVD]. United States: Magnum Pictures, 1989.
Robg. "Fright Exclusive Interview." *Icons of Fright.* Oct. 2005. Retrieved July 11, 2011, from http://www.iconsoffright.com/IV_Don.htm.
Robg. "Fright Exclusive Interview." *Icons of Fright.* Oct. 2004. Retrieved July 11, 2011, from http://www.iconsoffright.com/IV_Brad.htm.

•••••••••••••••••••••••••••••

Danielle Harris

Ask around as to who should be called "The Main Woman from *Halloween*," and Jamie Lee Curtis' name will probably pop right out the majority of the time. That's fair;

Curtis' Laurie Strode helped kick off the legendary series and its first sequel, then came back a few decades later for *H20* and *Resurrection*.

Still, there's another lady who should be in the running, for a few reasons. She managed to escape Michael Myers a few times in the series' first go-rounds, but came back as a different character when Rob Zombie started churning out some remakes in the 2000s. Plus, horror ended up filling a bigger chunk of her résumé than that of Curtis, or any other *Halloween* gal, at least as of the summer of 2013.

After three *Halloween* go-rounds, it was time to both change and stay the same. The third version of the saga had gone away from Michael and into a storyline about an evil toymaker, and it didn't work. So they did what horror film crews have a tendency to do when one well is dry: drill another with a new storyline.

With Laurie dead in a car crash (another tale that would be discarded for further film resuscitation in *H20*), Michael was now left to wipe out the family's next generation.

Laurie's young daughter Jamie had been adopted by her friends, and Michael saw one more opportunity to keep things all in the family. He started off the fourth installment by waking up in an ambulance after Laurie blasted the hell out of him in Part II, and went back to his old hunting grounds.

With just a couple of TV show roles starting out her résumé, Danielle Harris charged into her first big-screen role. "I wanted to hear [Curtis] in my head," Harris says. "I didn't want to go in there and copycat her."

With Jamie out trick-or-treating in an ominously familiar clown costume, Michael guns a city worker into the voltage substation to drop the town into darkness, then wipes out the entire police force. Dr. Loomis (Donald Pleasence, the only holdover from the first two films) gets Jamie and her friends inside the town sheriff's home, then goes on a hunt of his own.

After playing defense for much of her horror career, such as in two *Halloween*s, Danielle Harris went on the horror offensive in *Hatchet 3*.

"I was scared of the dark!" remembers Harris. "The whole thing was hard and weird. I was so young that I don't think I really understood what was going on."

With Michael on the attack downstairs, Jamie's lowered to the ground below, and Loomis takes her to an empty school. Michael disposes of him with the help of a glass door, then hides on the underside of a truck everyone's using to escape.

"I got to run around yelling and screaming in a Halloween costume, even thought it was really April," says Harris. "Basically, all the stuff you really look forward to as a kid. You really don't think about the fact that you're working, because you're young and having so much fun. The entire cast and crew made it a point, because I was so young, of making sure that it was fun and I knew that it was make believe. I never really had nightmares."

With Jamie's foster sister driving now, Michael gets blasted with the truck and flies into a ditch. Jamie makes her way to him, but Michael rises one last time before getting holy hell shot out of him by the cops.

"It was fun for me, tasting the fake blood and seeing how they did all the prosthetics," Harris says. "Michael running around chasing me with the knives, it was all fun and games for me." Not, though, for her character, or the rest of the family. Michael's gone for now, but his effects have addled Jamie's mind.

Running a bath for her foster daughter, Jamie's new mom sees something stalking through the hallways, both a flashback to the first-person perspective of the original film and a pitch-black foreshadowing of what's about to happen. One round of screams later, the now hardcore, stoic Jamie is standing at the top of the stairs, peering down at the terrified souls below, wearing a familiar clown mask and holding a pair of scissors, everything covered in plasma. Has Michael become Michelle? Is she ready to re-start the tradition that Michael began?

"The way *Halloween 4* ended, I thought I was going to be the killer," Harris says. "I thought it would have been fun to come back as the killer, or Michael's sidekick." That didn't happen when the sequel arrived a year later, although Harris would eventually grab villainess roles over a decade later, helping out the killer Chromeskull in *Laid to Rest 2* and doing the job herself in *Blood Night: Legend of Mary Hatchet*.

Still, Harris carried on a bit of Michael's spirit away from the camera, traipsing through her neighborhood for candy that Halloween in character.

"I went trick-or-treating in the clown costume," she laughingly recalls. "I was a bit of a demented child, and I thought it would be really funny the year that it came out, if I threw it on and covered myself with blood and got a pair of scissors from my mom's kitchen and went trick-or-treating in my neighborhood."

For part five in 1989, both Jamie and Michael were indisposed, she as a near-catatonic mute in a children's psych ward, him being looked over by an eremite who found him floating in a river, who he repays with the typical manner of murder. But the two are linked upstairs, as she can't help but feel his motives and imitate his movements.

Out of the hospital, Jamie's back on the run, with Michael lowering the local population before chasing her through the woods in a car. "When I was running through the woods and Michael's chasing me with a car," Harris says, "that was probably the only time I was really scared. I was actually the one doing the running in the dark woods. Our stunt coordinator mapped out a route for me to run around certain trees, so I had to remember to turn at this tree and that tree. I remember being scared that I wasn't going to remember which way he wanted me to go. There was just so much smoke, and it was late, and dark, so I was definitely a little bit worried about that." She helps Loomis lure Michael back to the house where it all began, but Michael beats Loomis and kills some cops. Jamie leaps down a laundry chute, but Michael stabs through it with a knife, cutting her a few times. She charges up to the attic, where he's hung the family dog, and Michael's upon her. The terrified little girl tries once more to find the humanity inside him that her mom couldn't, but touching his masked face sends him back to insanity once again. Then Loomis sweeps back in to save her.

"Michael Myers is your average guy, possibly the guy next door," she says, "a real man, unlike a Freddy or a Jason. What makes him creepy is he could be living right next door to you."

Harris would see just as much violence two years later in *The Last Boy Scout,* playing the daughter of Bruce Willis' Joe Hallenbeck, a disgraced private eye who stumbles onto mob corruption in pro football. With her daddy about to eat the mob's gun metal, her Darian shows up with a gun inside her stuffed puppet, then gives it to her dad for him to waste everybody. The scene's repeated a bit later, only with larger guns and more blood, her dad slaughtering a mass of people before her terrified eyes.

Harris' next jaunt into horror came in 1998's *Urban Legend,* one of the first such films to have a female behind everything (but not Harris—Rebecca Gayheart ended up as the villainess). Such *Legend*s are usually used by sadistic parents to keep their kids up at night, or young friends trying to send chills through one another. Stories about alligators in the sewers or rattlesnakes in arcade ball pits run rampant, right up next to someone getting passed a drugged drink in a bar and waking up with no kidneys, or a babysitter finding out that those threatening crank calls are coming from upstairs.

Then there's the one where a young woman comes home to find her roommate engaged in mattress action. Too polite to turn on the light, the lady grabs her things and leaves. But the next day, she returns—and the roommate's gorily slaughtered, with "Aren't you glad you didn't turn on the light?" written on the wall or mirror, usually in blood. As it turned out, she mistook physical gratification for slow, fatal brutality.

Harris played the promiscuous roommate to flick heroine Alicia Witt.

As Marion Crane's shower scene in *Psycho* showed us, nudity in films, Harris says, "is full vulnerability. In a movie, in a situation like this, as an actor, I was a disaster, because I was completely not in control. I am a total control freak. To shed your clothes, literally, in a room full really wasn't what freaked me out, it was more about what happened to me in this situation."

Rob Zombie brought back Michael in *Halloween* (2007), and Harris was along for the ride, playing Annie, the daughter of Haddonfield's sheriff and galpal of the new Laurie, Scout Taylor-Compton. "Annie is the most like me in real like," Harris says. "I remember saying, 'You know, Rob, I really relate to her.' [Zombie] said, 'She's [somewhere] between a slut and a good girl.' I thought, perfect, I have this one in the bag!"

As newbie Michael (Tyler Mane) runs rampant, Annie becomes one of the few women in horror history to get laid and make it out alive, "only" getting a beating from him before Laurie and Loomis (now Malcolm McDowell) take him out. But she wouldn't be so lucky two years later in the sequel.

"I was kind of reinventing myself as an actor," she says of the new films. "Everything's kind of come full circle. It was a euphoric experience, really cool growing up and transitioning from child to grownup actor because of *Halloween*."

In the first *Hatchet* movie, Marybeth Dunston (Tamara Feldman) is trapped in the swampish woods of New Orleans just a rock's toss away from Mardi Gras with her friends. She looks for Victor Crowley, the spirit she believes killed her brother and father (Robert Englund plays the dad). Tormented by youthful punks in his day, Victor was trapped inside a burning house, accidentally killed by his father who was trying to save him. But Victor's aura is back, and it's out for blood (Kane Hodder is both Victor and his pappy).

Victor goes to work much faster than Michael did, knocking off five people in a matter of moments. Marybeth and her new boyfriend Ben hop onto her father's boat and attempt to escape as Victor's body count rises, and Maybeth falls overboard. Reaching up out of the water to grab Ben's hand, she finds that it's just about all that's left of him. Victor's on the other end, his screaming, disfigured face inches from hers as the film ends.

Harris became the new *Hatchet* gal when the sequel arrived four years later. "I was definitely a fan of the first movie anyway and I watched it quite a bit before I did the film to kind of get the accent down," Harris recalls. "I am not sure mine was too similar to [Feldman's], but I think mine was definitely more put-on than hers."

Hatchet II literally picked up right where the first one had cut, with Crowley's hand wrapped around the new Marybeth's leg before she manages to escape and runs off to meet Rev. Zombie (Tony Todd). As is often the case with sequels, we get a bit more backstory here: that Marybeth's dad was one of Victor's involuntary manslaughterers, that his dad was diddling around with his wife's nurse, that the nursery mistress was Victor's mommy, and that both were cursed by the wife in her dying words—basically, that pretty much everyone involved deserves to die.

Marybeth, Zombie (secretly against her), and some others are back on the hunt, and Crowley's in his personal heaven, going to work on the group with hatchets, chainsaws, and a belt sander—to the point where Hodder repeats several of the murders he committed as Jason in his *Friday the 13th* go-rounds. He finally goes after Zombie and rips his skeleton out of his skin (?!), but Marybeth gives Victor some payback with the title weapon, punctuates things with a "*Fuck you!*" and blasts his skull in half with a shotgun. After relying on so many others to save her as Jamie, Harris got to go on the full offensive here.

In one film, Harris got to act alongside Nick "Chromeskull" Principe, be the daughter of Robert "Freddy Krueger" Englund, get saved by R.A. "Leatherface" Mihailoff, fight with Tony "Candyman" Todd, and blow the head off Kane "Jason Voorhees" Hodder.

If staying serious had been a struggle for her as Jamie, playing Marybeth took a toll on the tiny titaness. "*Hatchet 2* was probably one of the hardest roles I have had to date, just because every single day I was in distress. There was no building up to the moment, then all of a sudden I have to be a hysterical mess; I was a hysterical mess from the word go. I spent five weeks basically out of my head emotionally and I was exhausted. I will work all the way through a shoot, then two days before we wrap I will end up getting the flu. So I really think your body kind of holds it until you are ready to stop working."

In the third installment a bathed-in-blood Marybeth arrives at the local police station, huge gun and earthshattering confession ready for the local sheriff (*Gremlins'* Zach Gilligan), then near-catatonically waits in a cell. Her claims send some deputies back to the scene of the crime. Of course, Crowley's back, his decapitation fetish flaring like a wildfire.

She's the only one that can stop him, atonement for her dad's deeds more powerful than any shotguns.

Unlike Norman Bates and Jason Voorhees, this guy just wants his *daddy* back, and the elder Crowley's ashes are in the hands of another local (played by the legendary Sid Haig).

"She's got nothing to lose," Harris says, "but at the same time…, who does she have to help now? She doesn't care if she goes to prison or she gets the death penalty. It doesn't matter she lost her family. It's all over. She's just done. Nothing to lose."

Once again, things come down to a pint-sized princess up against a giant who's faced down more bullets and beatings than an army troop. "Now that I'm the final girl, I have to go through a lot more for a longer period of time as an actor," Harris says. "I have to go to hell and back again, and be completely just destroyed emotionally and physically for me to live. It's definitely a challenge, but I've been up for it for a while."

Dan. "An Interview with Danielle Harris." *GeekaDelphia*. Feb. 24, 2011. Retrieved Sept. 11, 2012, from http://geekadelphia.com/2011/02/24/hatchet-2-an-interview-with-danielle-harris/.
Farinella, Tony. "Danielle Harris of Halloween 4 and 5 Interview." *Matchflick*. 2013. Retrieved Sept 10, 2012, from http://www.matchflick.com/column/1498.
Harris, Danielle. Personal interview. May 2, 2012.
Natty. "Fright Interview with Scream Queen/Hatchet III Star Danielle Harris." *Icons of Fright*. Aug. 8, 2013. Retrieved Aug. 17, 2013, from http://iconsoffright.com/2013/08/08/fright-exclusive-interview-with-scream-queenhatchet-iii-star-danielle-harris-2/?utm_source=rss&utm_medium=rss&utm_campaign=fright-exclusive-interview-with-scream-queenhatchet-iii-star-danielle-harris-2.
Red Carpet News. "Danielle Harris Interview: Halloween and Action Stars." *You Tube*. July 9, 2012. Retrieved Sept. 10, 2013, from http://www.youtube.com/watch?v=47PksSy6344.
"Rob Zombie Interviews Danielle Harris." *AMC*. 2007. Retrieved Sept. 10, 2012, from http://www.amctv.com/videos/rob-zombie-interviews-danielle-harris.
"Video Interview with Danielle Harris." *Halloween Movies*. n.d. Retrieved Sept. 10, 2012, from http://www.halloweenmovies.com/DanielleHarris/DH.html.

Legend Alert: Rondo Hatton and The Creeper Films

When I was a news reporter, I always said that one of the best parts of my job was getting to tell the stories of people who didn't have the means to tell it for themselves, often for horrible reasons—like them not being *around* to tell it. As a writer in any capacity, you take on certain responsibilities when trying to let a group of people know about someone, particularly someone who passed on long before their time, and why they deserve to be remembered.

When a horribly painful and incurable disease tried to rob Rondo Hatton of the hopes and career he'd always intended to pursue, he simply changed his objective and made the best of a situation he knew he'd never fully escape. Rather than allowing an issue he couldn't control to overtake his life, Hatton stood up to it and fought as hard and well as anyone ever could.

Like fellow acromegaly sufferer Andre the Giant, Hatton's biggest acceptance was found in a make-believe world. He visited a land where pretending was normal, and cherished. And like all who knew Andre have attested about the Giant, Hatton was a gentle soul in an oversized form.

Hatton was voted the most handsome at his high school in Tampa, Florida, in the 1910s. But stepping before a camera was never a career goal for the youth; when World War I broke out, he was at the forefront of young American boys looking to fight in Europe.

Hatton headed to France to hunt Germans. There, dodging and firing bullets near Paris, Hatton was caught in the midst of some poison gas. His damaged lungs healed after hospitalization, but doctors soon found something even worse: acromegaly. A tumor that forces the pituitary gland to keep secreting hormones long after it should have halted, the disease causes grotesque overenlargement of the hands, feet, and facial features. It also sends blood pressure through the roof and weakens the heart, to the extent that few with the disease, even treated, ever make it into their 50s.

His dreams of continuing the athletic career that had made him such a big man on the high school campus dashed, Hatton headed home and approached the sports world from a different perspective, writing about it for the local papers.

An innocent victim of the agony of acromegaly, Rondo Hatton made his mark on the horror film world. Inspiration is rare in the genre, but Hatton's life story became one of the more uplifting tales in Hollywood history.

As his affliction started to turn his once handsome face into something out of a horror movie, Hatton found himself nearly overtaken by depression, a common side effect of acromegaly. One day in late 1929, movie director Henry King came to town to direct *Hell Harbor*, the first talking picture shot in Florida. Newspaper reporter Hatton stepped onto the set, camera, and list of questions in hand.

King signed him up for a role as an angry bartender. Receiving praise and compliments for his natural charisma and his unnatural looks (many passersby undoubtedly considered his appearance a great job by the makeup department), a stunned Hatton could see his new career on the horizon. It may not have been what he'd ever expected or wanted, but the acting world was the new right place for him.

Hatton didn't realize it right away; it took a full six years before his second wife persuaded him to pack up and head across the country to Hollywood. King hadn't forgotten his old find, placing him in *In Old Chicago* and *Chad Hanna*. For the long time being, Hatton's acting career mainly focused on spot gags and extra work, mainly walking around in the background of prison or construction scenes (he appeared as a participant in an "ugly man contest" in 1939's *The Hunchback of Notre Dame*).

The new trade kept pushing his star higher and higher. As his Hoxton Creeper helped evil Giles Conover race Sherlock Holmes (Basil Rathbone, generally considered among the best to portray the detective) to find a valuable pearl in 1944's *The Pearl of Death,* Hatton's character—like many he played, not intellectually gifted—eventually realized that his boss was just using him to advance his own goal. It was a role reminiscent of Jaws, the henchman who stalked James Bond through two films before being turned good by love in *Moonraker* (Richard Kiel, who played the Bond baddie, also suffered from acromegaly). It also called to mind the giant Fezzik that Andre the Giant became in *The Princess Bride.*

Just as they eventually would with Jaws and Fezzik, critics and fans went wild over the "new" man in Hollywood. He'd play the same sort of role a few more times over the next year—but *House of Horrors* (1946) would forever implant Hatton's likeness in the memory of horror fans.

A sculptor whose dreams of fame and fortune have been shattered by his critics encounters the Creeper and takes him home. The sculptor starts to create his latest artistic creation in Hatton's likeness. It might be the best sculpture he's ever done—and the Creeper, in his tradition of following without questioning, starts to rub out those who badmouthed his master. The artist begins to go mad with power (Sweeney Todd and Victor Frankenstein locked into one!), with a lady reporter the only one suspecting anything amiss. The artist wants her dead but, the Creeper allows himself to pick love over commitment, saving the gal at the cost of his own life.

Just as Boris Karloff had turned Frankenstein's monster into a sympathetic victim of a society too ignorant to take the time to understand the why's of his actions, Hatton makes the Creeper violent, even murderous, but still sympathetic.

To that point, a lack of formal training in the acting arts might have benefitted Hondo, as his characters were *supposed* to be lacking in feeling, in emotion. But for what would sadly become his final film, he'd been practicing for it his entire life.

Hal Moffat, a bright, handsome fellow in a college chemistry lab, finds himself disfigured into the Creeper after an accident early in *The Brute Man.* Just as Hatton's first marriage had ended in divorce, Moffat's lady leaves him. Just as the Creeper had done before, he made those responsible pay, through his typical murderous ways. Just as Francis Dolarhyde would in *Red Dragon* decades later, he takes the time to fall in love with a lovely lady not blessed with sight.

Right around Christmas of 1945, Hatton suffered a mild heart seizure, probably just his only one that's publicly known of. Just over a month later, he passed away after a sudden heart attack.

For decades, it appeared that people would never get or even want the chance to remember him. Then, when horror fans across America got reacquainted with King Kong, Godzilla, and the rest of the classic monsters of yesterday, Hatton's name and Creeper face were rediscovered. People got interested in the man, more perfectly created for the horror world than any other.

Then, in 2003, the Rondo Hatton Classic Horror Awards were created. Best movie, TV show, magazine, blog, and so much more are awarded, with statuettes in the shape of Hatton's infamously notorious mug being presented to the winners. Even if he wasn't the nicest thing to see, Hatton's face and name live on.

Pednaud, J. Tithonus. "Rondo Hatton—The Creeper." *The Human Marvels.* 2012. Retrieved Feb. 12, 2013, from http://thehumanmarvels.com/850/rondo-hatton-%2%80%93-the-creeper/disfigured.
Ray, Fred Olen. "Rondo Hatton: Monster Man." *Midnight Marquee* 37 (Fall 1988): 87–93.

Smith, Richard Harland. "Everybody Talks About Rondo, But Nobody Does Anything About Him." *Movie Morlocks*. Feb. 24, 2009. Retrieved Feb. 12, 2013, from http://moviemorlocks.com/2009/02/24/everybody-talks-about-rondo-but-nobody-does-anything-about-him/.

Legend Alert: Jackie Joseph and *The Little Shop of Horrors*

Jackie Joseph and the rest of a small cast and crew put together 1960s *The Little Shop of Horrors*. It then took decades for them to realize what an impact they had made. It's why she's been receiving fan mail for decades. It's why fans still visit her and the rest of the *Shop*-keepers at conventions and appearances.

Joseph was Audrey, the bombshell co-worker of lovesick Seymour Krelboyne, stuck in a dead-end job at miserly Gravis Mushnick's flower shop. But unlike the Audrey that Ellen Greene later played on the Broadway stage and in its 1986 movie version, Joseph's girl didn't get to belt out "Somewhere That's Green," "Downtown," or even "Suddenly Seymour."

In the last months of the 1950s, Joseph was finishing up a stint of musical comedy in *The Billy Barnes Review* in New York. One phone call from her agent later, though, she was on her way across the nation. "They told me to come home," she recalls. "They were offering me this movie. I had to shoot it in two days, to get a script and memorize the whole script." Something about the leading lady alongside a detective, she understood.

"I accepted because I was in my 20s, and I was asked to be in a movie," Joseph says. "When you're a drama major, you slide into working in the theater, and then you get a few little crazy beginning jobs, little movies or TV shows. But this was a real motion picture with a real part, and you don't even care what it is! You never think it's anything untoward. It was just about 'I'm going to be in the movies!'"

Back in the Golden State, Joseph glanced over the new version of the script. Things had ... changed a bit.

There was still a detective, but he and a male partner now had small parts. She'd still be the heroine, but her partner was Seymour, a good-hearted nebbish without the guts to look such a beauty in the eye. Crimefighting? No, this was about selling flowers.

But all of that was nothing new. What set this apart from any other, ever, was the film's protagonist: a plant that learned to talk—and eat people.

"We didn't really know it until we got the script," she recalls. "But we couldn't be discerning or have an attitude, because it was like a snowball—there was no way it was going to stop. It was, get the job, do it, and goodbye."

Along with Jonathan Haze, who played Seymour, Joseph put together the relationship of a man, a woman, and a carnivorous plant that would come between them.

"Jonathan came over to my apartment," she says, "and we drummed each other through the script and helped each other learn the parts. It was us being gaga. We had a couple of days alone where we just read the lines and worked out where we were supposed to stand. There wasn't time to do anything else, unless we were working with a physical prop, like the plant."

She managed to find a bit of Audrey in herself, and used it to move forward fast.

"My automatic tendency was to inhabit this girl, to see what her situation was and lead it into an honest situation," Joseph says. "This is where she worked. Nothing was questionable to her. Everything was how it was. I don't think she was dumb; she was just so truthful in this middle of this situation. All I knew was that she had no wiles. She wasn't manipulative. She was just a really good person with questionable tastes in men."

Seymour wasn't a bad guy, but his situation would push anyone toward the edge.

Faced with losing his job, the fellow shows Mushnick his new creation, a combo of a Venus flytrap and butterwort, two of the natural world's hungriest meat-chompers. He's even named it—Audrey Jr.

Many might have an issue with being named after a plant that literally devours its prey, but like Joseph said, the thrilled Audrey didn't know how to have an attitude, giving Seymour a little piece of her heart.

Seymour can't get the plant to sprout, until one ominous night when he pricks his finger, and the plant comes to life. It's a vampire with leaves. Choosing between his platelet count and employment, Seymour starts opening the veins, and not just his own…

Whereas we're amazed today if films go from start to finish in a month, Joseph, Haze, director Roger Corman, and the rest of the group had to move like Olympics track stars: The entire filming process took two days.

The most common and likely explanation lies in the root of all evil: the folding green itself. At 12 a.m. on the first day of the 1960s, the Screen Actors Guild's new rules would go into effect, including required residuals, payments to actors when their work was replayed on small screens. Getting things done early would save someone quite a bit of money.

"We didn't know what residuals were," Joseph says. "We were childlike, wanting to be in the movies, but we had to make a living. It was using the passion to be an actor. We worked in 1960, and realized we had [the residual] privilege when they ran [our work] again. It was a lot of naiveté, but it was funny.

"I had to change my dress in a carpenter's booth on the set, so when they were lighting, getting the new set ready, it was one, two, three, and I had to be ready to go. There was a lot to do. I felt like I was in a play. There was a rehearsal, and this was my part, and my job was to fill up.

"Roger Corman directed it with four cameras. If there was a shadow on you, too bad. Throughout the movie, there's a pretty good shadow on us at times. I figured that everybody that worked on a movie set was a professional and really knew about doing movies, and I should just learn and listen to and respect everybody who worked behind the scenes."

One day, Haze appeared in the scene where Seymour goes to the dentist. Forced to pretend to *be* the doctor, Seymour attends to patient Wilbur Force, who doesn't really mind a little extra agony. By the time Wilbur leaves, his masochistic grin could only be found in a horror movie.

Having worked with Corman the year before in *The Cry Baby Killer,* the fellow who played Wilbur was in the same boat as Joseph and Haze, just looking for a rope to grab to stardom. Yes, even Jack Nicholson once had a tough time in the business.

"It really went so fast," Joseph says of working with the man. "This was before he was *Jack Nicholson.* He was just a young player. He got our attention because we were all just young people who were hanging out around Hollywood. We kind of knew something was stirring with him because he wasn't a boring young man. But he just did his scene and disappeared, while we were probably changing our costumes at the time. He was just one of the kids." Elsewhere in the cast was Dick Miller, who played Burson Fouch, the flower shop regular who turned Mushnick's plants into his lunch. He'd later come back into Joseph's acting life.

With reality no longer a concern, the film now gives Audrey Jr. a voice, demanding more plasma from wherever (it was voiced by screenwriter Charles Griffith, who ironically became his own victim, playing a robber tricked into stepping inside the plant). But unlike Frank Oz's musical, this tale doesn't have a happy ending, as Seymour becomes its final meal.

Joseph and the rest moved on. Away from the cameras, she served on both the board of the Screen Actors Guild and the American Federation of Television and Radio Artists before the groups merged in 2012. Acting-wise, she appeared in a few *Police Academy* films and voiced everything from episodes of *Scooby-Doo* to *Josie and the Pussycats*. In 1983, she and Miller played husband and wife in the music-ruled comedy *Get Crazy*.

The next year, the two would play the same roles in a slightly different sense: they'd be Mr. and Mrs. Futterman, early victims of the green-skinned reptilian title critters of *Gremlins*. It would take longer for Joseph to film one scene as Sheila than she had for the entire production of *Little Shop*.

"I knew that was going to be a big picture, with Warner Brothers doing it," she says. "It was just about being cast without having to go through the interview process. It just tickled them to have someone from *Little Shop* in their picture. They had fun with the humor, having the original Audrey come in and be Mrs. Futterman." Six years later, the two would come back for the film's sequel.

In the early '80s, Joseph noticed more and more mail arriving from her fans. Spurred on mostly by Nicholson's stardom, the first *Little Shop* was released on video several times. Right around then, word started getting out about the show moving to off–Broadway stages, rewritten with lyrics. People may have gotten the film to check out young Nicholson, but they noticed the film's female lead as well. "It was years before we started hearing from the fans that were developing," Joseph recalls. "I got a piece of fan mail, and the whole rim of the stationery looked like it had black vines that were dead all over it, and it turned out it was from a *Little Shop of Horrors* group of fans." Her appearance at a theatrical production was front-page local news, the original Audrey seeing the new one.

Then, in 1986, came the remake, with Oz in the director's chair, Greene as Audrey, Rick Moranis as Seymour, Bill Murray playing Nicholson's role, and Four Tops lead man Levi Stubbs voicing Audrey II (no longer Jr.) all the way to an Oscar nomination for the tune of "Mean Green Mother from Outer Space." (The film was also nominated for visual effects, but didn't win in either category.)

"The film was adequate," Joseph recalls. "I don't think it could come up to the stage version. It would have been nice if it had been a big wonderful, forever kind of musical. I didn't dislike it at all: it just wasn't gargantuanally wonderful. It was just okay."

She, Haze, and the rest of the original's cast and crew still gather to meet and greet fans, over half a century after she spent less than fifty hours becoming Audrey.

"We get to witness a miraculous happening," she says, "a fluke of culture, meeting the people that got hooked on that silly little thing. It [tickled] a lot of people's funny bones of all ages, and it's just something that gets into their beings. When it came out on video and you could watch it, it became popular, and you go to the memorabilia shows. I sit at the tables, usually with Jonathan. We're all a little eccentric. It leaves its mark. People at those shows dress up like monsters, with blood dripping off them, terrible scars and tattoos, and then they come up and sound like the boy next door. You soak it up. It's amazing."

Joseph, Jackie. Phone interview. Feb. 12, 2014.

Michael Karnow: *Incident at Loch Ness*

How much preparation is needed to play oneself in a film? As Michael Karnow found out, sometimes a great deal.

A writer by trade (he worked on the too-short-lived John Leguizamo sketch comedy *House of Buggin'* and several other shows), Karnow was asked by his friend Zak Penn to play a role in Penn's 2004 mockumentary *Incident at Loch Ness,* yet another search for one of the world's most famous mystery monsters. Karnow would use his own name and his own look.

"With writing," he explains, "you're writing, you're re-writing, you're developing material, you're pitching an idea, you're so many steps away from actually shooting anything. [Acting] is the opposite end of the spectrum. People who get involved in acting have to go through a lengthy process. I was just lucky. I had never taken an acting class. Zak was directing, and, for whatever reason, he thought I'd be perfect for the part. I didn't have to go through the process that most people do."

Indeed, he'd "only" have to transform into a cryptozoologist, one who studies animals that currently exist only in myth (Bigfoot), or are thought to be extinct (dinosaurs). Karnow got to incorporate a few bits and pieces of his own personality into the role.

"The main thing that I did was read this book called *The Encyclopedia of Cryptozoology,*" he recalls, "which I found very amusing, because the point of view of the book was that all this stuff existed; there wasn't any ordinary skepticism involved." Apparently, Nessie and her colleagues are still all too real to some, such as the publishers of the 2005, nearly-600-page reference work.

"I adapted the voice of that book, and it became the voice of the character that I was," Karnow continues. "If you crack your character and you know who they are, and you start to channel them, then they kind of write themselves. Once I got into a groove, and knew where he was and where he was coming from, there wasn't any work to do. No matter what came at that guy, I knew how he was going to respond."

Even before traveling to Scotland where the movie would be shot, "I just came up with things that I thought were funny," he says. "[My character] was kind of like a desperate, deluded guy. I was imagining that in the back of his mind, he knew that [the monster was only a legend] but that he can't admit it because he would have nothing else in life. There was this underlying desperation to this guy. From there, I just starting making up all sorts of things. Did he have a source of income? Once you figure out who this person is, if you have a central comedic premise for the character, then it comes up."

Michael Karnow (left) and Werner Herzog (right) survey one of the world's most legendarily and mysterious bodies of water in *Incident at Loch Ness.*

That's one of the biggest issues in working on a flick based almost completely on improvisation; it's up to the performers to create their characters. This can be both an asset and an obstacle; if the character's humor and other personality aspects work (like Sasha Baron Cohen's *Borat* title character), the performer's talent quickly becomes obvious. If the character's not convincing, then its creator comes off badly.

"You have to follow your own lines and create your own character," Karnow says. "I like to do pranks. I make weird prank phone calls. When you're doing a prank, all you have to do is convince somebody that the information you're presenting to somebody, and who you are, is true. If they believe you, then you've done your job." Apparently acting and pranking are branches from the same tree (more on this in a moment).

Penn asked Karnow to show up at the audition in character and discuss the practice of the cryptozoologists with one of the film's special effects officials. "[The official] didn't know I was an actor," he recalls. "He thought I was a real cryptozoologist. I gave him more and more shit and became more and more difficult. He'd draw what he thought the Loch Ness Monster looked like, and I'd say that that was totally wrong, that if he did that, the entire cryptozoological community would be up in arms and he'd have a real shitstorm on his hands. He believed me, so I thought I'd done my job."

The movie scenes sets in bars, on the banks, even between the waves were all done by computer, he claims.

"It was all filmed in a studio, with a blue screen," he insists, tongue nearly audibly moving into cheek. "The technology was so advanced that they can do that. Werner [Herzog] wasn't even there; it's a computer composite of him that we created with a very inexpensive program, not even his voice. Really something you could have made on a Mac."

And if we believe that, he has a Loch to sell us.

"I'm just kidding," the jokester admits. "Sorry, I couldn't resist. We were on Loch Ness."

Early in the film, Zak Penn (nearly all the main characters go by their real names) tries to draw longtime filmmaker Herzog into his new project. Herzog's a bit of a skeptic when it comes to the Scotland creature. He tries to quit and head home, but Penn somehow manages to keep him around. As the expedition comes to a close, it appears that the group will find the same thing as so many other Loch investigators: nothing. But the journey may end before anyone would have wanted it to; the boat stalls on a foggy afternoon, leaving everyone stranded in the middle of a big wet nowhere. The tension between Herzog and Penn that's been building throughout the film finally comes to the surface.

"We had this weird boat that made fog," Karnow says. "People on shore were saying to call the fire department, because they thought it was on fire."

Suddenly, something crashes into the boat. The crew tries to force each other to believe that it was a log or something equally harmless, but Penn has made off with the lifeboat, and they're stranded.

Then the boat, in a flashback-to-*Jaws* fashion, gets whacked again, and Karnow topples overboard. Werner and the rest of the group shout for him to swim back to them, but a giant fin rises from the water to show that he's not alone.

Maybe it's the Loch's notoriously cold, dark waters. Maybe it's the ungracious resident. But either way, Karnow's makeshift cryptozoology career has come to an abrupt end.

"That particular part called for pure realism," he says. "I screamed a lot and splashed around. It was cold, but I liked the opportunity to get in the water. I had a wetsuit underneath my clothes so I wouldn't freeze. We went water skiing out there, and it was bizarre to water ski on Loch Ness." The fin, he admits (truthfully, this time!) was all special effects.

"I'd like to see what it would be like to do a movie with real lines," he says. "One thing I learned about improvisation is that you really have to spend a lot of time to develop characters and develop bits, then try them out and shoot them."

Karnow, Michael. Phone interview. Feb. 17, 2010.

•••••••••••••••••••••••••••••

John Kassir: *Tales from the Crypt*

Writing this profile, my only regret is that it's impossible to imprint sound into a printed page. It's tough to get the full effect of John Kassir's work without being able to hear him.

He voiced Buster Bunny on a kids' cartoon and he spoke for the Cryptkeeper. Do you need any further proof of his diversity?

So how does a fellow train the old voice box to do what his does?

"It's something I started and continued to develop as a kid," Kassir shrugs. "Being an actor allows you to create the right voice for the right character. It's great because you don't get typed out because of your look or your age, and you get to play all kinds of things you'd never play based on how you look." And no, he doesn't *look* anything like the characters he has voiced. He's worked on *Pocahontas* and *The Simpsons* and played a psycho Smurf (the guy's *name* was Crazy!) when the blue beings made their way to the big screen in 2011.

After starting out as a comic book in the early 1950s, *Tales from the Crypt* first made its way to the big screen in 1972, featuring two-time Oscar nominee Ralph Richardson as the Cryptkeeper, telling a group of visitors (including longtime horror star Peter Cushing) of their own deaths that unbeknownst to them have already occurred. Kevin Yeager, who worked on Freddy Krueger's makeup for three different *A Nightmare on Elm Street*s, made a Cryptkeeper puppet for the HBO series *Tales from the Crypt* in the late 1980s.

Waiting at Yeager's studio to try out for the character's voice, Kassir recalled that he had read the *Tales from the Crypt* comics as a youth. Then he saw the *thing* he'd be voicing. It had the same burning baby blue eyes that had given Chucky from the *Child's Play* movies so scary.

"I went in there, and just by the way he looked, I came in and improvised."

And what a vocal smorgasbord he tossed together. He yanked in shades of Jerry Lewis' and Henny Youngman's comedic tones. He tossed in small impressions of the speech styles that Alfred Hitchcock and Rod Serling had used to ominously introduce viewers to their respective TV series.

It's highly unlikely that anything anywhere near such a vocal combo had ever been put together in entertainment history. But it worked. After one more tryout, this time in front of Yeager, producer Joel Silver of *Die Hard* fame and director Richard Donner, Kassir had the role. He'd spend the next seven years speaking the Keeper lines through dozens of *Crypt* episodes on HBO and in syndication on Fox.

"It took a little while," Kassir says, "but I found a place in my voice that worked well

The author (right) and his friend Jennifer meet John Kassir (left), who clearly doesn't resemble the Cryptkeeper he voiced.

with it. I had to slow it down a little bit in the first season, because the puppet worked slower because the motor was slow, but after that, it was pretty easy. I would go off of what they wrote, and then they started developing my personality."

The Keeper wasn't an active participant, only the narrator on the outside looking in, emitting a cackle that made the Wicked Witch of the West's sound G-rated, and tossing one-liners at the characters and audience like a fire-spitting machine-gun ("It only 'hearse' when I laugh!" "See you next time, boys and ghouls!" "Frights, camera, hack-tion!"). He even added a bit of Marlon Brando's *Streetcar Named Desire* accent.

"They'd write the wrap-around to go with the episode, and they'd see how the episode was developing," Kassir says. "Sometimes I'd do one or two episodes at a time."

Over the next seven years, everyone from Brad Pitt to Demi Moore to Whoopi Goldberg would show up at the *Crypt*. Some of Kassir's favorites were 1993's "Death of Some Salesman," in which Emmy nominee Tim Curry played a mother, father, and daughter that tormented and killed traveling salesman Ed Begley, Jr., and the second season's "The Man Who Was Death," with William Sadler as an executioner who gets a taste of his own medicine. The series allowed actors Michael J. Fox, Michael Keaton, and even Arnold Schwarzenegger a chance to see things from the other side of the camera.

"What's not so easy about animation is that you go into the studio and you don't know what the character is going to look like," says Kassir. "You have to use a lot of your imagination, and it's great to see what they finally end up with. Sometimes you go, 'Hey they really went off of what I did,' and sometimes you think, 'Wow, I wish I would have known that, I would have done it a different way.'"

Kassir, John. Personal interview. May 25, 2013.

•••••••••••••••••••••••••••••

Camille Keaton: *I Spit on Your Grave*

Schadenfreude.

Many have said that violent films (and video games) beget violence in those who watch them. We get pleasurably excited by bloodshed. Explosions become bursts of adrenalin inside. We don't just want the good guy to win; we want the bad guy to pay. To suffer, and for us to see it all. To see him get some bloody comeuppance.

That's schadenfreude: taking pleasure in the misfortune of those who have wronged you. Not only doing well on your own, but enjoying the sight of someone else falling flat on their face.

One film basically asked its audience, "Just how far are you willing to be pushed before you start feeling sorry for the original bad guys? How long can you go before our heroine goes around to being the villain? Is your violent nature enough to want to see these guys punished this badly?"

The movie's seeds were sown in the young adulthood of Meir Zarchi. Driving home from a tennis match one day, he and his friends saw a lady being assaulted. After helping her out and taking her to the police, Zarchi started to think about what a victim of this horror might do if she could get the chance.

Would she go to the police? Maybe so, but back then, and to an extent today, victims of sex crimes sometimes get blamed for what's happened. How many times have we heard some rapist use the excuse "She led me on!" or "Dressed like that, she was asking for it!" This doesn't just happen on *Law and Order;* it's for real. And for rape victims, it can be a nightmare.

But taking matters into one's own hands? Showing that even after a rape, labeled by some as the ultimate act of obscene control, charge could be taken right back,

Camille Keaton showed film audiences a new and full-blown brutal side of female aggression in 1978's *I Spit on Your Grave*.

even violently or dangerously so? If we could get these cretins where we wanted them, in a place where we would be the only ones to decide what happened, and what they felt … what exactly would we do? Zarchi put together *Day of the Woman,* which sounds like a feminine-rights fundraising event title.

Getting the lead in any film is attractive to many actresses, but it's likely that the subject matter of this flick probably caused a few starlets to say, "That doesn't need to be my big break!"

Fresh off a stint of acting in Italy, Camille Keaton was in Manhattan when she read in a magazine about an upcoming audition for a movie role.

A distant relative of the legendary comic Buster Keaton, she headed to the tryout. Then she got a look at the script.

She read the story of Jennifer, a woman at a countryside lake cabin, looking for a bit of privacy to write a book. A group of young men starts prowling around her area, like sharks circling an unsuspecting swimmer. Then they attack, and in a much more obscene manner than any great white. Over and over, the men use her as their unwilling sex slave. Rape after rape, Jennifer's will and body are shattered.

"I began reading the script," Keaton recalls, "and thought, 'Oh dear, how are we going to film this or that?' I started to worry about it then." But she still took on the role. By now, the title was *I Spit on Your Grave.*

With no ominous music in the background, the gang-rape scene goes on forever. "You don't think, 'How did I feel when I got raped by four men?' because that didn't happen," Keaton says. "You have to say, 'Someone's beating me up! Someone's scaring me. Let's get this over in one take.'"

With her life in shambles, Jennifer's torture continues long after the men leave. Would law enforcement chalk it up to "boys will be boys"? Might she face retribution from them or their families if she were to go elsewhere for help? Jennifer knows that she's got to go somewhere, physically and mentally, she never dreamed she'd have to visit, and somewhere she might not get back from.

"I did like when the woman gets revenge," Keaton says. "The chance to show her as a victim and vulnerable, then allows her to turn around and say 'Okay, now I'm going to empower myself' and show a darker side of herself. How would I as a woman react to being victimized this way? In that respect, it was all just generated out of my own emotions."

There's a tough scene of Jennifer in a church; she's asking God to help, and hopes that He'll understand if she doesn't go the "turn the other cheek" and "love thine enemies" route. Many of us could never consider taking another life until we're in a situation where the unavoidable occurs; think of a solider unwillingly pushed to the front lines with an M-16 in shaky hands.

Of course, in that type of killing, pure politics are controlling everything from behind the scenes. This, on the other hand, is personal, and Keaton and Jennifer went into uncharted territories.

Luring one of the men back to her cabin—the slow-witted virgin who took forever to rape her—Jennifer appears to be most forgiving, seducing him under a tree. Then a noose drops around his neck, and he flies upward, never to come down alive.

The vengeful lady picks up another perpetrator in a car, then entices him to the cabin. But it's too good to be true for him as well, as she goes for the non-sterilized form of castration and leaves him to bleed to death. "I saw the first half as being very, very real, as real as it can be," Keaton says. "The second part, when I get my revenge, or my justice, it looked more like a fantasy…. You can't condone what she did, but back in the day, a woman would talk about herself being raped, and get blamed for it."

An axe to the back puts an end to the rapist days of another of the men, and now it's just Jennifer and the last one. Knowing what she's done and what she intends, the man begs for mercy. But Jennifer's gone too far to turn back now; punctuating her final act with, "Suck it, bitch!" (the words he said to her), she guts him like a fish with a boat motor, and triumphantly speeds away.

"Looking at it, I felt like I was seeing someone else up there," Keaton recalls. "I didn't feel like I was looking at me at all…. It was a difficult film, don't think anybody really enjoyed making it, but I drew on my techniques and what I'd learned with directors in Italy. The worst thing was that I was afraid my parents and grandparents would ever see this."

Not many people did see it, at first; *I Spit on Your Grave* wasn't a big hit at the ticket booths, and critics abhorred it for its violence. Even over three decades later, legendary critic Roger Ebert held it out as one of the worst films ever.

But it still maintained a below-the-radar spot in the film world, usually amongst young teens looking to prove their manliness, or women in a really, really bad mood. It became a wonderful excuse to experience the guiltiest of pleasures. It showed up on the age-restricted shelves of video stores, banners on the box blaring about the film's deviance.

Steven Monroe made a new version in 2010, this time with Sarah Butler in the leading lass role. Zarchi, married to Keaton for a few years after the original came out, was a producer. As remakes tend to be, this one was quite a bit more graphic, as Butler's Jennifer boiled one of her rapists in a lye-based bathtub, castrated another, helped birds eat off a third guy's face, and ending up killing the last two with a single shotgun blast.

Three years later, a sequel followed, with Jemma Dallender making her screen debut as Katie, an aspiring model who's kidnapped to Bulgaria and tortured by another group of dirtbags before following in *Spit* fashion with bloody revenge. The guys' mom gets in on the suffering this time, giving Katie a payback chance that her predecessors didn't get.

"Horror News Podcasts: Camille Keaton." *Horror News.* Sept. 19, 2010. Retrieved March 27, 2011, from http://horrornews.net/podcasts/09.19.10_Horrornews.net_podcast.mp3.
Keaton, Camille. Personal interview. April 20, 2012.

Nick King: *Sinister*

Many believe that the devil is the true personification of evil, darker than any minion who ever wandered the earth; his homeland a land of eternal suffering.

Still, there might be someone—some*thing*—just a little stronger. A little smarter. A bit more menacing. Someone who goes just a little more below and beyond to snare his inhabitants. Someone who wasn't the main character in *Sinister*, but personified the adjective in pitch black capital letters.

Many who believe in Hell believe that those who end up there do so by choice, that our fate isn't fate, but free will gone the wrong way. That we're in control of our soul's final destination.

Nick King had done some stunt work just a year before on *Paranormal Activity 3*. There's a pretty substantial line between stunt work and performing, and it was time for him to find a way across it. "Not many people in the stunt business get to do a character like that," King recalls of his *Sinister* persona, "except the ones that do Jason or Michael Myers." Indeed, the many men behind those masks had been faced with the tasks of scaring without speech or facial expression. Still, at least they'd been human, at least for a while. King's guy was something else.

Ethan Hawke's Ellison Oswalt, a horror writer anxious to recapture his glory, arrives at his new home with his family in tow. He's the only one who knows that a family of four was hanged by the tree out back, and that that fiend who did it also took the family's daughter, probably to kill later.

Films in an attic box tell Oswalt the stories of other unfortunate families. One group was drowned in a pool, another burned in a car. Still more had their throats slit in bed, or were mutilated with a lawnmower. Every time, one young innocent from each unit was stolen, never seen again. If Oswalt can find out where they were taken and get it on paper, a Pulitzer might be in his future. Some young lives might be saved too, but a man has to have priorities.

A figure in the darkness watches from the woods in which the hanging took place. Then he watches from the bottom of the fatal pool. Who is this presence? A human, or a former one? A vengeful former resident? The figure's not moving much, or doing much at all. Just observing for now. But his features show us and Ellison that this is no angel of mercy.

Getting ready for the role, King sat down and checked out some of his horror predecessors, from times even before Voorhees, Myers, and Krueger.

Nick King became Bughuul and teamed with Clare Foley to terrify us all in *Sinister*.

"For the acting aspect of it, I got really into old horror movies," he recalls. "I watched them, studied them, learned how their body language was, and how they played the whole role."

Eventually, Ellison meets a local professor—funny how often a member of academia with all the answers just *happens* to be working nearby in these films—who tells him the story of a dark pagan divinitarian who specializes in killing families and taking young souls. Its name is Bughuul. Its life and work would be King's new job.

"I was uncomfortable in the mask," he recalls. "I was in it for fifteen, sixteen hours a day. I had this whole persona of being alone, being isolated, not being able to talk to anyone. It already put me in that environment, feeling spooky and all that stuff."

The spirits of the missing children start to torment Oswalt and his daughter Ashley. With Bughuul closing in, the family flees back to their old place. But the box of films has somehow managed to accompany them, and Oswalt, his own mind holding on by the slimmest of strings, can't help but sit back and watch the director's cut of this tale.

He sees the missing kids committing the deeds themselves: killing their parents and siblings, with not the slightest emotion. And he can always see Bughuul in the background, there to oversee the doings of his minions. To thank them and congratulate them. Indeed, the children weren't kidnapped, at least not physically. It was their souls that were stolen. Their hearts and minds were taken away to Bughuul's dark world.

Perhaps Bughuul is one up on the Underworld Overlord. According to most faiths, Satan only brings home those who make the choice to break the laws of faith. Bughuul finds those too young to know the difference between good and evil and takes them as part of his foot soldier army, showing them the "right" way to be before they're experienced enough at the whole "life" thing to make up their own mind.

"I was with the kids the whole time," King recalls. "I watched them and how they acted. I tried to make sure we had chemistry between us all."

As the films end, Ellison can't focus. Not just because of what he's seen, but because it appears something may have been slipped into his drink. His mental and physical facilities gone, he goes down. Awakening, he sees his wife and son nearby, apparently identically incapacitated. Then Ashley appears. In one hand, she's got an axe. The other's holding a video camera. She's making the next entry to Bughuul's personal horror section.

Bughuul's something stronger than her dad. He owns her now, and the family is now the next set of victims. And certainly not the last.

Bughuul was just too strong for Ellison or anyone else to save the child from. It's horrifying and heartbreaking at the same time. *Sinister* strikes the chill of fear into our heart, then freezes it until it breaks. Few things can ever hurt parents more than knowing their children can't be saved, that they're somewhere we couldn't stop them from entering, no matter what we tried.

By this time in filming, Bughuul's aura was starting to reach out of the filming and into the crew, King recalls. "Every time I would walk by someone, they would get freaked out," he says. "Even people like the production assistants, who'd been on the set the entire time, got freaked out. The whole persona of set was deep and dark. I liked that set a lot."

Clare Foley played Ashley. Having *lived* for less time than some of her co-stars had been *acting*, the ten-year-old's horror debut came as the cinema world's newest, and smallest, mass murderer.

"I have *not* seen it!" Foley asserts. "Maybe when I'm older!"

King, Nick. Phone interview. Sept. 18, 2013.
"L.A. Screening: Clare Foley." *Trailer Addict.* 2012. Retrieved Sept. 22, 2013, from http://www.traileraddict.com/trailer/sinister/la-screening-clare-foley.

•••••••••••••••••••••••••••••

Brandon Lee: *The Crow*

Irony can be a funny thing, both in the sense of ha-ha and the why-the-hell-does-that-happen? It can bring a sense of justice. It can bring a sense of redemption. It can bring a sense of humor.

Or, as in the case of Brandon Lee, it can tear your heart out.

Like his father Bruce two decades before, Brandon was a young, budding martial artist (not quite on Bruce's level, but neither was anyone else) with an eye for acting. He'd done some small action films, but now he appeared to be on the verge of a blockbuster. This film could have sent him into the upper echelon of marketable men in Hollywood. And while action-first stars tend to have shorter careers than their dramatic counterparts (it's tough to hit those eight-foot high-kicks and backflips in your forties), Lee wanted to be seen as an actor first and a martial artist second, to take the chances, and the roles, that his father never got to enjoy.

And then, just as it had for his dad, everything fell apart for Lee and those who were rooting for him. Just like his father, Brandon fell far too young, showing that even the strongest men in Hollywood are still human, and that death can sneak up and take who it wants, when it wants.

In spring 1993, leading up to the completion of filming *The Crow*, Lee couldn't wait to show his work to a generation of fans too young to remember the first Lee. In the supernatural thriller, he'd star as Eric Draven, a man led by the title character to avenge the murders of himself and his wife. If everything had gone as planned, *The Crow* might have even been turned into a series of action films.

"If you died, and a year had passed since you died, you have to assume that the people you loved and the people who loved you would have had to come to terms with having lost you," Lee said. "And now suddenly you are given the chance to come back for two days.... Wouldn't you feel a responsibility not to trammel in the lives of the people who have had a year to deal with that loss? And you would see the world from a perspective no one has.... That's one of the wonderful things about playing this character: There are no rules about how a person who has come back from the dead is going to behave."

To get ready for Draven, the same rules, or extreme lack thereof, applied to the man becoming him, continued Lee. He lost some weight for the role, and, given that his character was a musician, looked to similar performers like, appropriately enough, Black Crows star Chris Robinson. He also spent time in single-degree weather (filming in Wilmington, North Carolina, wouldn't be much warmer), and read a book his father had written for motivation. He also had to learn to work with birds, as the title character's appearance on Draven's shoulder became one of the film's lasting images.

"[I wanted] that real skinny, gaunt, rock-and-roll look," Lee explained. "Also, because he is the man that comes back from the dead, I felt he should not have a real robust, healthy appearance." Lee forsook the weight room, instead heading out for cardio-related activities like rope jumping and using a Stairmaster.

Showing shades of Tim Burton, director Alex Proyas bathed the film in darkness. The

Brandon Lee's best performance was tragically also his last in the superb *The Crow*.

majority of it takes place over a period of one night, mostly held in a slummy part of town. Draven's crazed-clown face makeup, and the flashbacks he shares with his wife Shelly (a debuting Sofia Shinas), are some of the film's few literally bright spots, showing that there's still good even in the darkest times and places.

"The makeup Eric ends up putting on when he assumes this persona of the Crow is his reaction to being pushed to those limits," Lee said. "He cannot deal with what is going on, and by assuming this persona he creates someone who can. If you've ever found yourself pushed to the limits of your tolerance … you find yourself doing some things that, from the outside, can be seen as quite insane." Lee dropped brief moments of insanity into his crew's lives early on, sneaking up on co-workers during his first day dressed in character.

Draven's craziness was evident throughout; his howling cackles after being shot through the hand, his snappy one-liners just before gorily dispatching another victim, even his pontifications that he knows something that no one else does. In the midst of Draven's revenge spree, he's held at gunpoint by Officer Albrecht (Ernie Hudson), who tried to save Shelly's life after her attack. But the cop doesn't yet recognize his old pal. "I said, 'You move, you're dead!'" barks Albrecht.

"And I say, 'I'm dead,'" Draven snips back gleefully. "And I move." Seconds later, he's gone, off to continue his mission to take out who took him. "I hope that any wicked, dark sense of humor Eric exhibits," says Lee, "comes out of the fact that he'd been pushed to the point where it seems quite sensible to say some of the ridiculous things he says."

> Guess it's not a good day to be a bad guy, huh?!
> —Brandon Lee as vengeful Eric Draven in *The Crow*

The very first day of filming *The Crow*, a carpenter was shocked and burned by power lines. A cast member found an actual bullet in the firearm he was to use in the film. Sets were damaged by a raging storm.

One night, the crew shot Draven's murder scene, when he's shot after interrupting a gang burglarizing his house and raping his wife. With a grocery bag in his hands, Lee strolled through the door of his home and straight into a hellish nightmare. Drug dealer Funboy (Michael Massee) fired at Draven, and he fell, the bullet appearing to rip through the bag.

"I'd never seen anything like it," Shinas recalls. "I remember thinking, 'Wow, what a great actor. This is so theatrical.'" Everyone kept going on in character. But when the "Cut!" cry rang out, Lee didn't get up. Because this time, he wasn't acting. The gun had blasted part of an empty cartridge through the bag, and it plowed into Lee's stomach. He held on through five hours of emergency surgery, but died the next afternoon.

No one knew how to react—that night, or any time shortly thereafter. Shinas left the set, along with many of her colleagues.

"We were all just stunned, having known Brandon as a wonderful person," said Shinas, whose role, originally intended to be much larger, had to be shortened. "I just became a recluse for the next six months. It taught me to understand and realize my own mortality."

The cast and crew met several times. Everyone talked. Some wanted to shut the film down. Some wanted to quit. Some wanted to keep on. No one, in any capacity, can ever prepare for this sort of thing, and no one could ever know what the right or wrong thing to do would be. It will be debated forever.

They soon decided that, yes, maybe Lee would have indeed wanted the film to be finished. But beyond that, he deserved to have it be seen. The effort that he put into becoming Draven, and the talent that he had as an actor, millions deserved to check out. Brandon Lee's name would live on for many sad reasons, but the work that he had done should have been displayed, to be appreciated by those he'd worked for.

<blockquote>It can't rain all the time.—Draven</blockquote>

On May 26, 1993, nearly a month after the accident, filming continued. For several scenes, especially the one where Draven first returns to his apartment after his resurrection, doubles were used. Massee finished his role, and then took a year off from acting in general. "It absolutely wasn't supposed to be happening," he told the TV tabloid *eXtra* in 2005. "I wasn't even supposed to be handling the gun until we started shooting the scene, but they changed it. I don't think you ever get over something like that."

Unlike the mysterious coma that killed his father in 1973, this accident didn't set off an explosion of conspiracy theories. It wasn't Massee's fault, or the prop manager's fault, or anyone else's fault. It was just the worst kind of surprise. That actually makes it seem even tougher. It would be easier if there was someone to blame. It just happened.

"This film deals with the concept of a solution being struck between good and evil," Lee said. "I must say I've never done anything where I felt that the violence was as justified as it is in this [movie]. The man I'm playing was murdered; the woman he loved was raped and then murdered. And he has come back to settle the score. I truly feel that if I were in the same situation, I would do the same thing." Heartbreakingly, he was planning to marry Eliza Hutton a few weeks after filming (Hutton wore her wedding dress to Lee's memorial service).

As a film, *The Crow* has been underrated. It offers more than the cookie-cutter whiz-bang action and dark humor that so many other such blockbusters are content with; *The Crow*, like Draven himself, is dark and disturbing but heartfelt, a film filled with violence that few filmmakers or stars have the guts to try. It's an emotional film that plays with the word "hero."

Draven's in a position that no one can understand and he's there, as we hear in the film's opening monologue, "to put the wrong things right." It what makes the film so surreal; it blends impossibility (not the usual impracticality—we're miles past that point) with something that so many of us wish we could do, or be.

"This is the best role I have had the opportunity to get my hands on," Lee said. "Because we do not know when we are going to die, we get to think of life as an inexhaustible well and yet everything happens only a certain number of times, and a very small number really. How many times will you remember a certain afternoon of your childhood? An afternoon that is so deeply a part of your being that you cannot conceive of your life without it? Perhaps four, five times more. Perhaps not even that."

After watching Draven, after remembering Brandon Lee, it's a safe bet that audience members sat back and appreciated the things we do and have that are too easy to take for granted, realizing that everything (and someone) that we love can disappear in a second, sometimes with no warning, no reason, nothing.

"I don't know if I was destined to play this role, but I feel very fortunate to be doing so, said Lee. "It's only if you lose a friend, or maybe have a near-death experience, [that] many events and people in your life suddenly attain real significance. When you take into account the fact that that could have been the last time I would ever see that person [or] do something so mundane as go out to dinner.... This is [where] this character is coming from. [He realizes] how precious each moment of his life is."

> A building gets torched; all that is left is ashes. I used to think that was true about everything: families, friends, feelings. But now I know that sometimes if love proves real, two people who are meant to be together, nothing can keep them apart.—Rochelle Davis as Sarah in *The Crow*

And now for the young woman who became to *The Crow* what Ishmael had been to *Moby Dick,* the person who ties everything together, whose lines start and end the film, who makes it mean just a little bit more.

Sarah is the adoptive child that Eric and Shelly didn't get to have just yet, the one that Albrecht mentors throughout.

The film had been Rochelle Davis' first time before the camera, but it was far from her first acting job. "When I was about two, I started putting on plays for my mom," she remembers. "It came very natural to me. As soon as I was in school, we were doing little plays in kindergarten. I was always given lead roles because I could remember parts, all the lines from things."

Just before she was about to head into the dredges of middle school, a shot at being Sarah made Davis wonder if she could make a career out of this sort of thing.

"I was an old soul at that age," says Davis. "[Like Sarah,] I didn't have my father growing up. He wasn't really much around, didn't really want to be involved in our lives. I'd been through a lot in my life, and it was easy for me to understand the character."

Walking into the first official tryout of her acting career, Davis combined being the part with looking it. "I tried to read the role and get the impression, the attitude of who I was going to be playing, and then tried to dress accordingly," she says. "I was wearing very baggy sweatpants and a T-shirt, with a bandana on my head. Dressing like a hoodrat was the role. It's not about looking nice, it's about looking *her*."

Through four callbacks, she stepped farther and farther into Sarah's dark, sad world. She was asked about being able to ride a skateboard, as Sarah does throughout the flick, and about being scared of heights, as Draven's enemies hold her captive atop a building. "The more that they called me back and the more signs I got, the more exciting it was," she says. "I was thinking that this could be mine, the part that I get to play. I tried to improve a little more in each audition with what I thought Sarah's essence was. It took a lot of putting together a person named Sarah, to make them point at me and say, 'That's her.'"

One day, having waited as one potential Sarah after another tried out ahead of her, she strolled into the room. Then she reached into her pocket. Davis pressured a small monkey figure, eliciting some squeaks from it and some laughs from her judges. "I'm not nervous," Davis recalls. "You could feel the tension in the room like a knife, and I think they needed that to lighten up. It was tedious, with them auditioning the next girl, and the next girl, and the next girl. I showed them I had this personality they hadn't seen before."

It worked; not long after that, she learned she'd been picked. "I think my eyes rolled back into my head and my head started spinning in circles," she says. "I screamed at the top of my lungs."

Rochelle Davis became Sarah, the cornerstone of *The Crow*, the young lady who ties the whole story together from the background.

She checked out the comic book on which the film is based beforehand, getting an idea of who Sarah was. She stepped farther and farther into character. By the time she headed to North Carolina, Proyas knew she knew what she was up to. "He just said, 'You know what you're doing. Go do it. Walk from here to there, say these lines, do it the way you do it and that's all I want from you.'"

Though Lee didn't have a tremendous amount of experience himself, mentoring was a new, welcome experience for him. The protective nature that Eric shows toward Sarah throughout the movie crossed over into filming. For the graveyard scene where Sarah says her final goodbye, "I couldn't remember one of the lines for the life of me," Davis says.

For one of the only times during filming, Lee sat down with her and rehearsed it. By the time it was time to film, Davis, "couldn't get myself to stop crying…. They'll yell 'cut,' and they'll be looking for me to do it again, and I'll be around the corner wiping my eyes because I couldn't stop crying for some reason." It ended up being her favorite scene of the film.

Not having Lee around for the last part of filming made things unbearable for the young actress. Her narration was only added to the storyline after Lee died. As for Sarah's soliloquy, as she wanders around the Draven loft with a cat as a partner, "was supposed to be [a conversation between] me and Brandon," she says, "sitting at the fire where he was burning up pictures of himself. We were talking, with him explaining to me why he was doing this, and why he couldn't be too close to me."

> If the people we love are stolen from us, the way to have them
> live on is to never stop loving them. Buildings burn,
> people die, but real love is forever.—Sarah

Baiss, Bridget. *The Crow: The Story Behind the Film*. London: Titan Books, 2004.
"Brandon Lee's Final Interview." *The Crow: Believe In Angels*. 2002. Retrieved April 15, 2010, from http://inner_mercy.tripod.com/Last_Int.html.
"Brandon Lee's Last Interview." *EW.com*. 1994. Retrieved April 15, 2010, from http://www.ew.com/ew/article/0,,302196,00.html.
Davis, Rochelle. Phone interview. March 20, 2013.
Goodson, William Wilson. *A Tribute to Brandon Lee: Martial Arts Legends. Brandon Lee's Last Interview*. n.d. Retrieved April 15, 2010, from http://stickgrappler.tripod.com/articles/brandonlast.html.
Sofia Shinas. *The Crow—A Dead Man Visits You*. 2007. Retrieved April 15, 2010, from http://deadman.crowfans.com/crow_shinas.html.

••••••••••••••••••••••••••••••

Michael Reid MacKay: *Se7en*

With so much time in the makeup chair, there was little to do but wait and think.

Think about that life-changing moment in the halls of his junior high school, when the drama teacher had walked by and offhandly asked if he'd like to be in a play, the unofficial kickoff to his acting career.

"My response inside was 'Who, me?'" MacKay recalls. "I had never been in a play, so I guess I didn't feel popular or anything. But I was in the play, and I knew then and there that this was what I wanted to do."

For a big chunk of Michael Reid MacKay's acting career, he has been buried under loads of makeup or costume, usually unable to speak and/or move.

Once again, it all started for MacKay back in junior high, which led to an acting award

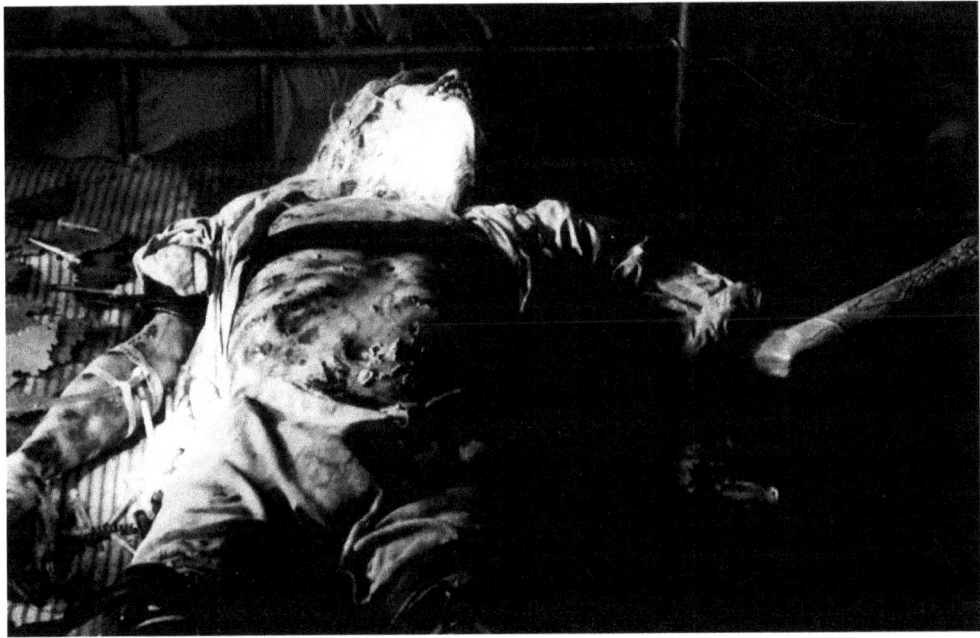

As the horrible demonstration of the sin of sloth, Michael MacKay didn't need to even move to terrify us in *Se7en*.

in high school and then some education in the field (he got an early taste of realistic horror with a small role as Charles Manson in the TV film *Summer Dreams*). Then one day, a friend saw a casting ad in *Variety* magazine. "They were looking for someone very skinny, on the verge of anorexic," recalls MacKay. "I answered the ad and went to the studios, then auditioned with gestures."

That's because his character couldn't speak; being wrapped in bandages has that effect. MacKay was trying for the mummy role in *The Monster Squad,* the 1987 story of a group of young horror film fans who suddenly find themselves in a neighborhood war with Dracula, the Wolfman, and, of course, he of the bandaged sort. He didn't spend as much time as Boris Karloff had getting ready to become the creature decades before but, after already becoming Frankenstein's Monster, Karloff had at least known what to expect. Sitting there, MacKay saw, and slowly felt, himself starting to change.

"Once I was in makeup and they started wrapping me, my character started to develop," he recalls. "You get directions from the director: walk slowly, turn a certain way. You feel inside of the character. You feel the creature, or whomever you're playing. Once you're in makeup, you become that person, that creature, that entity. You totally get into it. You start to feel like the makeup, and the more they put on, you feel totally enveloped. Your character starts to come out of you. That's one thing I really love about acting."

After he and his comrades were vanquished by the Squad, MacKay went on to 1991's *Highway to Hell,* the story of Rachel (original *Buffy the Vampire Slayer* Kristy Swanson) who's kidnapped by one of hell's deputies, and the man who goes down to get her. Featured in small roles are Ben Stiller, his dad Jerry, and Oscar nominee (not for this film!) Richard Farnsworth. MacKay endured Arizona heat while being turned into the lady's demonized form. "I was in that suit for fourteen hours," recalls MacKay, taught by Swanson how to walk in the creature's high-heel–like hooves. "I knew what I was going to be looking like and what I was going to be doing. I wasn't going to be a person. Once I was fully enveloped in the outfit, I started to transform into this creature. I felt like the demon. I *was* the demon."

He was next involved in one of the signature scary events of the 1990s. No, not getting cold-cocked by Jim Carrey and turned into an impromptu fur coat in *Ace Ventura: When Nature Calls,* but the same year. MacKay's agent called to tell him about an upcoming movie about one of the brutal serial killers in horror film history, a fellow who truly believed in the theory that pain is the best purifier of sins, even the seven deadliest. "I thought this was terrible," MacKay admits, "really horrific, reading what this guy had done to these people." Still, getting a chance to get bossed around by David Fincher and scare the hell out of Morgan Freeman and Brad Pitt was worth it.

It would have been very easy for *Se7en* to degenerate into meaningless gore, to allow the bloodshed to wash away the strong storyline that made it a landmark in film history. But, it's elevated by Fincher's skill at taking a dark, dank, depressing atmosphere and giving his audience a reason to hang out there.

Right off the bat, we know this one's going to be tough on the eyes: An obese man is forced to eat himself to death, then has his organs ruptured by a kick in the side. A lawyer forced to literally donate his own pound of flesh. Soon enough, Freeman's Detective Somerset learns that they've just seen demonstrations of the ultimate payment for the sins of gluttony and greed, just two on the list of the unluckiest of seven.

Fingerprints are found on a wall at the lawyer's office, spelling out "Help Me." They're traced to a man named Victor, a pederast the lawyer helped escape. Piling into his apartment, a SWAT team, with Somerset and Pitt's Detective Mills along for the chase, has him trapped on a bed, covered up in fear. But when they pull back the covers, it's the epitome of an unpleasant surprise…

Laying down for his audition, MacKay saw one person with a camera, another giving out directions. "They said to stand up, turn to the right, sit down, and do what I wanted to do, but don't turn away from the camera," he remembers. "I lay down with my head away from camera, then turned my head really slowly and looked dead-eye directly at the camera, perfectly still. It was very short."

But good enough; he soon found out he'd gotten the role and he was back in the makeup chair.

"It was the longest job I ever had," he says. "It was fourteen hours of makeup. I got there really early in the morning, and went to work late at night. They painstakingly airbrushed me and gave me gelatin sores. I was lying on this table all day while they made their creation. By the time they were finished, I felt really scared."

Good—that way he could share it with the others.

As the cops reveal him, their search is far from over. Victor's not the killer: far from it. He's cuffed to the bed, the hand used to plant his fingerprints amputated. His veins are visible. There are open sores and calluses on his body. The stench is sulfurous. He's been there for a long, long time.

Looking around, the detectives notice the word SLOTH scrawled on the wall above him. That's the sin of laziness, and Victor was its forced model. Even if it was punishment for his crimes, this victim's death is a mercy killing.

"I felt pretty bad," MacKay says. "My real preparation was on the set. When I got onto that bed, I was told not to move. It's really important that I couldn't see or breathe. It's imperative to be completely still, and it was very difficult, because they were spraying me with water, and I was trying not to shiver. I had to really tuck in my breath and pull my body tight."

Things start to calm down a bit, the cops sadly realizing that they're back at square one in their investigation. A SWAT man leans close to Victor's disfigured face.

Then comes the explosion.

"I cut loose and start screaming," MacKay says. "I let it all out, and when you do something like that, you just have to go for it."

Victor's not dead. Cops with years of experience at seeing and feeling all sorts of shock and pain, including Somerset, are freaking out, screaming at the top of their lungs, no clue in the world what to do about this.

"I'm epileptic myself," MacKay says. "I know what it's like to have a seizure, so I imitated that. That scream was a release, just a bloodcurdling, gut-wrenching scream, then a wild seizure mode. I didn't have words to say; with all that air saved up, I held the scream for as long as I possibly could, and kept it up until David said cut. I didn't do a lot of takes on it."

Fans might have been more grossed out by other parts of *Se7en*. Kevin Spacey's uncredited performance as the killer, whose moniker never goes past John Doe, along with his brutality that culminates in the heartless, shocking murder of Mills' pregnant wife, pushed the film even farther into horror legend. Still, it's highly unlikely anyone was as far out of their seats as at Victor's moment. Including, as the flick made it to theaters, MacKay himself.

"I was watching it, and the people I was with kept asking when I was going to be in it," he remembers. "I'm thinking I'm all slick, this is what I do."

Then he saw himself flip out, and found himself wondering how he managed to suddenly get to the other side of the theater.

"I jumped up out of my seat, like everyone else in the theater," he says. "I scared the hell out of myself. I didn't expect this, but I scared myself. Then it's over, and I'm like, 'Oh my God!'"

MacKay, Michael Reid. Phone interview. May 30, 2013.

••••••••••••••••••••••••••••••

J. Mallory-McCree:
Cloned: The Recreator Chronicles

If we met ourselves—I mean, not just someone like us, but *our very selves*—well ... how would we like them?

Would we like them? Would we want to hang out with them? We're the same person, so it's unlikely we'd have much to chitchat about, but would they be our friends?

What if we didn't like them? Perhaps we'd realize just how tough we are to be around. Maybe we could learn quite a bit about this. Cloning's always going to be a controversial topic, but it might be the epitome of a scared-straight project.

On the other hand, what if they *were* just a little different? What if they weren't ourselves, but perhaps a little *better*? They'd be us, but they'd be the people that we wish we were.

A few years ago, long before their flick lit up screens (the movie was made in 2009, but wasn't released for three years), a group of up-and-comers came face to face with a new opportunity ... and themselves.

"I went over the script and did all the type of preparedness that I would do for a theater role," recalls stage veteran J. Mallory-McCree of his biggest film role. "I would make sure I understood exactly what was going on. Like with any film, you shoot out of order, so I wanted to be as clear as I could about each moment that was happening, whether we shot the last scene of the movie or the first."

In *Cloned: The Recreator Chronicles*, a group of pals go into unfamiliar territory for a camping trip. In other words, basically they walk around with signs on their backs that screech, "Hey monsters! Come kill us!" And there are monsters here.

While his friends Craig (film rookie Alex Nifong) and Tracy (Stella Maeve, in her sci-fi debut after roaring off in the Oscar-nominated *Transamerica*) try to find a way from platonic to romantic in the relationship sense, Derek is left to wonder just what's going on here.

Things start to get crazy. A storm traps the three inside someone else's cabin, only to be caught by the owners and forced to bury bodies that bear more than a striking resemblance to the owners. But before the trio becomes the next grave residents, another group shows up to save them.

It's them—Craig, Tracy, and Derek. But it's not really them. It's a bit more. It's a version of them that they, and we, can't help but admire. They know a bit more than us. They have a rapport with each other, a closer relationship than most people have with their best buds.

Their self-confidence exudes like an aura, and makes them intimidating without them so much as speaking.

As the "old" versions get to know the new ones, it's clear that the newbies are here to wipe them off the earth, ready to take their place. Derek is flying off to Iraq as soon as the vacation's over.

Armed with the enthusiasm of taking the first steps toward film success, Mallory-McCree charged into Derek, both of them.

"Three go in, and six come out!" Mallory-McCree says of his sci-fi debut. "I thought this would be a lot of fun. It played against type. I just threw myself in there and said, 'How much fun can I have with this?'

"I wanted to make a difference between Derek One and Derek Two. I listened to certain music to really understand why [Two] was that way, why he was such a maniac. One just wanted to have fun."

Barely able to pull their attention away from the gorgeous sights of the Adirondack Mountains, Mallory-McCree and his co-stars got to know the town of Tupper Lake in northern New York.

"We spent about a week there before anything was shot, and we got a chance to go to the schools and the church, all the local places in Tupper Lake," he says. "We even went to a high school football game.

"I had to learn how to canoe. I'm not a strong swimmer, but on days when we shot, the water was freezing and choppy. It was raining, with thunderstorms happening. I had to learn quickly, because I had to do all my own stunts. Now I actually do it as a hobby."

Derek was the only black character in the film. Mallory-McCree met some Lakers who could relate. "There were three black kids at the high school, and I did some interviews to see what their experiences were like, being the only black people in the town. It gave me a lot of inspiration."

As the clones methodically plot their attack, he had to go about becoming his own worst enemy, literally. Mallory-McCree drew two sides of the same coin, the lightheartedness of his original self and the ominous persona of the clone's heart. "I tried to find what triggered Two, the evil one," and he was the most fun to play: more quiet, more intense and focused. I was trying to figure out what his ticks were. I started running and did a lot of physical training. I wanted him to be stronger, faster, smarter.

"There's a scene where I had to punch myself and kill myself," Mallory-McCree says. "Especially when I punched myself, I did that with a green screen and a pole. It was the first time I had done that. That's technology!"

Mallory-McCree, J. Phone interview. May 3, 2013.

·······························

Meet Some *Massacre* Men

Leatherface wasn't killed at the end of the original *Texas Chain Saw Massacre* (1974), leaving the door open for a sequel. The next man to put on the Leatherface mask had never checked out the original.

"I never saw the first one before my audition," says Bill Johnson. "I got the call to audition, and then I went out and rented it. It was eerie. Very deeply disturbing. Unsettling, unnerving. And inspiring."

Johnson would have a bit more to work with than Gunnar Hansen, the 1974 Leatherface. First off, there was the backstory of the first flick; both the characters and ticket buyers had some previous knowledge of who (what?) Leatherface was and why he did this sort of thing. Secondly, there was a moniker; Leatherface's Christian name showed up as Bubba Sawyer early on.

Thirdly, some star power was on hand; Leatherface would be the prey of detective Lefty Enright, uncle of the first film's traumatized victim. Dennis Hopper, the next thing to a household name since the days of *Easy Rider,* would be chasing the baddest guy.

Finally, there was love, at least Leatherface's version of it. Things start out the same as before, with some kids out gallivanting in the Deep South. They're suddenly attacked and killed by a guy with a chainsaw.

The next day, Lefty's on the case, but his highers-up feel that he'd take it just a little too personally. Undaunted, he teams with the lady DJ with whom the kids were on the phone when they were attacked. They hit the killer straight in the ego, playing her tape of the murder and taunting the killer.

Many have stepped behind Leatherface's false face in *The Texas Chainsaw Massacre* saga.

Enraged that someone would have the audacity to mock their murderous ways, Leatherface and his brothers descend upon the radio station. But just as he's about to send the DJ the way of his previous victims, Leatherface decides that she's just too lovely to slaughter.

"Leatherface is no longer anonymous," Johnson explains. "He had a name. He was melancholy, rebellious, distressed by a terrible wrong he'd done. He was mad, bad, and dangerous to know. Now he was going for being more humane. He wasn't out to kill everyone; he wanted to explore the typical *American Graffiti* life: cruising for chicks, looking for thrills, bitten by the modifying spark of humanity. He was looking for love, so he was willing to risk it."

For probably the first time in his life, Leatherface hides something from his family, falsely convincing his brothers that the DJ's been killed. Back at the family house, now a dilapidated amusement park, he ties her up, then, in an honest attempt at an expression of affection, skins a friend of her and places the man's face on hers.

"Since there were no lines, I had to really study the script to look at the special world," Johnson explains. "Also, I was going over my mime and pantomime exercises, working on crisp, definitive, unitized body movements and gestures, looking for symbolic movements and gestures that were in essence, in relating to the subject matter. I took martial arts classes. I worked out pretty hard because I thought I'd be working hard, and I certainly was.

"We were in the middle of a very hot summer, and in the underground scenes, it was like 125 degrees in there. The crew rented 40-ton portable air conditioners and brought them in between takes. Being in a suit, a wig, a mask, gloves, and shoes, the only places that were left open for any kind of perspiration were my eyes, the lips, and the tongue. A lot of people got sick. I got pneumonia."

Like Hansen, Johnson had to work without words or facial expression. But unlike Hansen, Johnson had to act out more emotions than anger and family devotion. Leatherface falsely convinced his brothers that he'd killed the DJ. He defied them when ordered to kill her once again.

Just as it's difficult to imagine Leatherface caring one way or the other about religion, his artistic side was probably eternal unexplored territory as well. But it was that sort of thing that Johnson used to put a new inner spin on the monster who took a big step toward simple manhood.

"I read poetry," Johnson says of getting ready for the role. "I was looking for something other than an outraged frenzy. There was something else here. Leatherface was split and torn, torn between the family and safety he had always known and come to believe in, and the pheromone called action. What was he going to do? Which way was he going to go? Was he going to sit on the fence? Did he have to hop it, or saw his way through it? It was pretty exciting. It was nice to do something that was humane, rather than following sadistic human impulses of modified monkey flesh."

As the DJ slips towards the edge, she's placed in the same position as her predecessor, surrounded by the family for another dinner, brothers and Grandpa included. But just as she's about to become the main course, Lefty bursts in, sets her free, and takes on Leatherface in a chainsaw duel.

"Poetry is a very condensed, compact purse," Johnson says. "It's often romantic. It's certainly passionate. It's a form of communicating some of our experience, of what's going on inside. What's going on inside of Bubba Sawyer to cause such a change inside, to make him want to risk the wrath of the family, the expulsion, maybe even death itself? I was looking for the masters of poetry to bring the depths of heart and soul together."

As the DJ escapes—physically at least, as her chainsaw-wielding, screaming dance, reminiscent of Leatherface's jig at the original's conclusion, shows that she may never be the same again—Lefty impales Leatherface on his saw. In a bizarre twist of events that would make Rube Goldberg do cartwheels in his coffin, the grandfather hurls a mallet at Lefty, who ducks. It hits Leatherface, who drops his chainsaw, hitting a brother hiding under the table with a grenade. The miniature bomb goes off, apparently taking everyone out for good (unless, of course, the film was a big box office hit).

"Emotionally, Bubba has really invested a lot to keep [the DJ] alive," Johnson says, "and to see her in danger of being cannibalized and turned into filling for croissant sandwiches was a hardship. That was emotionally difficult in terms of character. We leave the realm of cognitive logic and go far into the right brain, the kind of chemical bath of pheromones and adrenalin and fantasy. I wanted to have a real rich tapestry in my tank, to have that in place for me for the character. It would have been easy to get just hard as nails, and just a machine, which is a one-trick pony that doesn't reveal much. It's just very interesting."

Leatherface's character continued to develop in the third installment, to the extent that 1990s Part III was named for him. He'd show a new sort of caring this time around. There'd also be a new, albeit hidden face on the character (Hansen was in talks to reprise the role, but a deal couldn't be reached).

"I was a big fan of the first two [*Massacre*s], as well as a lifelong horror fan," says R.A. Mihailoff. "Science fiction, fantasy, and horror have always been some of my favorite genres. Being cast as Leatherface allowed me to fulfill my childhood and adult ambition simultaneously. When I was a kid, I thought about how fun it would be to play those characters, like Frankenstein or the werewolf.... My adult ambition was that once I realized that acting was a career option, I started working toward becoming a movie star."

One of his first steps in that direction was appearing in the 1982 Civil War drama *Divided We Fall*, with Jeff Burr and Kevin Meyer at the helm. Eight years later, Burr and Mihailoff reunited for *Leatherface*. (The studio had previously wanted Peter Jackson to take the directing helm.)

"I had seen both [*Massacre*] films during their theatrical runs, so I was very familiar with the character," says Mihailoff. "Once you get into makeup and wardrobe and grab a chainsaw, the process becomes in a sense automatic. When you come out of the real world and step onto a movie set, it's almost like falling down the rabbit hole. You leave the real world behind and you come into a rarified atmosphere, and the magic starts to happen."

The flick opens with a young couple halfway through a cross-country trip, making their way past a mass grave in Texas (the film was actually shot in California, unlike its predecessors). Stopping at a service station, they encounter a fellow named Tex.

Like the second *Massacre*, this one had some star power behind it as well. Tex's star, however, had only just started to rise: Viggo Mortenson, who, over a decade later, would be seen by millions as Aragon in *The Lord of the Rings* trilogy and score an Oscar nomination for *Eastern Promises*.

Tex gives the couple some directions. Little do they know that their final destination will be the man with the chainsaw: Tex's family member Leatherface. Evidently, the heartbreak at losing his first love was enough to both overcome the physical agony of the explosion in the second film, and shove him back into the mindlessness of mass murder he exhibited through the first one.

"Once you begin the physical process, [preparation] almost becomes instinctive," Mihailoff says. "When you put on the mask and grab the chainsaw, 50 percent of your work is done. When the set is lit, dressed, and the actors take their marks, the creative juices flow, sometimes without a whole lot of effort. You know what the intent of the scene is, you know where your character should be, physically and emotionally."

Leatherface traps the male half of the couple in a beartrap, slicing into him with the chainsaw, and using him as a meathook ornament. His beloved flees to a nearby house. A little girl is there with her doll.

It's made of bones from a smaller previous victim of the family. Indeed, it's a trap, and Tex shows up to grab the lady and nail her to a chair. As Leatherface and the rest of the family gather, the youngster shows off her natural ability and persona, using a lever to blast the man's face. Leatherface taught his daughter well.

Whereas family love ruled Leatherface in the first film and that of a girlfriend in the second, here he's trying out the paternal side of things. "In our world," Mihailoff explains, "we were a normal family that just happened to eat human beings."

As the family sits down for another dinner, a hunter shows up with his trusty machine-gun, blasting holy hell out of the family. Tex and Leatherface chase him outside as the prey frees herself, but the hunter pours gas on the ground and lights it. Tex dies in the inferno.

As Leatherface and the woman grapple near a swamp, the hunter shows up to free her, but Leatherface sidelines him with a good whack. She blasts Leatherface in the head with a rock. As she makes it to a car, the hunter miraculously joins her. But just as they're about to escape, another brother shows up.

Much like the heroines of the first few films, she's had just about enough of this, and shotguns him. But as she and the hunter drive off to freedom, Leatherface is still around, comforting his little girl that this one got away ... but more will follow.

"There's nothing you can do to me on a movie set, short of killing or maiming me, that is worse than anything I've endured in my real life," Mihailoff says. "It's acting, it's portraying, and it is one of my biggest pet peeves when actors bitch on a movie set. You're living the good life, you're being paid well to play characters, and you have the unmitigated gall to bitch about it. Acting to me is pure joy and pure fun."

Then came *The Texas Chainsaw Massacre: The Next Generation* (1994), the tale of a young girl named Jenny on the run from the maniacal Vilmer and his family of cannibals, including Leatherface. There's a re-enactment of the forced dinner scene and Leatherface's end-credits dance, and a cameo by Marilyn Burns, one of the victims from the original. Jenny was Renee Zellweger. Vilmer was Matthew McConaughey. Both would be household names before the decade ended. Leatherface was Robert Jacks, who passed away in August 2001 at age 41.

"My first night on set I had to use a chainsaw for a couple of minutes," Jacks remembered. "[The crew] had showed me that it just cuts like butter through these tree limbs. I tried it, and that was it. So I was up for my scene—I had to cut through these saplings to get to Renee—and I had to do this sort of viciously, and then run myself out of camera."

The enthusiasm he poured into Leatherface freaked out more than his fellow characters, he continued. "I was hacking through these tree limbs, and suddenly everybody in the entire company leaves their posts because they thought I had gone insane," Jacks said. "Absolutely everyone except for ... the cinematographer, who realized that I knew what I was doing. Half of them still think I really went crazy and the other half thinks, 'Wow, this [man] can really do this.' That was pretty funny because I hadn't heard of anything like that happening on a movie set before."

In the 2000s, an "Age of Remakes" swept across the horror film world. Some called them tributes, others whined about lack of originality. New versions of *Friday the 13th, Halloween, A Nightmare on Elm Street, Predator,* and others showed up.

Fittingly, *The Texas Chainsaw Massacre* would follow suit in 2003. Andrew Bryniarski led the way that time, then again three years later with *The Texas Chainsaw Massacre: The*

Beginning, which gave us Thomas Hewitt: The Pre-Leatherface Days. To be fair, by the time yet another *Texas* incarnation rolled around in 2013, it was getting a bit hard to differentiate. Was this a sequel? A remake? A remake of a sequel that had itself been a remake?

To its credit, 2013's *Texas Chainsaw* (no *Massacre* here) a 3-D film, put a different spin on the Leatherface legend. It made the monster with the human face (or other humans') a bit more human than ever before.

Like Hansen *his* first time around, Dan Yeager was new in the film world.

"Nothing in my actor training really prepared me for the role," he recalls. "Acting schools don't cover wearing a mask of human flesh and chasing folks with a real chainsaw with the intent to kill them."

Yeager started buffing up with some extra weight room time. Perhaps aided by the mind-cleansing rush that workouts can provide, he dissected horror's eternal connection to its audience. "I realized that horror itself is kind of an odd form of entertainment," says the lifelong *Massacre* fan. "I kind of studied what the emotional connection that we have with horror is and … got into the history which is rather convoluted. I tried being silent and I think that the most horrifying thing about this character is his silence. I think it informs his mental state more than anything else. Just that fact that he doesn't speak. He has his mask and he has his saw and that's his connection to the world.

"I've acted in a mask before on stage and it's just a matter of being aware that you have to physically move if you want to convey anything," says Yeager. "You can't show it in your eyes, you can't show it with a wry smile. It's got to be a physical move and so you just make those moves meaningful. You go from your head down to your head up and it's got to mean something in the context of the story. And people will infer from what you're doing, what it means. It's a different challenge. It's like learning to deliver your lines, it's just very physical."

The film starts mere moments after the "first" one (i.e., the one that Hansen had starred in). Cops and self-appointed bounty hunters descend upon the house, the Sawyer family trapped inside—including Jedidiah, known to them as Jed and, quickly enough, to us as Leatherface. The place gets torched, taking out everyone … they think.

"I am the older version of Gunnar Hansen's character," says Yeager, who also got ready by watching the original *Massacre* one hundred times (so he claims, perhaps an exaggeration) and reading several Hansen interviews. "I started with him, with that complete character that he had already created and then a lot of things happened in Leatherface's life. Our movie starts at a very pivotal moment in his life where his world is turned completely upside down and by the time you see me on the screen, he's gone through twenty years of radically different life to become the updated character that I portray."

After spending his entire life as the family follower, the main man was now out on his own, thrust into a scary new world, with no one to look after or to look after him. "In the original he had no self-determination," Yeager says. "Everybody told him what to do and he liked that. He was very much an instrument of the will of other people, so he didn't have to think for himself at all. And when he did think for himself, he had nothing but good thoughts. He loved his family, and he worried about them.… When the kids unwittingly unlock the cellar, he's lived in the cellar for 20-some years under completely different circumstances. And he's become older. He's gotten a little crotchety, a little grumpy. He now has a will, but he still sees the world as 'you're either family or you're food.'"

Boss Sawyer, who tried to save Jed at the beginning, was played by the original Leatherface. "It was a surreal experience to walk through the real Sawyer house with all the bone furniture and everything," Yeager says, "and then to walk through the house with Gunnar and be able to talk to him."

Just as those who had played the role in the past attempted to do, he thought about the man-thing behind the human skin mask. What had Leatherface been doing for those nearly two decades he'd spent alone on the Sawyer estate, with no one to order him around? "I think he liked fairly simple barbeque," Yeager says. "It was his grandma's cooking that he lived on for all those years. He was almost a prisoner down there.... He liked to make things. He's very childlike still. He plays with stuff like a kid does. His life experience is a bit limited. He has a television, but he probably doesn't see a lot of it and doesn't relate it to anything because he doesn't have the context. It's just images. It doesn't mean emotionally to him what it would mean to a normal person that lives a normal life. I don't think he could read, but he does like to make things." Remembering the leg injury that Leatherface had suffered decades before—both in real and reel time—he gave the character an awkward stroll, very clear in the chase scenes.

Meanwhile, young beauty Heather (Alexandra Daddario) finds her world flipped when she finds out she's adopted. The upside: She's just inherited a large chunk of property. The downside: There's an unwelcome gift in the bargain. "The last time *anybody* got away, my entire family was slaughtered," the new Leatherface recalls, "so I don't take it lightly when more people try to escape."

Just about as soon as Heather and her friends arrive, some not-so-subtle tributes to the original work start appearing; Leatherface's first-ever introduction is recreated in a full-body shot that culminates in him bashing in an unwelcome face (the hitchhiker, who becomes a robber this time). Just as Hansen did, Yeager got to impale a victim on a giant hook, then chop someone in half. (Today's audiences were tough enough to actually *get shown* these things, rather than the simulation of the original.) The scene where a corpse popped out of a freezer gets redone, only this time the victim's still alive—until a startled policeman inadvertently puts a bullet through her skull. We even get to see Leatherface's dime-store surgeon skills, removing a victim's face and sewing it onto his mask.

"If you ever get the opportunity, and someone tells you to get a chainsaw and go chase somebody like you want to kill them, you should do it," Yeager recalls dreamily. "There's no more powerful feeling that I had ever had. It was a sensation."

During a carnival chase scene, Leatherface happens upon a pipsqueak wearing a pig mask, much like Jigsaw's from *Saw*. The pig person runs off in terror. Looks like someone wanted to send a message about who the *real* scarers are in this world. "When you're chasing a woman with a chainsaw," Yeager says, "it just makes you want to kill her more."

But there's one big difference between this version and all the rest. Eventually, Heather finds out that this big bad killer is actually her cousin, the only blood family she has left and the one who saw his family slaughtered—her adoptive parents helped in their own "massacre," killing her biological mom. And despite all the lives he's taken, sawing her friend in half before her eyes, and that he was trying to dismember her just hours before, she decides to be there for him, helping him escape and get revenge on those who killed his—their—family.

The Leather man had a big heart after all.

"That's kind of the pivotal moment that sets up the payoff of the whole movie, that it's all about family," Yeager says. "Forget everything else. You do have to overlook the flaws of your family members. There had to be some kind of emotional connection for Heather to decide to stay. She had to see something human in Leatherface or she would just get the hell out of there. That moment has to happen, that, Jesus, he's really this pitiful creature under that mask but he's also dangerous as hell, still. And the simple hand on her arm, those little subtleties mean something."

"Exclusive—Interview with Dan Yeager." *Horror Pilot*. 2013. Retrieved Sept. 10, 2013, from http://www.horrorpilot.com/exclusiv-interview-with-dan-yeager-texas-chainsaw-massacre-3d/.
Frances, Laura. "Interview: Director John Luessenhop And Leatherface Actor Dan Yeager on 'Texas Chainsaw 3D.'" *Screen Crave*. Jan. 3, 2013. Retrieved Sept. 10, 2013, from http://screencrave.com/2013-01-03/interview-director-john-luessenhop-leatherface-actor-dan-yeager-texas-chainsaw-3d.
Johnson, Bill. Phone interview. March 25, 2012.
Luessenhop, John. *Texas Chainsaw 3D* [DVD]. U.S.: Lionsgate, 2013.
Mihailoff, R.A. Phone interview. March 9, 2012.
Nemiroff, Perri. "Texas Chainsaw 3D' Interview: Dan Yeager's Leatherface is a Family Man." *Screen Rant*. Jan. 2013. Retrieved Sept. 10, 2013, from http://screenrant.com/texas-chainsaw-3d-interview-dan-yeager/.

Chris McGinn and Ted Levine: *The Silence of the Lambs*

Through the first half of *The Silence of the Lambs*, we hear about some of the worst crimes that cinema has explored. Torture, cannibalism, it's all here. We even see a few snapshots of the victims of these unthinkable crimes. But it's not until we get a truly up-close and *far* too personal look at the work of a madman that we really understand why the law needs to go the extra mile to get this dirtbag off the streets—or better yet, off the earth.

Equipped with some of the dark clues Hannibal Lecter's handed out about Buffalo Bill, killing and skinning his victims in true Ed Gein style, heroine Clarice Starling goes to the autopsy of his latest victim. The woman died a brutal death, and in her throat is a moth, one of Bill's favorite pets. Its habitat is far from where the victim's body was found, and it heats up Starling's pursuit of a man she's starting to know.

"The character description was that they wanted women who weren't small and looked real," remembers Chris McGinn, who played the unfortunate woman. (One of Bill's trademarks is that his victims are heavyset, giving him enough fresh skin to make materials that would fit over his male form.)

"I went for the audition, and there were all these models: tall women, six foot, skinny models," she says. "What am I doing here? That played into my attitude when I went into the audition. I thought it was such a riot, something that I hadn't done before." Not having read the film's novelization, McGinn had tried out for the role of Bill's victim Catherine Martin before getting a different opportunity: A directing assistant asked McGinn to play dead.

"I left thinking, 'What a crazy experience.' They called an hour later and said I had the role. It revealed itself later because of me being dead, because of all the makeup prepping

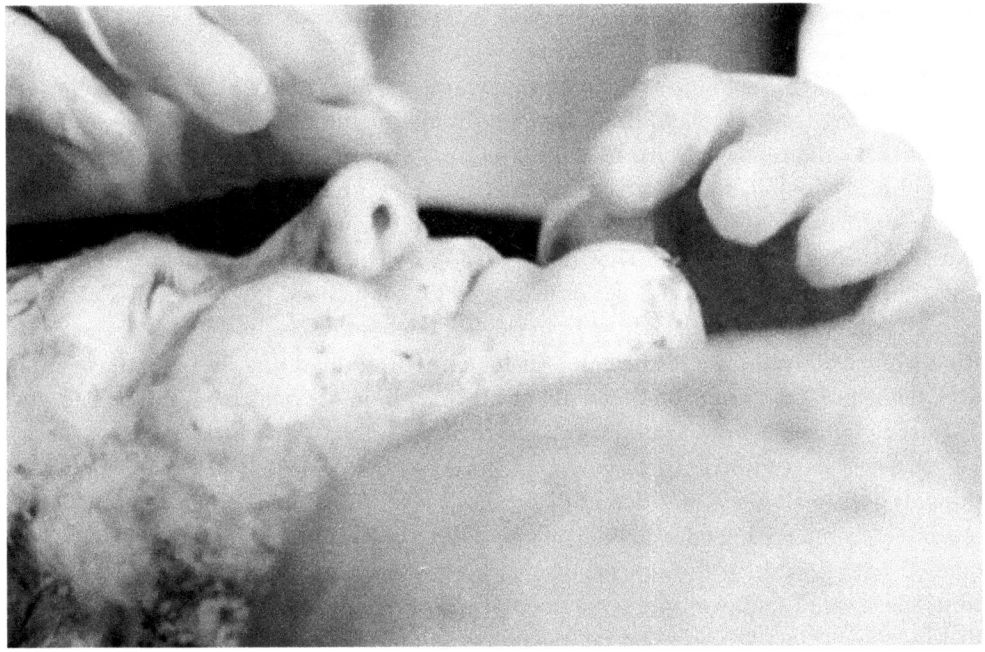

Chris McGinn became Buffalo Bill's first on-screen victim in *The Silence of the Lambs*.

that had to go on, they wanted a woman who looked real, not a model. They wanted someone with a good disposition. They didn't want someone who was going to have an attitude."

She read the screenplay and the book it's based on (up to where her character appears), and studied up on Foster and Demme. Then McGinn and the makeup crew went through some makeup tests and had a few plaster molds made of her.

"They created pieces that looked like skin to glue on to me," she says. "They put makeup on top of the skin pieces to look like I'd been filleted. They were taking Polaroids of my mouth and teeth, the angles they ended up using in the movie, to find the thing in my throat." McGinn had a birthday during the shoot; photos show her celebrating over a cake, surrounded by partygoers, in full makeup and clad in just a robe.

"My scene took two days to shoot," says McGinn, whose scene was shot in an old funeral home. "One day they were shooting me on one side, the second day turning me over. I knew everything that was going to happen. They had a room for me, a towel, and a sheet to cover me the minute they said cut. I didn't really feel naked in a certain sense. I was more naked with the makeup guys because they were gluing the skin to me, and putting makeup on it. I was walking around in my terrycloth robe, looking half dead on one side on one day, and half dead on the other side the next day. I couldn't sit down because the makeup glued to me would come off, and six hours of makeup would be wasted."

As for the butterfly, "[t]hey made it out of Tootsie Rolls so I wouldn't choke if it got stuck," McGinn explains. "I learned how to hold it with my tongue, to look dead, to be still, and for them to be able to pop my jaw. I learned how long I could keep it on my tongue inside my mouth before they opened it up and pulled it out." Both Foster and Demme praised her in promotional interviews.

Anthony Hopkins' Oscar-winning work as Lecter deserves as much praise as it gets, but Ted Levine's has never gotten nearly enough.

"It was intriguing to me, this complicated human being, an evil human being," Levine says of getting ready to play Bill. "I read up on material on serial killers. I saw a lot of images that I still remember. I read about Ed Gein, Jerry Brudos (the "Shoe Fetish Slayer" necrophiliac who killed at least four women) and the sense that I got from both of those guys in particular was that they were self-indulgent. They were addicted to this idea of sex and death being close together. They really got off on that. They fancied themselves as victims. Bill, aware of the hand he was dealt as a child, felt justified in what he did."

The film came under flack from both sides of the homosexuality debate—the anti-gay wing whined about a transvestite being such an important part of a Best Picture-winning film, while pro-gay groups blithered about making a homosexual character the bad guy. According to Levine, however, both sides were out of line.

"I never played him as being gay," explains the actor. "Male sexuality is a complicated thing. It goes in all kinds of different directions. I met with female impersonators. I went to some very interesting bars, looking at and talking to people about a side of life I wasn't familiar with. I came to the conclusion that none of that really had anything to do with this. The stance I took was more one of an acutely homophobic heterosexual man doing that mocking thing. I took it that he was imitating the way his mother might have talked to the poodle. By hearing that voice, he's talking to himself, his inner poodle as it were."

Bill wasn't into men, and his fascination with the female form came not so much from hating them, but wanting to *be* them. In his mind, women were so much more powerful, so much stronger, more domineering than he or any man could ever be. Bill's backstory shows a near-obsession with his own mother, and such feelings are not uncommon, albeit in a *much* more subtle manner, in men with this sort of fixation, as even famous guys like Elvis Presley and J. Edgar Hoover were shown to carry their own lifelong Oedipus complexes. Killing these women wasn't about something as petty as misogynistic hate; it was about using them to become something that strengthened him like a woman (not a misprint there).

"[Bill] got hold of the power that he perceived a woman possesses," Levine says. "I'm going to have you completely, and I'm going to skin you and crawl inside you."

Cross-dressing, even the "genital tuck" Bill uses in his unclothed state, he continues, are "things that anybody can do in the privacy of their own home, to check themselves out, to say, 'What would I look like if I was a girl?' It made it immediately accessible to me."

As Bill and Starling have their final battle, there's several spots where he could have easily taken her out—he's

Ted Levine's Buffalo Bill became the FBI's main target in *The Silence of the Lambs*.

equipped with night-vision goggles in pitch blackness, while 20–20 vision won't do anything for her here. But he doesn't do it, and it might just be because her wants one last taste of power over a woman. Being in control of one is more important, or at least just as much, to him as his own life.

Demme, Jonathan, Dir. *The Silence of the Lambs* [DVD]. U.S.: Orion Pictures, 1991.
McGinn, Chris. Phone interview. June 28, 2012.

Pollyanna McIntosh: *Offspring* and *The Woman*

As her minions did her dirty work, their impromptu matriarch sat back and enjoyed the results of her instruction. To those on the other side, the people being tortured and oftentimes killed might have seemed like innocent victims, people in the wrong place at the most horrible of times.

Not to her. And not to her family. These people were the enemy, the ones with the nerve to stand in her way. Every family deserves to live its own separate life of enjoyment, and those who dared to invade needed to be taken care of. Sort of beautiful in the most macabre of ways, the young woman sent others to do her murderous work, and participated sometimes. And like every worthy parent, this lady bestowed all sorts of rewards on those who did right in the family tradition.

Pollyanna McIntosh showed both the evil and moral sides of the woman in *Offspring* and *The Woman*.

Watching 2009's *The Offspring*, a filmmaker saw the family joyfully slaughter those who stood in their way. For all sorts of reasons, he noticed the female protagonist. She was lovely in an evil sort of form. He noticed her screen presence with small roles in *Land of the Lost* and other stories.

But beyond that, and most noticeably, she seemed to be enjoying the massacring. Not just as a parent setting an example for her youth, but getting a pleasure overdose from doing so. This woman seemed to *like* being in charge of the death and destruction. To her, it was fun. That evil smile that kept stretching out her countenance and those eyes that made us feel like a fly careening into a spider web ... was there more there than just a parental obligation?

What kind of person could possibly find this sort of thing pleasurable? He may not have known her by name just yet, but Lucky McKee had the type down pat right away—the sort that he wanted in his next film.

It would start off much the same as *The Girl Next Door*—evil scumbag kidnaps young woman and tortures her in his basement. Soon, the whole family joins in on the fun.

In 1989, Jack Ketchum had put the true story on paper, and it had made its way to the screen a few times—see Blythe Auffarth's profile for more information there. Then, in 2011, Ketchum and McKee's collective muse gifted them with *The Woman,* a new version of the sad story (Ketchum had also written *Offspring* in 1991). And unlike the first creation and the tragic true tale it told, this one wasn't confined by reality. Taking dramatic license to the darkest extreme, the two had put a whole new spin on the woman, the family, and the ending.

Like, what if that woman were to make it out? What if she could not only escape, but get a chance to turn things around and give everyone a taste of their own medicine? Keeping in mind that this lady already had all sorts of torturous tendencies, now she had a shot and a good reason to kick them up a few notches. There might just be worse than hell to pay.

And not only that, but after being terrified of and pretty ticked off at her for the first film, audiences might not want to cheer for her. She and her folk had brutally killed several women and children—and now we were being asked to wait around to see her human side? Did she even have one? Or would she *want* one, at least in the civilized sense?

One of the victims is stalked by her drunk, abusive husband, who gets as much torture as anyone else when he's found by the clan. Many fans might have just brushed it off as giving us just one more reason to hope that the good girl wins and the bad guy dies, but some of us looked a little closer. Intentionally or otherwise, the film might have been asking us: Who is really the villain here? The family that stays together, fights together, even dies for each other? Or the one that lies, cheats, steals, beats, even kills each other? Do the words "civilized" and "civil" mean anywhere near the same thing? Does being more evolved as a people make us better than those living in "simpler" times? Does an established society mean a more effective one?

"Modeling was just a happy task that came up that got me a lot of travel when I was still young, which was fun," recalls Pollyanna McIntosh, the Scotland native who kicked off her modeling career as a teenager in London. "[But] acting has always been something that I loved, storytelling, something that I saw myself doing from a really young age."

After a childhood filled with acting classes and teenage years peppered with theater and small films—not to mention a degree in psychology and drama before she was nineteen—McIntosh kept looking for the bigger and the better when it came to performing. And the looks that had gotten her so much attention in front of both still and filming cameras were forced into a 180 for the roles that pushed her farther in horror films than anything else to that point.

"She had kind of a clan," she recalls of our first glimpse of the main woman in *Offspring*. "She had a lot of children. They weren't all hers that she bore, nor were all hers that she was the legal guardian of, but she kind of took some kids. She kind of created her own family.... [S]he was the bad guy, but as an actor playing a role, I saw her as the good guy. And there was still an element of civilized against the uncivilized and the 'Who is right?' kind of thing." Like any good mother, her character was concerned about her kids. She helped them learn the skills needed to survive in this crazy land. She went to the ends of the earth (their definition of the world was clearly a bit different than most) to protect them, even putting her own life on the line at times.

It's tough to really pick winners and losers in *Offspring*; most of the "victims" survive, but it's clear they'll never leave this experience behind. The leader escapes, showing that someone had the inclination that she might someday be worth another shot on the screen.

But when McGee and Ketchum first offered her both the script and the spotlight with *The Woman*, McIntosh wasn't sure she could go back into character. "I was horrified at some parts," McIntosh recalls. "I was just like … I can't do a whole movie like this. What am I going to do with myself, you know?" Then she started rechecking things with the screenplay. She looked over Ketchum's book. And she decided to both resurrect and alter the lady.

"What I read in *The Woman*, with the Cleek family's all–American veneer," McIntosh recalls, "was something much darker, much more complex and, to be honest, much more challenging for me as an actress. I just knew exactly where I was going to go with her. I knew I wasn't going to be stopped from going to the places I wanted to go with her because we had four months of conversations on the phone."

As *The Woman* gets rolling, it seems as if the title character might still be the villain, perhaps getting a bit of deserved payback for her deeds. Out for a hunt, Chris Cleek notices her bathing and makes her his prey, knocking her out and tying her up in his basement, letting his wife, son, and daughters know that the lady will soon be "civilized." However, just as we got a taste of in the first film, civil and civilized can be light years apart.

While McIntosh had been able to pull off the woman's first portrayal without speech, now she'd have to work with hardly any physical movement as well. After being on the attack for most of the first film, she was playing defense. "I took everything that I'd worked on in *Offspring* and went back to that kind of animal research, spending time alone in the woods and feeling my body outside of our modern civilization as we've created it."

Off by herself for days at a time, sometimes in nearby woods, she learned about those who make such surroundings their habitat. "Studying animals such as wolves, big cats, and apes in nature documentaries and in zoos was a big part of it, as well as studying our ancient myths, especially with regards to hunting. I had to create a sense of my life if I were outside that cellar, what was most important to me, so I knew what I wanted to get back to and how I judged the family I was now faced with."

Being a model had gotten her used to the importance of physicality, but this was a whole new task in that department as well. "I worked out a lot, concentrating on the muscles she would use in her lifestyle," she says of the character. "This meant I was sometimes leapfrogging around the gym or hanging off the bars like a monkey. I also grew my hair out in every conceivable place.

"I felt very connected to the character. She marries my feminist side, my tomboy side, and my 'running around in nature like a wild child' side, all of which I've had since I was a little girl."

Now a stranger in a strange land, the Woman slowly starts to become the victim, not entirely without sympathy. Chris's son starts to show his misogynistic inheritance, harassing some of his lady classmates. His wife and other daughters stand silently by as he begins to "civilize" her though, like most abusers, his discipline is everyone else's cruelty (though she does land the first blow, chomping off his finger). With Chris's willpower looming like a raincloud over "his" women's lives, his wife is slapped for questioning his teachings on the woman. (Angela Bettis, whom McKee helped spring to stardom as the creepy lead in *May*, played the Cleek wife.) It appears that his daughter might be showing the signs of a far more sinister type of abuse, bringing a questioning schoolteacher into the equation.

All the while, the Woman refuses to give in all the way, and even those who saw *Offspring* are starting to reverse their sentiments towards her.

"I had to look into the Woman's life as it was almost before *Offspring* started," McIntosh says, "to her life with her family as well as her purpose and own sort of mythology along with the things that sustain her. The latter involves the hunt and her own territory and having those two things taken away from her and being locked in that cellar, which was the most difficult thing for the character. She then had to try to figure out how she was going to get out of there and back to what she craved and needed to survive. My character also had to figure out who this family was, what they wanted, and how their tribe worked. One of the neat things about this movie is that this supposedly civilized family ends up being much more messed up than my feral cannibal character."

Soon the family's civil disorder descends into absolute anarchy. Chris douses the Woman with boiling water, then blasts her with a power washer. The son starts to torture the Woman. The schoolteacher drops by, only to be fed by Chris and his son to the family dogs, her remains tossed into a wood chipper. Chris rapes the Woman.

Then we see that she wasn't the first; along with the two family pets lives a person treated as such, a woman-thing whose eyes have been removed and whose vocabulary has been beaten into animalism. She gets a few tastes of the teacher herself.

"Messed up" would never in a million years come close to describing this family. But there's still an ounce of redemption left, and it comes in the form of the abused daughter, who releases the Woman.

Now it's war. If she was an effective huntress before, the rush of adrenalin has pushed her to the point of invincibility. *No one* is going to stop her from revenge. And by this point, anyone and everyone on the outside is on her side.

"In many ways it was very liberating because I shed all my modern feminine expectations and found ways my body could live in a far more natural and powerful state," McIntosh recalls. "The mind follows and rather than feeling limited by the lack of language or the physical restraints of the role, I felt utterly alive and fiercely present and active throughout.

"The animalistic frame of mind started taking over my body. As a woman, you don't really get the feel that rawness state of mind, that kind of weight and power."

If she never got the chance to show it again, McIntosh helped the Woman take full advantage of this experience. The wife is the first to go, as the Woman makes her pay for setting such a horrible example for the young girls. Charging into the barn, she hacks the son to pieces with a blade.

Then, to emphasize the pain and destruction, or perhaps just to find out if the organ even existed to begin with, she proceeds to tear Chris's heart straight out of his chest. She makes a meal of it. An evil, darkly gorgeous smile of redemption stretches across her face as he collapses, for the first time in awed, agonizing terror of a superior force.

Forever a follower, the slave woman comes to her new mistress. The youngest daughter follows. The abused daughter hesitates, but then steps in line. Just about anything will be better than the previous life.

To them, the Woman's no longer just another person. She's someone who went through hell and came out all right. Something above all the humanity they ever knew. Like others did with another person who went through the epitome of pain purification, they're now ready to follow her. Or, by this point, Her. These women have been treated like tenth-class citizens their whole lives, but for the first time, they have someone who can show them how to be. How to live for themselves, rather than at the command of someone who had few redeeming qualities.

Granted, some of the women in Chris' family have already been beaten down by his authority, but it's a woman who saves Her at the end. It's a woman who helps Her get away. It's three women who go off with Her to start a new life—who allows Her to lead them to a new life. Perhaps She's found some new *Offspring*.

"It's very exciting for viewers to see how they feel about seeing a very powerful woman onscreen," McIntosh remarks. "A very powerful woman who's not using her sexuality to be

Alexa Marcigliano's slave (top) makes a meal of Carlee Baker in the climax of *The Woman*.

powerful. I think it is a philosophical movie. I do think there's so much about imperialism and control and abuse.... I think there are realistic characters and realistic reactions to what's going on. The reason I do this is so I can affect somebody and make them feel less alone and more human. I think this film manages to do that. It does that for me. If it allows someone to feel like they've been understood in some way, or less odd, then I'll be happy."

If the Woman herself had demonstrated a different kind of humanity, or lack thereof, the slave (not quite affectionately named Socket by the Cleeks) emphasized its loss. Who had she been? Where had she come from? How could she have been made this way? How can one go from human to animal, at least this far into it? Alexa Marcigliano had to show all that, without so much as the benefit of upright walking—and all in her first role.

As for stunt work, recalls Marcigliano, "It's been a lifelong dream of mine since I was little. I watched a lot of *Xena: Warrior Princess,* and finding out there was somebody who did all those cool moves sparked my interest. I've never been one to want my face on screen, which is the appeal of doing stunts—you're behind the scenes. The behind-the-scenes badassery of it all is what keeps me in stunts."

Being on the small side (Marcigliano is just over five feet) was a drawback.

"I got these casting calls in my e-mail," she recalls, "and they were never looking for someone like me. They were never looking for someone of my stature and my skill set." Downcast, she'd taken to pounding computer keys for the U.S. Fish and Wildlife Service.

Then one day, another message dropped into her inbox. "They were saying that they were looking for a five-foot tall, experienced martial artist female who could run around on all fours and play a dog character," Marcigliano recalls.

Marcigliano got hold of a video of a feral woman from the Ukraine who'd been raised by barkers. "She ran around on all fours and she barked like a dog, so I spent the next couple of weeks running around my apartment on all fours and barking like a dog, setting up obstacle courses. My roommate critiqued my form. I thought it was a novelty, but I'd been sitting in a cubicle for years. This was much more interesting."

At the audition, Marcigliano bruised her hands and knees. She barked. She growled and scowled. It's interesting to wonder about the criteria the casting crew used to judge the effectiveness of this sort of performance. "I didn't hear anything for weeks," she says. "Then I got a call saying I got it. They sent me a script. That's when I realized exactly what I was getting myself into."

She had the advantage of being able to ignore reality: The slave's world was nowhere near anything most of us could relate to. She didn't have to pretend to carry around the feelings, the emotions of a normal soul because she wasn't one. "I kept practicing running around on all fours," Marcigliano says. "I learned about violent moves, like attacking, rather than just jumping around. I used a lot of muscle during filming."

She spent about three hours in the makeup department every day, getting dirtier and bloodier. Finally, it was time to go teacher-hunting. "My mind almost went blank, and I had to let instinct take over as far as the philosophy we practiced, the marks I had to hit, and where we had to end up. I had to continue being ferocious, becoming a ferocious beast for a couple of minutes. Luckily, I had a day in between to de-compress from the ferocious scenes to the touching [escape] scenes the next day."

Marcigliano keeps going after her stunting goals, such as alongside Taylor Lautner in *Tracers.*

"When I got the role in *The Woman*," she says, "I went through the filming process and saw that this was what I wanted to do. Every day in a cubicle after that became impossible. I knew I needed to get out of there and have a career, with the skills and things that I could do with my own body for the entertainment of others."

Bain, Whitney Scott. "Interview: Pollyanna McIntosh, Star of 'THE WOMAN.'" *Starburst Magazine*. Oct. 31, 2011. Retrieved Sept. 17, 2012, from http://www.starburstmagazine.com/features/feature-articles/1246-interview-with-pollyanna-mcintosh-star-of-the-woman.

Eramo, Steve. "Savage Instinct: Interview with *The Woman*'s Pollyanna McIntosh." *The Morton Report*. Nov. 16, 2011. Retrieved Sept. 17, 2012, from http://www.themortonreport.com/entertainment/film/savage-instinct-interview-with-the-womans-pollyanna-mcintosh/.

Katz, Alex. "Interview: Pollyanna McIntosh, The Woman." *Flixist*. Oct. 13, 2011. Retrieved Sept. 17, 2012, from http://www.flixist.com/interview-pollyanna-mcintosh-the-woman-205170.phtml.

Manzetti, Alessandro. "The Woman: Interview with Pollyanna McIntosh." *Mezzotints*. April 11, 2011. Retrieved Sept. 17, 2012, from http://postonero.blogspot.com/2011/04/woman-interview-with-pollyanna-mcintosh.html.

Marcigliano, Alexa. Phone interview. March 12, 2013.

Smith, Nigel. "Meet Pollyanna McIntosh, The Woman Behind 'The Woman.'" *IndieWire*. Oct. 11, 2011. Retrieved Sept. 17, 2012, from http://www.indiewire.com/article/interview_pollyanna_mcintosh_the_woman_behind_the_woman_on_sundances_most_c.

Thambounaris, Amanda. "Interview with Pollyanna McIntosh." *The Celebrity Cafe*. Oct. 31, 2011. Retrieved Sept. 17, 2012, from http://thecelebritycafe.com/feature/interview-pollyanna-mcintosh-10-31-2011.

....

Zoe Naylor: *The Reef*

Before *Jaws*, even before films in general, the sea has always been a place of mystery for us landlubbers. It's enormous. It's mysterious. It's a land of the unexplored, the impossible to explore. It's unrelenting. And it has a darkness, in many senses of the world.

Hollywood has never failed to capitalize on our fear of the waves. Ever since a Creature with gills and a hankering for the ladies emerged from the Black Lagoon back in the 1950s, viewers have been more and more scared of the ocean.

Sharks average just a few kills a year around the world—but attacking silently, coming from nowhere, usually at nighttime, tearing a victim apart with unimaginable strength in seconds.

Because of *Jaws*, at least in large part, the great white species is the unofficial symbol of ocean prowling. In movies, humans are strangers in strange waters, and the sharks, whatever their real-life reputation may be, are licking their monstrous chops, just looking for their next meal.

In July 1983, three people were nearly lost off the coast of Australia's Townsville when their boat capsized in tiger shark–infested waters. After over a day and a half in the water, one was found on a reef. His friends had been taken long before by a water resident. By 2010, after American audiences had contracted aquaphobia from four *Jaws* films, *Deep Blue Sea*, and others, the story of the Australian shark attacks was brought to the screens—and it was called *The Reef*.

Acting has never been the only thing on Zoe Naylor's plate; she's in high demand as a motivational speaker and journalist across the Australian continent. But she snared a big

Kate (Zoe Naylor) looks desperately for a way through the strange land of the sea in *The Reef*.

role on the award-winning TV drama *McLeod's Daughters* and become the host of *Gladiators* (a near-exact replica of America's *American Gladiators*) in 2008.

The Reef wouldn't be her first film role, but it would be one of her biggest. Not only that, but it provided a different type of challenge: the chance to keep an audience entertained for over an hour, with just three other people and endless waters for company.

The sea, says Naylor, "is a huge, massive area, and something that we still know so little about. We really don't have a full understanding about this enormous body of water that surrounds us all. I think everyone, in the back of their mind, has to have some fear engrained in them from movies like *Jaws*. When you put that together with a script like [*The Reef*], it makes a great thriller."

Naylor played Kate, on an impromptu sailing trip with her ex-boyfriend, brother, and future sister-in-law. But off the coast of Indonesia, their boat meets a reef at high speed and gets the worst of the deal, literally, capsizing and slowly going down, miles from their last location.

"For me, when it comes to taking a role, the first thing I look at is the script, whether it moves me, excites me, scares me," Naylor says. "The next thing for me is the character and story. As a woman, it's rare that you get a role with such range, and that was a scary and exciting challenge to me as an actor."

As the foursome make their way towards the island, the area's true landlord shows up, and it's ready to dish out some final eviction notices. It's a great white, and they can only pray that he doesn't follow the pattern set by his predecessor from *Jaws*.

Always comfortable in the water, Naylor added a few more freestyling laps to her workout, then hit the local yoga circuit (part of Kate's backstory is her love for the outdoors). "I did a lot of extra research," Naylor says. "I watched all sorts of thrillers, some genre films to really work out what performances I resonated with and what I didn't want to do. I didn't want it to be unbelievable in any way. Making sure that it was really truthful was important to me."

And she learned from those who'd been there—or similar spots—before. "I read a lot of survival stories," she recalls. "Obviously, you pull as much as you can from personal experiences and observations, but this was one of those abnormal, freakish happenings. That was another really interesting thing that I found: reading extreme survival stories, I was able to gauge people's reactions and what people did to survive. This informed the choices I made for the character."

Still, she did have one *small* thing from her past to look back on: On New Year's Day a few years ago, Naylor was out surfing with a friend. "Something felt a little bit wrong," she recalls. "Then I saw a fin about a hundred meters away. I was out of the water like *that*. I have never swam and paddled so hard *in my life!* I never found out if it was a dolphin or a shark, but I didn't wait to find out."

In the waters off Fraser Island and Bowen and Hervey Bay in the Queensland neck of Australian waters, she sent the same feelings through Kate. "This was the toughest shoots I've ever done," Naylor admits, "spending ten hours a day, six days a week in the water. Nothing could prepare you for that."

Australia has had its share of shark attacks; a great white had been caught in Hervey not long before filming. Sometimes the skies would cloud over. Sometimes the water would darken. Sometimes Naylor and the rest of the cast and crew wondered and worried if they'd have some unwelcome company.

The shark scenes were filmed apart from the actors, up and down the Australian coast and all the way to the Great Barrier Reef. A scene where a shark bit the camera was left in the final print.

"Everyone worked so hard on this movie, so to see it with all the CGI, I felt so proud of the crew," Naylor says. "They took this film to another level. That's what I love most about filmmaking: It's not just one person, there's a whole team of people, all doing their jobs to the best of their abilities, coming together to tell a story, and that becomes the final thing."

Unlike the true story, three people are killed in the journey from shipwreck to island, and Kate is the final survivor.

"At times we were dropped out in the middle of the ocean and left there to swim," she says. "As soon as they yelled 'cut' I can't tell you how quickly I wanted to get out of that water! My mind was playing tricks on me regularly."

Naylor, Zoe. Phone/E-mail interview. August 26, 2011.

•••••••••••••••••••••••••••••••

Lyla Hay Owen: *Interview with the Vampire*

"Here's the downside to this role," the ad could have read. "The film's over two hours long, and you only get to be in a few minutes. You'll have to put on some very uncomfortable costumes, and hang out with two irritating poodles for the most of it…. But hey, you do get to make out with Brad Pitt!"

"At the time I interviewed for *Interview with the Vampire*," recalls Lyla Hay Owen, "all my girlfriend actors on the West Coast, everyone in New York, everybody I know had been interviewed for the role."

In the end, though, the producers happened to pick someone already living in New Orleans, where the first part of the film takes place. At a party for the Big Easy's elite at the Destrehan Plantation, Pitt's Louis tries to adjust to the requirements of vampirehood (i.e., one must murder to survive). He's new to the lifestyle, and something draws him toward the Widow St. Claire. There's a tint to her voice that grabs a young man's attention and a gleam in her eye that lets him know that she's got something planned for later.

In her first tryout, Owen remembers, "I started reading the role with a French accent. They said, 'No, no, no, if you're doing that, then everyone will have to learn a French accent. Just do it straight.'" She agreed, and got a second callback. The next time, she was in front of director Neil Jordan, one of the main reasons that she'd tried out for the role.

"In the middle of the audition," Owen says, "he said, 'Lyla, don't you think she'd have a French accent?' Without missing a beat, I said *absolument* ("absolutely" in French), and then I went on with it."

After landing the role, she and the crew got to work creating the character. "A wonderful British woman did the costuming, and another did the period makeup," she says. "I had some input into the character. I don't look like the Widow St. Claire, not one bit." She remembered her days of attending the Mardi Gras in her youth (her grandmother had made her a piece similar to the Widow's as a young girl).

The young widow appeared to be well-off in the dollar sense, but she'd never appeared to have experienced the fruits of motherhood, and may have felt like she'd missed out. "I improvised the scene where she bends down and kisses her dogs," Owen says of St. Claire's poodle pals. "The dogs were her children. They ate from her plate, from her hands. Anyone would react if something violent happened to their pet, but these were her children."

As she and Louis slip away from the crowds (Tom Cruise's evil Lestat is nearby, pursuing his own human prey), the Widow starts to show her animalistic side.

"I could tell that she was decadent and very sensual," Owen says. "That was what I concentrated on, that she was very self-indulgent and sensual. Whatever she wanted, she went for. In the kissing scene with Brad Pitt, Neil Jordan said, 'Lyla, I want you to be a little more aggressive with Brad!' I told Brad, and he said, 'Well, okay.'"

Her charms seem to work; Louis knows that a vampire can only survive at the cost of other lives, but he can't bring himself to do away with a lady he only just met. His solution doesn't make things much better; the dogs become his dinner, and she loses control, resulting in a quick kill by Lestat. "I kept saying, 'Why didn't you turn me into a vampire?'" Owen recalls. "I could have gone to Paris and met Antonio Banderas!"

While her own screen work has always been sporadic (twelve roles since 1973), Owen's taken home a multitude of awards for her stage shows. Now she's just as concerned with helping others follow the same path she embarked upon as a youngster. She's a common sight on the theater teaching circuit, mainly instructing up-and-coming grade-school–age performers.

"We get to have this energy," she says, "and if it's not addressed, they won't know what to do with it, and it can lead to difficulties, socially. I've found that when they have this area of themselves being fulfilled and utilized, they do better in every aspect of their lives."

And yes, she still uses her *Vampire* appearance to inspire her students—and maybe even to gloat a little. "I tell them, 'I had a kissing scene with Brad Pitt, and I got paid for it too!'" Owen says. "The actresses start screaming!"

Owen, Lyla Hay. Phone interview. January 9, 2011.

Katie Parker: *Absentia*

The woman's husband had been missing for seven long years. No one knew what would happen next, if anything at all. No news, in this case, was the worst news of all.

But suddenly, one thing after another started to happen. Her sister, intending to come home for comfort, allowed her past inner battles against drug addiction and religious identity issues to flare back up again. People throughout the neighborhood started to vanish—people the family knew and cared for.

Visions of her husband ran rampant through her mind. Was he back? And even if so, was he the same man who'd won her heart before, or were demons similar to her sister's now ruling him as well? Was it her imagination finally giving in to the tension? Was it all a series of dark coincidences? Was fate torturing her, making her pay for sins she'd never realized she'd committed?

Off the screen, however, the pressure was just as present, only in a different form. The cast and crew didn't have much time to get this done, and there were people waiting for them on the other side. People who expected some serious bang for the bucks they'd donated. People who'd given up some cash despite the unstable economy, and damn sure deserved something to show for it.

Rehearsal, reshoots, time for cuts, editing ... not in *this* world. It was get it right the first time or risk losing it all.

"It started out as a little movie that Courtney [Bell] and Mike Flanagan and I were making," Katie Parker recalls. "We were just going to fool around with the camera and make some reels, which are footage of yourself acting in scenes to submit to casting directors and agents." The recipient of a theater degree from Christopher Newport University in southeastern Virginia, Parker had peppered her acting résumé with small roles in theater, indie films, and television (a small role on *Young and the Restless* had been her most-seen work thus far), and her tiny group wanted to show the highers-up in the film world that they had some serious initiative.

Flanagan expanded their impromptu production into a screenplay. The group turned to the Internet for funding. In less than a month, over twice the film's original $15,000 budget had been collected.

Now came the hard part. Investors wanted to see some results—fast. With little experience either in front of or behind the camera, Parker and her friends, all of whom were waiting tables at the time, tossed out any semblance of stability in the lives of both themselves and their characters.

"After Mike wrote the script, we were in production like the next day," she recalls. "We shot almost everything in Mike and Courtney's apartment. There was no rehearsal time.

Forces from within and without tortured *Absentia*'s main woman Callie (Katie Parker).

If we knew we were shooting a scene next while other actors were filming, we would go into a bathroom or even the closet and run the lines."

She also found the blueprint to Callie, the visiting sister and recovering drug addict who inadvertently unlocks the dark key to the mystery surrounding her sister Tricia (Bell) and her family. "Mike and I came about with the Christianity and the drug problem," she says (Tricia utilizes a great deal of prayer and meditation to help her inner turmoil, which Callie's uncomfortable with). "I'm an atheist and I've never done drugs. But I have a lot of family members who suffer from addiction, so I understand that subject matter from an outsider's perspective, so it was interesting to dig into that place inside of me. I called some of my family members who had substance abuse problems and tried to make every word in the script come from a place that existed inside of me. This was a character that's got an internal struggle going on."

"A lot of it was shot in one take," she says. "Almost every take. All of the scenes were physical in the sense that there was no preparation. It's a really amazing feeling when you can look into your scene partner's eyes and trust them and know that the lines are going to be there, and that you're going to respond and listen honestly."

The short appearance of Doug Jones of *Hellboy* fame, there for a quick cameo as a crazy homeless guy who begs Callie for help in an ominous tunnel, momentarily gave the *Absentia* crew even more hurdles to cross. "This was friends getting together and seeing if we could do it," Parker explains. "The only real professional days we had were when Doug Jones was on set. We had a Screen Actors Guild actor, the guy from *Pan's Labyrinth* in our movie." As an SAG member, Jones could work "only" a 12-hour maximum day, a luxury that the rest of the not-yet-professional crew could only dream of.

As Tricia finally starts to get on with her life, including her love life, her husband comes back. Or does he? It might just be all in Callie's ravaged imagination. Dark forces start to take over the house and the tunnel—literally, as Callie and Tricia constantly find themselves enveloped in suddenly lightless environments, uncertain whether they'll emerge.

They try desperately to escape, but this is a new villain. One that can't be seen, understood, or fought. Will they manage to break away, or…?

"The scene that both of us hate the most is when we fight and she slaps me, when she finds my box with my drugs," Parker says. "We shot that in one take, at about 4:30 in the morning. We were both wrecked. Most of it's a blur because it was so fast."

The gang finally reached the finish line, but things didn't slow down for *Absentia*. Once the horror fans got wind of the show, accolades started to pour in, as the flick popped up at film festivals across the world, taking home the top prize or finishing near it at several.

"It snowballed," Parker says. "We had no idea how much it would explode in terms of the horror circuit."

Parker, Katie. Phone/E-mail interview. May 2, 3, 2012.

Elizabeth Pena: *Jacob's Ladder*

His practices hadn't worked so well back with Job, but the devil had another chance to reach out and grab another soul to drag straight down. Temptation isn't known as one of the seven deadly sins, although it's led many to commit just about all of them. Satan was at war with his heavenly enemy over the eternal prize of souls, but to make himself his own representative would drive anyone away, and upwards. Devils, demons, the monsters associated with Satan's hometown wouldn't make it a welcoming place.

The King of Hell needed someone to go out and do his dirty work. A scared, lonely man with no direction home was the perfect choice.

His target was Jacob Singer (Tim Robbins), his mind so addled with the hardship of losing his son in an accident (Macaulay Culkin, before he was tormenting burglars), and memories of traipsing through the dark jungles of Vietnam—it wasn't PTSD, as viewers will know—that his marriage had fallen apart. He was trapped in a directionless job. Little's left in Jacob's life but hope, and it's the one that his gorgeous postal office colleague Jezzie might just give him a little piece of her heart.

"To me, it was an interesting character because she was filled with secrets," says Elizabeth Pena of her horror debut in *Jacob's Ladder*. "I just liked that she had a whole bunch of information that [Jacob] didn't have. For me, as an actress, keeping a secret, even from the audience, makes it really interesting.

"When I found out I had the role," she says, "I picked up every single book about the afterlife, and demons, about dying, the process of dying. I read too much. By the time I got to set, I was overwhelmed with education. I overdid it."

On the first day of filming, director Adrian Lyne brought a box into Pena's dressing room and told her he was collecting all of her "homework." He took all her books, all her notes, everything she'd written, and put it in the box, saying she would get it back when filming was over. According to Pena, "He said, 'You have all the information. Just be.'" Both she and the director had Francis Bacon paintings in their dressing rooms, using their illusory imagery for inspiration, particularly during the film's infamous "face-shaking" scenes.

Early in filming, Pena flew to Toronto to have a body cast made of herself for a scene in the movie. "It was a really weird feeling," she recalls. "I had to bend way back for about an hour. I'm very claustrophobic, and they had to seal my head and face off."

As Jacob tries to readjust to life in the mail service, his life and mind start to slip out of control. People's faces begin to disappear. It's impossible to tell whether he's dreaming or awake.

Along the way, he becomes involved, perhaps even infatuated, with his fellow mailperson, whose name, like Singer's own, has a bit of Bookish significance (in the religious sense, the Ladder is a creation of Jacob's mind as he dreams of a way to reach Heaven). "I'm a great believer that we are not just of this flesh, that it's all part of a nice ride," explains Pena, whose naturally sultry voice aided her in creating Jezzie's dark temptress. "We keep going on. To me, that was what my character was about: letting go of the flesh. [Jacob] is technically dead in the first five minutes of the movie, and his struggle of letting go, I just found very fascinating."

Eventually, the two hang out at a party. It's the film's strongest scene. Surrounded by hundreds of friends and soon-to-be-acquaintances, Jacob tries to relax as some rough music plays. Then we see Jezzie, and she's *feeling* it. A look of near-ecstasy on her face, she's rocking back and forth to the beat, stealing the show, the spotlight, and Jacob's full attention. "I was pretending I had taken an acid trip," Pena recalls. "I think that people on acid are in their body, but not, and things around them are altered. I spent the entire scene, between takes, twirling myself in circles to feel disoriented. I didn't eat all day, to give myself a hallucinogenic feeling."

Just before the scene began shooting, Pena headed to the back of the large warehouse where the "party" would be held. Stepping into a large room, she found herself staring into her own face. She turned, and there she was again. Everywhere she looked, she saw herself. Had she stumbled into a mirror maze? Had her exhaustive mind-control practices worked a bit too well? No, the actress had encountered all the artificial copies of herself.

"It was like the *Twilight Zone,* because I saw five me's," she laughs. "I literally freaked out, it was so weird."

As an intimidated Jacob watches Jezzie let it all go on the dance floor, he sees something unthinkable. With strobe lights flashing like a visual machine-gun and music blasting everywhere, Jezzie's surrounded by dozens of people, but she's all alone in her mind. Then a lizard tail appears to slip down behind her, and Jezzie seems too into things to notice. Did someone drop something? Is she playing a joke?

No—it's far worse than that. Perhaps she's being possessed by the devil, and it just may be a welcome event.

A pair of reptilian legs launch behind her, and Jezzie tips her head back, looking as though she's about to be overcome. Something starts to edge its way out of her mouth. For a moment, the audience sees a close-up of Jacob, horrified. Then we're back to Jezzie—and a huge horn emerges from her mouth.

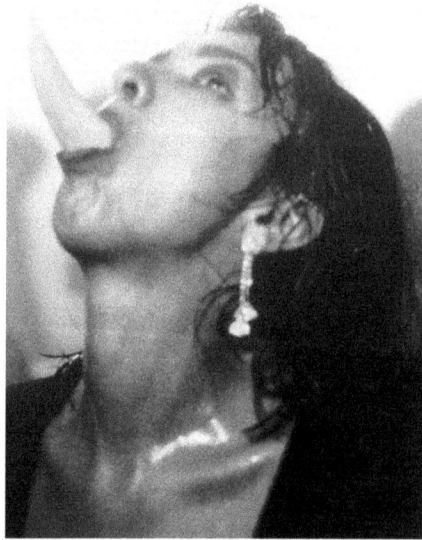

Jacob's gal Jezebel (Elizabeth Pena) finds herself overtaken by the dark forces in *Jacob's Ladder.*

Jacob loses it. He starts to scream and falls backward, and others rush to his aid. Soon, it's obvious that no one else noticed Jezzie—if she was ever there at all.

"When the whole horn came out, it was a dummy's head," says Pena. "Two people did the animatronic tail, and the 'legs' were the arms of a bodybuilder hanging upside down. It took a long time in an uncomfortable situation. I went home that night and didn't get up for ten hours."

As Jacob's mind slips farther out of control, he's committed to professional care. Surrounded by a group of demonic medicators, he notices a familiar face. That's where we find out what's really going on, and why Jezzie's beauty wasn't the only reason she was too good to be real. As Jacob and Jezzie meet in a dark house, she reveals herself to be someone else's tool, as Jacob sees his face become hers. He wouldn't have followed himself to Hell, but he certainly would have let her lead him there.

"Jezzie is really a collage of many women, any woman he's ever been with in his life," Pena says. "She's a little bit of a child, a little violent, very much a woman, she's the enemy, she's the friend, she's the perfect lover, she's the antithesis of every lover in the world. She's his wife, she's his child, she's a little complicated."

The movie concludes with Jacob walking up a bright stairway with his dead son, showing that they're going a bit past the second floor. The original, however, had Jezzie appearing as a demonic angel, ready to take Singer to his new home.

"I think the deliciousness of being an actor is to access what we all have," Pena says. "We can all be the serial killer, the whore, the angel, the mother, the child, the best friend, the backstabber. We all have that in us. We may not access it in real life, but we have it in us. I think most actors really relish the chance to say, 'Oh, man, I'm going to get to access this part of me!'"

On October 14, 2014, just weeks before this book went to press, Elizabeth Pena suddenly passed away. We send her friends and family our deepest condolensces and thanks for her help.

Lyne, Adrien, Dir. *Jacob's Ladder* [DVD]. U.S.: Carolco Pictures.
Pena, Elizabeth. Phone interview. Dec. 3, 2009.

Nick Principe: *Chromeskull* Films

Making his way towards Hollywood, Nick Principe had horror on his mind. But not just the field itself; Principe was into specific folks. Kane Hodder, a participant in some seriously scary stuff for the past few decades, was the role model for Principe. It was a sure bet that another *Friday the 13th* and/or *Halloween* would come down the pike sooner or later, and Principe just knew that he'd get the call to play the man behind the mask.

Eventually, Principe soon realized he'd need to make his own mark on Hollywood horror—and just as Hodder had with Jason Voorhees, and so many others had with Michael Myers, he kept looking for a break, and found it in the stunting neck of the woods.

"Basically, I did some research," he remembers, "and thought to myself, 'How do these guys get cast to play the monster roles? Do they take any big guy? What's the deal here?' So I looked into it and it seems they usually hire stunt guys, because most productions don't want to pay an actor to do the acting and then a stuntman to do the stunts, so they just hire a stuntman to do both. So I figured, if I want to play a monster, I guess I have to be a stuntman!"

Not that this would be totally unexplored territory for him; Principe has a black belt in kenpo and still does mixed martial arts to stay in shape. "If you've never punched someone in the face, then had no fear of prison time afterwards," he quips, "I *highly* recommend it."

But the door to stunt work wasn't wide open either, and a few months after arrival in Hollywood, Principe was biding his time working at a music store, undoubtedly around others dreaming of being Hollywood's next big star.

On a lunch break one afternoon, he noticed large vehicles across the street.

"Everybody always told me that if you see a bunch of trailers and trucks, that means they're shooting a TV show or a commercial or something like that," Principe recalls. "I just walked over there and ignorantly and blindly, I looked for the first person with a clipboard and a headset."

Spying one, he strolled up to the fellow and, in an impromptu audition, coolly asked if he might be of some assistance. "This guy replied, 'What are you, a PA?' [production assistant]," Principe says. "I didn't even know what a PA was, but I said, 'Yes I am.'" The fellow told him to go fill out a tax form and get to work.

With Principe's career in the retail field at an end, stunt work and small acting jobs started rolling in, including a small role alongside longtime horror queen Danielle Harris in *Hatchet II*.

"My love for horror and sci-fi is simple," he says. "Fantasy. Sure, there have been much worse childhoods than mine, but it's always been the sense of make believe, the unknown, the escape. No other films have ever been able to make me forget whatever it is that is bothering me for 86 minutes than genre films, to literally be taken to another world, to be scared

It's tough to believe that what's under Chromeskull's mask is scarier than what's on it as Nick Principe brought him to mass murder.

of something pretend." Little could he have known that his main jump into horror would be of the realistic kind, considered by many to be the scariest of all—after all, these things could actually happen.

Soon came 2008's *Killer Pad,* and Principe jumped at it. Not because everyone thought it would cause a stampede to the ticket booths, but because of the man in the director's chair. Robert Englund (the movies' Freddy Krueger) had been terrifying us in front of the camera for decades; for this flick, he was behind it. That's where Principe had a meeting that would change his horror career, running into a fellow in makeup named Rob Hall. "I said to him how much I loved doing creature work, but I'm dying to be a slasher, as that is my favorite sub-genre of horror."

About a year later, Hall had scraped together enough folding green to tell his own screen story. With Principe's near seven-foot height, Hall figured he'd be perfect as the genre's newest fear figure in *Laid to Rest.* And like the many merry men who were Michael, Jason, and so many others, Principe would have to do his scaring without voice or face work. There would be no background (at first), no personality, and a name that rose from the fellow's getup: Chromeskull.

Sort of like a much more evil version of G.I. Joe's enemy Destro, Chromeskull would have a built-in headguard, an ominous silver skull covering his chromed dome.

Principe incorporated some of Michael Myers' soundless prowling. He grabbed a bit of methodically violent replicant Roy Batty from *Blade Runner.* Even *American Psycho* title character Patrick Bateman made a mental appearance for Principe.

But Principe knew that slashers of one form or another had been rolling through Hollywood for decades. In order to keep Chromeskull from getting lost in the sauce, he'd have to reach into the darkness of his own persona.

"For about three weeks before, all I did was work out, read serial killer profiles by FBI agents, and blast hardcore and grind music. Music is the key for me. Plus, all I watched was slasher films, like *Just Before Dawn* or *The Prowler* or *The New York Ripper,* and *Maniac* and *Relentless.*" Intending to make the character something of a psychotic psychiatrist (and we thought Hannibal Lecter had the market cornered in *that* department!), he decided on a dark turtleneck; Chromeskull wanted to look dapper, even as he made the blood spatter. Principe came up with Chromeskull's stiletto skills, adding extra blades to a Bowie knife and spiking some brass knucks to show the man's true devotion to his work.

Eventually, even before anyone else got a chance to meet Chromeskull, Principe felt himself taking a backseat, or at least a passenger one, to his character. His girlfriend, he remembers, "actually even said to me 'I'm scared to be around you,' which really hurt at the time, but fuck, it just means I did my best ... I started hating women, which is insane because I was practically raised by my mom and grandmother. I started hating myself. It was fucked."

The movie starts out normally enough: A lovely young woman finds herself in a strange place; her mind, addled with amnesia, sees the Skull man brutally slaughter another person and she runs off, with him in hot pursuit.

The killings continue, as Chromeskull cuts off one man's face, and slices open a lady's stomach. Eventually, the girl and a fellow make their way to another man's house, where a web search tells them that they're the next prey in a spree that has already taken dozens of lives—with all of them on film.

As big a boon as technology has been to researchers and schoolchildren across America, it can also bring out the worst in us. It's given criminals new ways to rob and harm us, and made it all but impossible to for us to prevent children's eyes from seeing things that would make even an adult's stomach turn.

America's fascination with the dark and macabre has always been present, but electronics have pushed it closer to the surface, making it easier to access than in print, or even in televised sort. People like Chromeskull really do exist, and there are many out there that see them as people worth following.

"Chromeskull is not supernatural," Principe says. "He doesn't lumber about, he's not out of his mind, he knows exactly what he's doing, and he's very clean cut ... I see him as vain as possible; he's the worst kind of monster because he's human. Some people don't like that, but it's why I love him."

He keeps lopping off heads. He blasts a kid's cerebellum in half with a shotgun. He plants a knife in another guy's heart. He fills a fellow's head with sealant until it explodes.

"Add the fact we shot for 28 nights in Maryland," says Principe (filming was done in an abandoned mental hospital). "Working nights with that mindset just simply fucked with my head. I won't say what actor, but at one point during a lighting change I bent closer and whispered in her ear, 'I wish I could do this for real to you.' She won't speak to me to this day."

A gun and knife couldn't stop Chromeskull, but he'd eventually be done in by his own hand. Feeling himself incomplete when his mask is knocked off in a brawl, he uses glue to paste it back on. But it's actually acid, and his face melts off. One baseball bat to the Skull later, the girl appears to have reached her happily-ever-after ending.

Certainly one "death" wouldn't be nearly enough to put Chromeskull out for the final count. "One thing we agreed on was that we did not want to go supernatural with Chromeskull for a sequel," Principe says. "I love the fact that he's still a human monster. That makes him way scarier to me. A lot of people don't like this actually, that we're breaking a 'slasher' code because he's not disheveled, he's not dirty, he's not lumbering, he's not mentally disabled. Instead, he's very calculated and clean. That's exactly why I like him! He's not like any of the other 'slashers' other than the fact that he's silent."

In *Chromeskull: Laid to Rest II*, some dedicated law enforcement and medical personnel toss their personal feelings to the wind, demonstrating the Hippocratic Oath and all the professionalism it requires, putting the Skull right back together.

"The biggest thing for us was, how are we going to bring him back from this?" Principe says. "So I did a lot of research on the Internet, and I found this story about a guy in Russia who was hunting bears and a bear pretty much took off his face from above his lower jaw to his forehead, and they were able to reconstruct a fake face for him to snap on. So right there, we thought, okay, there's actual medical proof that if this did happen, someone could survive it as long as there was no brain damage and they were able to immediately get the help they needed."

With music in his ears again, Principe got ready to add even more emotion to a character that soullessly took one life after another in the opener. And right away in part two, there's some insight into Chromeskull's mind and soul. We'll never see his face, and after what he went through, that's a good thing. But as he stares into an unseen mirror, the emotions come out as almost never before, as it suddenly becomes his next shattered victim. Here's where we really find out why that mask was so important. Not because he was a big Halloween fan (the holiday, not the series).

"I just figured this guy only wore a mask because he's so fucking vain," Principe says, "and now he has no face, so he is just pure rage. I always said that Chromie was Rob's son and my stepchild."

As his backstory keeps getting written, Chromeskull finds someone to take it all out upon. Like we eventually learned about *Saw*'s Jigsaw, Chromeskull has minions—willing servants to do his bidding. And just as with Jigsaw, one of them's a cop who can't wait to follow in his master's footsteps, practicing by quickly taking out the one who got away in the first flick. Just as in *Saw,* another assistant is a gorgeous young woman—it's Harris; after playing defense for most of her horror career, she was now helping do the scaring. As Chromeskull continues to speak only in texts, the group sets its collective sights on another young woman—of course, many more will violently get sliced and diced along the way!

"It kind of establishes that the guy's a multi-millionaire," Principe says of his creation, "and for me, him having a crew like that to do his cleanup work was a statement saying that if you have money, you can buy anything, including people. You can make people look the other way for a price. If this guy has been doing this for so long and has killed this many people, how does he not get caught? Well, he's probably in bed with political figures, police figures, government. That's how he makes things go away, because he has so much money. That's a really, really scary truth. If you are super rich, you can probably get away with whatever you want in this world and there are no repercussions."

The truth about making it in acting, in just about any genre, he continues, might be a bit less painful, but it can be just as frightening. "The level of delusion in Hollywood is uncanny," Principe says. "I mean, through the roof. So if you have some talent, people will see it. Never give up! It is a refusal of defeat that will be the deciding factor. Then, once you're at the level of auditions and doing the agent shuffle, you need to be able to look yourself in the mirror and say, 'You suck.' You don't, but get used to hearing it. Casting agents and directors and producers can be straight cruel. You need to grow a thick skin and say, 'Well, you don't like me … but the next group will love me! So fuck you!'"

Coe, Terry. "Nick Principe." *The Horror Asylum*. Dec. 1, 2010. Retrieved Aug.14, 2012, from http://www.horror-asylum.com/interview/nick-principe/interview.asp.
Galluzzo, Rob. "FRIGHT INTERVIEW—Nick Principe (Chromeskull of 'LAID TO REST')!" *Icons of Fright*. Oct. 27, 2011. Retrieved Aug. 14, 2012, from http://iconsoffright.com/2011/10/27/fright-interview-nick-principe-chromeskull-of-laid-to-rest/.
Layne, Staci. "Nick Principe in 'ChromeSkull: Laid to Rest 2'—Exclusive Interview." *Horror*. Sept. 9, 2011. Retrieved Aug. 14, 2012, from http://www.horror.com/php/article-3664-1.html.
Principe, Nick. E-mail interview. June 9, 2012.

Lorna Raver: *Drag Me to Hell*

The horror genre can be tough for actors to break away from.

Once a performer's name gets associated with the instillation of fear, the film world—never known for being long-sighted—has a tendency to keep it there, particularly those who do the scaring.

Anthony Perkins became indistinguishable from Norman Bates for as long as he ever acted. No matter how many times we've seen Robert Englund's natural visage, we'll always be subconsciously adding Freddy Krueger's scars to it.

But what about those who act for a while, then get suddenly thrust—fired like a cannon might be more appropriate—into the terrifying spotlight? How about those who spend the first few years of their careers doing what they can, then suddenly finding, or even being forced into, their niche in horror?

Over the past few years, Lorna Raver has found herself on the same path. After a series of small roles on TV and the big screen, Raver got the same shot at scary stardom that so many others have turned into a career.

"When I first auditioned for [*Drag Me to Hell*], I didn't really know the full skinny on the film," she recalls, "because while I knew of [Sam Raimi's] work from other films, I was so ignorant of the whole horror genre that I had never even heard of the *Evil Dead* [films]. I was definitely interested in doing it because of Sam Raimi, but I was not fully aware of exactly what I was getting myself into until it happened."

Raimi, the man who'd brought Spider-Man to the big screen, was taking a foray back into horror. Equipped with more CGI and other special effects weaponry than had been available during his first few zombie flicks, Raimi was looking for someone to star. He had his heroine in place, Allison Lohman, but what of her tormentor? What of the one who shoves Lohman's Christine Brown down the darkest of paths, both physically and mentally?

Well, that would be Sylvia Ganush, the victim of Christine's new cutthroat nature, the sad, broke old lady that Christine dumps on the street to make a few extra dollars for her agency. It would be Raver's next quest. "What I liked about the character was that she was

Sylvia Ganush (Lorna Raver) swears revenge on the evil world that destroyed her in *Drag Me to Hell*.

powerful," Raver says. "It was fun to have the principal villain be a senior citizen, and a woman, which I thought was kind of cool, because seniors are often depicted as either being kind of pathetic or objects of ridicule. [Ganush] was a troubled lady, but she was a woman with some power. She took action." Her powers went far beyond anything Christine could have ever imagined.

"The character is supposed to be Hungarian," Raver says. "When I met with a lady from Hungary, I was almost spot-on without really quite knowing it, because I didn't really have any resource before I did the audition. I could also pick up some phrases to use in the film from her."

Without health, money, or hope, Ganush grovels and begs. But Christine doesn't care. After all, it's part of the job, and in this economy, we do what we must to get and stay ahead. Sometimes people get hurt, but we tend to forget them. But Ganush isn't going down without a fight. There's not much else for her to live for, and revenge can be quite the feel-good action.

The two square off in a car in a brawl rivaling the Ultimate Fighting Championships.

"We spent a week in a parking garage just doing that, and then we revisited the scene on set," Raver says. "It was really interesting and grueling. Allison and I wanted to do as much of our own physical work as we could. Anything that we could, Allison and I did."

Ganush's false teeth fly out, and Christine manages to knock her out of the car. But this lady appears to have been through this sort of thing before: one cinder block through the window later, the battle is back on. Even when Christine pounds a ruler down her throat, "Szajha" is Hungarian for bitch and Ganush fires it off a few times here.

Then she rips a button off Christine's coat and recites the curse that sets the tone for the remainder of the film. If she can't beat the younger girl physically, she'll destroy her from the inside. Placing the button back in the surprised young woman's hand, Ganush leaves. For good? Maybe, maybe not.

"Being from the organic school, it's helpful for me to feel it physically, and not just pretend physically," Raver says. "You're pretending that this is happening so that they can accommodate it and integrate it. It was interesting to see how they put it all together."

The best horror films are about more than just fear and death, and Raimi's flick went far beyond both, allowing for more character development than many such films try for. Again, Ganush is undoubtedly Christine's antagonist, but that doesn't make her a villain. Her methods are the epitome of unorthodox, but it's hard to say they're unjustified. Lohman, on the other hand, made Christine a bit black and white in the first part of the film, but brought out her emotions (i.e., remorse) in the second part, although never to the extent that we really feel as much sympathy for her as we do for Ganush. Not even when Ganush appears in Christine's bed, and vomits a load of bugs into Christine's open mouth. (Actual bugs were used, and Lohman admits she got an impromptu snack during filming.) And especially not when a repentant Christine shows up at Ganush's relative's house, only to find it in the midst of Ganush's funeral. Or when her body somehow manages to attack Christine, pinning her to the floor as unsympathetic relatives hand out the deserved mocking.

"I had a lifecast done for them to build the makeup and the dummies of me," Raver says. "That was actually the scariest part of the whole movie, because I'm a little claustrophobic. So having that cast on, I was not looking forward to it, but the special effects guys were very sweet to me. They made it an easy process."

But even with Ganush dead, the evil force keeps coming. With her job, even her life, starting to slip away, Christine turns to one fortune teller after another. Now nearly in He-Woman mode (new for Lohman), she goes to Ganush's grave to become the ultimate re-gifter, handing back the button for a curse refund. And everyone lives happily ever after. Or maybe not. Maybe Ganush's curse, like so much else in horror, can't even be stopped by death....

Of all the good things that can come to a performer who appears in a horror flick, perhaps the best is the appreciation. Perhaps more than any other genre fans, horror fans join together to show their thanks for those that kept them up at night. Conventions, award shows, books and magazines—frightening films and their fans put more of these together than just about any other movie connoisseurs.

Raver's been experiencing it since her first *Drag*. In 2009, her flick took the top honor at Spike TV's Scream Awards, a mini–Oscars for the genre. (She lost the Best Villain honor to Alexander Skarsgård of *True Blood*.)

"I didn't go into it thinking, 'Oh, I'll get to scare everybody!'" she says. "I was kind of surprised at how the horror fans loved this character, and I think it's wonderful. But basically, I was playing the woman. Here's a woman who's got problems, and she makes decisions about how she's going to address them. It may be a little unconventional, but I didn't think of it as trying to scare people; it just kind of evolved as we went along ... I think it's funny that now that I'm an old lady, I'm known as a horror star. I think it's a hoot."

Raimi, Sam, Dir. *Drag Me to Hell*. [DVD]. U.S.: Universal Studios, 2009.
Raver, Lorna. Phone interview. Dec. 16, 2011.

Silje Reinåmo: *Thale*

Getting ready for this role was going to be a piece of the tastiest cake ever put together. Just one thing to do, hardly a trifle. The definition of simplicity.
Silje Reinåmo would just have to step into a different world.

Nothing to it, right? Just become someone, something, that had evolved in a land far from Reinåmo's home in the small northern Norwegian nook of Mosjøen, far from her place on *Earth*. A land where everyone communicated without speaking, and attire was awkward as hell.

Early in her career, Reinåmo took on the title mark in *Thale*, the story of two men who stumble onto a lady whose looks are out of this world. Few guys would mind that, but this is a literal thing.

Thale's a huldra, haunting the forests of Norway, helping wandering hunters or fishermen, occasionally seducing them. Huldras were not known to be malicious, but sometimes tricked men into a random sexual encounter and showed up with a child out of nowhere, usually to blackmail them into marriage.

Of course, that was done back in the huldras' hometown. Thale's trapped in the foreign world in which we live, and she's as lost as we would be in hers.

If these beings were to show up here in everyday reality, some might not mind—just

Silje Reinåmo brought to life Norway's mysterious myths of the huldra in *Thale* (2012).

as, chances are many of us would be okay taking a swim with a gorgeous mermaid. Others, as E.T. found out, might get taken away by evil authorities, studied and perhaps killed in the name of safety or science.

Reinåmo's stage debut was as a dancer as a teen. "I had great movement understanding and musicality," she recalls, "but I always knew that I wasn´t good enough to become a professional dancer. On the other hand, I always stood out when it came to my communication skills and the way I expressed myself on the stage."

So not being able to speak in *Thale* would be the least of her concerns; forming a backstory and trying to develop a character that existed only in song and legend would be another matter entirely. Without much rehearsal time, Reinåmo pored over story after mythological story of Norwegian lore. She learned about the personality of a huldra, and what it would be like to stroll around silent, nude, and with a huge tail, like that a cow or horse waves around.

But there was one source from which she couldn't derive much: the film's screenplay.

"[Thale] has no text in the script, meaning there is not a lot to build on except from what all the other characters say about her, obviously." Reinåmo says, "But here is the crucial thing. Since she can't speak, she listens intensely all the time. In many ways she has the qualities of an animal. So the listening, the body language, the *being present* became even more important for me.... Everything had to be intuitive with this character."

The creature doesn't show up for a while in her own flick, as we first meet a pair of criminals. One, barely into his thirties, has lung cancer, and the other finds himself estranged from his daughter. In a hidden basement they find all the trimmings of a mad scientist's lab: weird-looking jars, unlabeled tubes, and a small bathtub filled with something looking like old milk.

And something else: Thale rises out of it, sustained through air tubes and with no clue how to go on. The person who placed her there is gone, and these humans are the only ones around now. She can't speak to them or them to her; with no human language to toss back and forth, there's no way to find out what anyone's thinking or wants.

"I see even more now how important listening to the other actors is," Reinåmo says. "I believe it´s all about the reacting and not necessarily the acting for an actor. I think when you truly pay attention to your co-actors, the interesting reactions and scenes appears. Perhaps we tend to forget that when we always think about our next line. Everyone asks me if it was difficult to play a role with no text. I would say it is just different. But right now I am thinking that perhaps it is more difficult with all this text for actors, especially on film where this subtle reactions means everything."

Through flashback scenes, we see her enjoyable relationship with her keeper. But with some tapes he left behind, it turns into an illusion, as it looks like he was just keeping her around to grow up enough to be stolen and held until death. It makes Thale's early attack on one of her finders understandable; the only other human she ever knew was using her the whole time.

Eventually she calms down, but the tapes also reveal that some people are coming to get her, to take her away, to study her at the expense of her physical safety.

"When it comes to the role," Reinåmo explains, "everything about Thale was or became appealing to me as the process went on. She is the heroine, she is vulnerable, you feel for her.... At the same time she can be scary as hell and she has got extreme power. She has so many layers and it is exciting for an actress."

And yes, she's naked. But she couldn't feel discomfort, or at least not show it—because this was about being and staying in character. And Thale would have no idea about the human definition of modesty, and the role fashion plays here.

"The nude scenes were definitively a challenge," she says. "You feel very naked and self-aware, and Thale shouldn´t be self-aware at all. In the final result you see just bits, but on set we see everything. And I mean *everything*, which can feel very strange and make you feel extremely vulnerable."

Her character felt the same way, especially when the hunters arrive. The men hide her, but get taken themselves. But with one terminally ill and the other far from his family, there's little for them to care about any more. And when a couple more fellows go back to search for Thale herself, they find out exactly what they're up against. Super speed, super strength, near invisibility. Huldras were never known for being angry or malicious, but when their back is against the wall, their non- and superhuman sides flare up, and no one's going to keep them somewhere they don't want to be.

Time and again, Thale makes very short work of them, and rolls off to her homeland (the flick was actually made in Mosjøen). But we see her helpers, themselves having gotten away from the bad guys, and her magic seems to have rubbed off on them; one guy's family is back with him, the other a sudden medical miracle.

"I think the result goes to show that in this digital world you don't really need all that money or fancy equipment to make a great movie," Reinåmo says. "This role has taught me so much. I think if you want to make it in acting, you have to want it so bad that you lie awake just wondering how on earth *you* can make it…. As an actor and if you love acting I think the genre you act in shouldn't really matter that much, at least not in the beginning. Our job is the same in every genre: create a believable and complex character."

Even if that character means stepping outside of your species.

Reinåmo, Silje. E-mail interview. January 10, 2013.

••••••••••••••••••••••••••••••

Julianna Robinson: *Wasting Away* (*Aaaah! Zombies!*)

Ever since *Night of the Living Dead* a few decades ago, our dear departed friends have been coming back to haunt, taunt, and slaughter us.

Still, once in a while, someone has the guts to swim against the horror mainstream. To take the original storyline and toss a few kinks into the equation. Usually, it's worth the effort.

Shaun of the Dead (2004) was one of the first to deviate from the zombie film repetition. The flick didn't so much change the storyline of zombie invasion—just as about all the other times, the dead came back to murderous life, and the humans dealt with it—so much as it just altered the narrative form of the story. *Shaun* added all kinds of comedy. It worked.

A few years later, another group went another different way when it came to resurrective horror. It's easy to see the zombies as the bad guys, the villains, and it's even justified,

Julianna Robinson prepares to tell the zombies' side of the story in *Wasting Away*.

considering they're usually trying to turn humanity into a post-midnight snack. But what if we looked at things from their point of view? Zombies should have a chance to tell us the full story. *Wasting Away* presents the old story from an entirely new perspective.

Wasting Away was the film's title in development. When it went into release, however, the crew decided to switch the title to *Aaaah! Zombies!,* as such a title made the film easy to find, particularly online. The repetition of the letter "A" makes it pop up at the beginning of any search. Since the film came out, it's been seen under both titles. In this profile, we'll stick with *Wasting Away*.

Now let's hear from someone who helped us see the world through the eyes—wild, unfocused, discolored though they usually are—of the creatures themselves.

Coming out of the curtain call of her most recent theatrical jaunt, Julianna Robinson ran into a few fellows looking to put their names in the Ranks of Romero (George, the chap that kicked off the modern zombie genre with *Night of the Living Dead*).

"I thought it was unprecedented," she remembers. "No one had done that before. We wanted to feel like we were pioneers in film." They were going over the same ground as *Dawn* (and *Day* and *Shaun*) *of the Dead*—only this time, the zombies would be the protagonists. Not necessarily the heroes of the piece, but the main characters.

She was up for the female lead, an attractive spot. After darkening her light locks to Vanessa's brunette levels, Robinson thought about what had happened to her before audiences would come to know the heroine.

"I do the same thing for all my characters," she says. "I sit down and do a lot of writing. I create a character's backstory, a character's family, a character's needs, a character's secrets. I take pieces from the script, like point of view. What are other characters' points of view towards me, and what is my point of view towards them? I put all that together and try to create as real a person as I can on paper. Then I try to let some of that stuff go and live in the moment on set with the other actors. If you do a lot of work beforehand and build a life for the story for the character before you go to work, you can forget about that stuff, because it's sunk in and it's a part of you. Then you can be free and live in the moment and have fun."

Hanging out in a bowling alley one night with her friends, Vanessa's enjoying one of her last night of freedom before the prison-esque demands of a law career kick in. When a friend talks up a new ice cream topping, the group can't want to do some serious sampling.

But that topping has some unknown, unwelcome ingredients—specifically, some secret serum from a failed military experiment, leaked into the alley after a recent truck crash. It's poison, and they're all dead instantly.

Except—they're not all the way dead, at least not conventionally so. They can't understand why everyone who sees them runs away screaming. Now we learn what life's like for one who doesn't know she's lost it.

"We were shooting in the middle of the night," Robinson remembers. "We were tired, we were punchy, and a lot of times shooting at night, your inhibitions are down. You just feel more comfortable, less wound up than during the day. None of it felt like a chore." So when one guy suddenly discovered how tasty other people's brains truly are, it didn't seem too unusual. When Vanessa has to kill a few people and then help her ex Mike re-attach a hand that an attacking human sliced off, it's no big deal.

"Once anybody gets [the zombie] get-up on, you really start to get in character," Robinson says. "It's like at Halloween, when everybody becomes an actor. They get dressed up to be these characters from different time periods, and they really embody that. It's everyone's typical actor moment. The first time we had that makeup on, got dressed up, played around with walks, physicality, things that were special to us, and little voices we would make up, we had fun with it.

"As far as being a zombie, that was just the most fun thing to play. Having the opportunity to wear the mask of a zombie, wearing the contact lenses, the makeup, it really helps you feel free in your body and in your expression to take risks that you might not be able to take if you were playing a normal character. We all commented on that being our favorite part, being set free to fly."

As the unknowing zombies start to rack up a body count, a new fellow arrives, secretly in on everything. But even knowing that their superhuman strength and recuperative powers are a result of loss of humanity doesn't make them give up and die. As more and more people start to chow on the affected icy treat, the group's ranks rise, and it's getting to the kill-or-die (again) stage, with Vanessa one of those leading the way.

Vanessa, Robinson theorizes, "felt more in control than the other ones. I think she felt like she was the caretaker for some of the other characters. Even when she was getting chased by the zombies, I think she felt like she had some nurturing, mothering for the other characters. Some of the other characters felt more lost than she did. She had moments of taking control. When the other characters go off into battle, she's responsible for organizing it."

As Mike, lacking a hand and head already, sacrifices himself as a final distraction to those mean humans who want to make zombies extinct, Vanessa and most of the troops escape to their own desert town. Chances are, viewers are already firing up conspiracy theories for a sequel—what is daily life truly like for a zombie?

"It's not just a movie about zombies," says Robinson. "It's about friendship and people sticking together, no matter what. It's a love story."

Robinson, Julianna. Phone interview. March 18, 2013.

•••••••••••••••••••••••••••••

Felissa Rose: *Sleepaway Camp*

Horror film fans are used to the twist ending. We know that there's always going to be something at the end, some secret, some connection, something hidden revealed.

For the first nine-tenths of 1983's *Sleepaway Camp* we watched young introvert Angela slowly climb out of her social shell, and we had a pretty good idea that she was the one knocking off her tormentors throughout. Finding out that she was the killer wouldn't be a surprise ... but the rest of the story, well, that was a tornado.

"I couldn't wait to get to the set and have fun!" recalls Felissa Rose, in middle school when she became the newest scream queen, or at least princess. "I wanted to meet boys and get out of school for two months."

Rose's representative informed her that Robert Hiltzik was putting his own spin on the "kids killed at camp" storyline that had been established a few years before with *Friday the 13th*. "When I met with Robert," she says, "he really just wanted me to do some improv situations with him. I remember he had me sitting on a chair and told me to pretend that

Felissa Rose, so horrifying in two *Sleepaway Camp* films, shows the author her skills.

I was eating a candy bar and just completely stare into space. So I thought that was so hilarious; I mean, I was only 13 years old, but I took that as something really bizarre. And I sat there and pretended to eat a candy bar and I started picking my teeth with my fingers … and for some reason he enjoyed that. And then we did another improv with [producer Jerry Silva] where I think I had to pretend to be on a beach with some guy and I really didn't want to be there. We played out that whole scenario and it was a lot of fun."

She later got a call-back.

"When I walked into the room," Rose says, "there were a bunch of 'snotty' girls there and they were all staring at me. But I felt really confident. In fact when I walked out of the call-back, this overwhelming feeling came over me, and it was like I just knew that I got the part."

She was right, and it was off to camp…

Angela's introversion was easy enough to understand; as the film opens, we see the youngster and her brother Peter hanging out with their dad in a boat. It flips over, and the three head for shore where the father's boyfriend awaits. (The film was much more cavalier about homosexual parenthood than many of the time, and even today.) Suddenly, another boat crashes into them, killing the father and young boy. Angela's sent to live with her "eccentric" (in movie-speak, that's PC for totally friggin' nuts) Aunt Martha and her son Ricky.

Now it's eight years later, and the pair arrive at New York's Camp Aarawak. Almost immediately, Angela's targeted by the bullies we find in so many of these films, led by counselor Meg and camper Judy.

"With being 13 on the set," Rose says, "I didn't get to party a lot. I didn't get to go to all the crazy parties they had in the motel."

In character, things start happening. The head cook, obviously there for the children for all the horrible reasons, suddenly gets bathed by a pot of scalding water. One guy who tormented Angela is drowned under a canoe; another is fatally attacked by bees in a bathroom stall.

"My mom was on the set with me the whole time," Rose says, "so she was very involved in things that I was allowed to do and things that I wasn't allowed to do. They wanted me to do all the killings, they wanted my hands, and my mom right away said that she really didn't want me to do that because she felt like it would kind of disturb me at age 13."

Meanwhile, Ricky's friend Paul chats Angela up with stories of the pair's troublemaking youth, and she finally speaks, if only for, "Good night." But when he tries to get to the level of "affectionate," she can only flash straight back to watching her dad make out with his male companion, and heads off. "I was directed to just sit there with an intense stare," Rose says, "so I did the best I could."

By now, *Camp*'s dark and disturbing to the extreme, even more so than the first *Friday the 13th*. Meg and Judy toss Angela off a pier, and some nearby little brats throw sand at her. Then Meg's forced into a *Psycho* remake, sliced open in the shower, but it's Ricky that falls under suspicion, as he might be doing this to get back at those who bothered Angela.

For Meg's murder, Rose says, "they wound up using Jonathan Tiersten's [Ricky] hands, which worked out perfectly! And I think it also added to the whole film because I have very little thin hands, so if they used my hands, you would probably know that it was my, Angela's, hands rather than suspecting that maybe it could be Ricky or maybe it's not."

Up until now in the film there's been nothing earth-shatteringly new. The camp owner gets an arrow to the throat, much like Kevin Bacon did in *Friday the 13th*. But now it goes where, still today, few are comfortable.

First off, the children who bothered Angela are found hacked to death with an axe. Judy gets jumped in her cabin, punched out and violated to death with a curling iron.

Judy was originally to be played by Jane Krakowski of *Ally McBeal* fame, but she quit after objecting to Judy's gruesome death. Krakowski's replacement, Karen Fields, didn't like the scene either, so it was actually cleaned up a bit—and if being fatally raped with an inanimate object was the *tidier* version, it really makes you wonder what the hell was first going to occur.

Now in a panic, the campers prepare to leave. But there are still two missing…

Suddenly brimming with self-confidence, Angela leads Paul onto a beach, telling him to undress. A few campers approach, and she seems to be cradling him and serenading him to sleep. Then Angela turns around, and so does the film. The twist ending we expected turns into a corkscrew from Hell.

In the flashbacks, we learned that the crazy aunt already had Ricky, so another boy wouldn't work for her. She dressed and raised her new arrival as the daughter she never had. That's right—it was Angela who died in the boat accident. She's a he. The Angela we've been watching is actually Peter.

Covered in blood and screaming like an animal, Angela stands and drops Paul—or at least his head, because that's all that's there. She stands up in full altogether view, her eyes and mouth wide open and threatening like nature's most prolific predator, and the film suddenly ends.

That one was tough on everyone. Plans for Rose to wear a prosthetic member were made and discarded. Then they decided to make a fake Angela face and plant it on a guy—who just happened to have the body of a thirteen-year-old girl!

"It was a long and arduous process," Rose says, "but they found someone at Albany State College. He got paid well and got really drunk before they filmed the scene."

Back home, Rose and her friends headed off to a local showing of the flick. When people died, some probably screamed, while others cheered. But when Angela's secret showed, everyone gasped, including her.

"The movie theater was packed in my hometown," she says, "and I think everyone was pretty shocked. I remember closing my eyes as the last shot appeared. I had never seen a penis!"

Rose attended New York University rather than reprise the role in the film's first two sequels. Pamela Springsteen (sister of the Boss) snared the role, and turned Angela into a conniving vixen of evil. But decades later, *Return to Sleepaway Camp* arrived in video stores across the nation. At another camp, someone was trying to set a record for murderous brutality amongst the campers and counselors.

For audiences that had already been through several *Saw*, *A Nightmare on Elm Street*, and *Friday the 13th* films, gore and horror were all the norm, and the new film didn't disappoint. A young man was castrated by a truck, another eaten by rats. A girl got hanged from a basketball hoop, and a man was skinned alive.

And in the end, it all came back to Rose's Angela, who'd been posing as a sheriff throughout the film. As she again finished things off with a maniacal laugh and a triumphant glare straight into the camera, the *Sleepaway Camp* killings came to an end.

For now.

"You just dive into the character and think about what the psychological ramifications are for that person," Rose explains. "When are you getting chased by a person in a mask? When are you being sliced and diced? Never! So we have to create it!"

Rose, Felissa. Personal interview. April 20, 2012.
Rollans, Scott. "Angela's Slashes." *Fangoria* 262 (April 2007): 66–69.

•••••••••••••••••••••••••••••

The *Saw* Films

Throughout the first decade of the 2000s, arguably the most terrifying "real" killer haunted our dreams and waking moments. With his gravelly, "James Earl Jones in a dark mood" voice and experiments in pain that would have scared Nazi doctors, Jigsaw used the *Saw* films to show us the worst in human pain and suffering, his treatments for victims who pay for not living their lives to the fullest. I use the word "treatment" instead of punishment because his tactics show, by the greatest force, a new lesson in morality. It's about spiritual cleansing, and there's no more effective purification than pain. It's a certainty that the few who escaped Jigsaw had a new appreciation for life, and learned a lesson about being careful what we wish for.

The man whose voice has been edging its way into the ears and psyche of millions of viewers—weren't we all afraid to pick up a cell phone after hearing him ask, "Do you want to play a game?"—took a warp-speed step into horror icon-dom.

Jigsaw (Tobin Bell) gives his protégé Angela (Shawnee Smith) some advice to carry on his work in the *Saw* films.

Off the screen, he's a little league baseball and flag football coach—with a delightful sense of humor.

"They don't!" Tobin Bell jokingly asserts when asked how his young charges feel about their coach being the *Saw* killer. "My son's amused by the fact that his dad is playing this guy. People recognize me, and say, 'Hey, that's Jigsaw!' We have a lot of laughs about it."

Laughing has been about the last thing on viewer's minds as they've watched Jigsaw force people to saw off their own feet, rip hooks out of their skin, and gorily slaughter each other. "I really don't think about terrifying so many people," Bell says of his mindset during filming. (It's so surreal to hear Jigsaw showing his friendly side, especially when transcribing a taped conversation!) "I'm up there trying to make the lines seem like they're happening for the first time.

"People have asked me what it feels like to be a horror icon; I'm not thinking about that. I don't take myself and put myself on the other side of the screen and into the audience when I'm doing what I'm doing. Sometimes people have trouble separating what they see on the screen with reality, but I never project myself into the results. I try to do the best that I can at the time, in the scene, in those moments. Watching the film and seeing how people react to it is always fun, but I frankly don't spend a lot of time looking at myself on the screen."

The first *Saw* flick debuted in 2004, with Leigh Whannell acting out his own screenplay as Adam, the ignorant voyeur who suddenly finds himself trapped inside a bathtub, then chained to a wall. Across the room, he notices Dr. Lawrence Gordon (Cary Elwes), imprisoned by a chain around his leg.

And in the center of the area, the pair see a man lying face down, blood spurted across his head from an apparent self-inflicted gunshot wound. Over the next hour or so, the two men receive messages from the outside on a cell phone, wondering what's going on, what will happen next, and whether they'll be physically or emotionally able to make it through to the end.

The man in the middle of the room isn't dead: He's the killer, the gamesmaster. With about a minute left in the film, the audience and Adam find out the shocking truth.

"Not many films are about three people lying alone in a room," Bell said. "When I read the script, and I saw that that was going on, it struck me as very theatrical, very stage-like. That my character lay in a pool of blood did nothing to lessen my ardor for the piece, because I've long since learned the strength of silence." (Bell had been doing stage work in New York for years.)

"The character was developing and being developed in *Saw*. It just left a great deal to the imagination. If you walk down a corridor in a cloak, and you're getting shot from the back, you've got to know a whole lot more about the guy. How you walk down that corridor in that cloak is very much affected by the decisions you made regarding the character. It's not just an issue of exposure to the camera; it's how you're exposed to the camera, if you can tell a tale or a story with the smallest details."

It's a story he got to tell again and again: by 2011, the *Saw* franchise had spawned six sequels (all but one opened at the top of the American box office) and grossed roughly $800 million worldwide, making it the most successful horror franchise of the new millennium.

"It's important to keep the scripts and the story as solid as you can, and it's important to keep the bar up on the story," said Bell. "It was a very confined situation. One of the things you look for as an actor is a two- or three-character play because of the energy that you develop in a three-character play, as opposed to an ensemble piece with twenty or so characters. You can really develop the role, and the action is very compressed."

Fortunately, he was given some space to free Jigsaw up. In the second film, the character (whom we'd eventually come to know—and fear—as John Kramer, a former engineer, now suffering from cancer) played mind games with Detective Eric Matthews (Donnie Wahlberg). Not surprisingly, there's a gory backstory involving a group of people (one of whom is Matthews' son, Daniel) trying to find their way out of a home alive.

"When I was shooting *Saw,* I thought it was an interesting piece, and I wanted to work with Danny Glover," Bell said. (In the original, Glover played Detective David Tapp, who met an untimely end.) "Aside from that, I had nothing in mind about it going beyond the original *Saw.* But when it did, of course, I had an opportunity to flush this guy out in terms of who he is, what he's doing, why he's doing it. That's a marvelous opportunity, and the question is, 'Can it be done? Can it be done in an entertaining way?'"

It was; *Saw III* allowed Jigsaw to show his past, filled with love (stay tuned for this one), joy, and even humor. But just as the audience wanted to put its collective arms around the sweet old man and say, "You know, you're not such a bad guy after all!" Jigsaw's dark side came back out, just before he himself finally was killed (in a sense—it's been proven that the only thing certain about *Saw* is that nothing's for sure).

"On *Saw II,*" Bell recalled, "Donnie Wahlberg and I got a chance to recraft the dialogue, along with the help of [director Darren Lynn Bousman and Whannell], and keep a lot of the ideas in there, regarding appreciation of blessings and survival of the fittest, such as, 'If you knew the moment of your own death, how would it affect the way you live your life?' It's about how something is said and how something is done, and Donnie and I worked very hard to make those scenes a cat-and-mouse game. You cannot just have two people sitting at a table without the stakes being very high, and without the level of drama being very high. When I look at that film, and look at those scenes, it's a gratifying thing to see, because what you experience on the set and what you shoot isn't always what ends up on the screen. In this case, it did."

Bell called upon Tommy Lee Jones' performance as real-life murderer Gary Gilmore in *Executioner's Song* and Marlon Brando's vengeful Kid Rio of *One-Eyed Jacks* as inspiration.

"With characters such as those," Bell said, "you understand why. You understand where he's coming from. It doesn't mean that you think he's right, or that you would do that, but it gives layering. It gives different color to the character. The most interesting people in the world are the people that are not just one thing. As actors, we strive to let the horrific and the sublime aspects of being alive and the humanity exist in the same place."

That's because his people may not be the nicest or the most heartfelt—but they're still people, and people don't always act in kind, generous, respectful ways.

"I don't think in terms of good and evil. No matter what character I play, whether it's a priest, an astronaut, a mathematician, or a police officer, I'm looking for the human elements. I approach every character the same way; I try to explore his humanity, because if you're not interested in the character—if he's all just one thing and one-dimensional—then you're not going to be interested in him. We were all children once. We all had parents. We all had hopes and dreams and aspirations, and you want to see those hopes, dreams and aspirations in the eye of whatever character you are playing. I try to work against the obvious, and try to bring out the qualities that may not be there if I didn't."

There would be quite a bit more to Jigsaw as the series went on. "I always try to go the opposite way with him, to express his humanity," Bell says. "The experiences that people have will speak for themselves, but only I can speak for him, and I looked forward to expressing that character in a way that impresses me."

Here's one more stunning fact about one of Hollywood's scariest: he's not really into horror flicks! Well, not to the extent that most of the Kramer-inspired Clan is; Bell's quick to point out that doesn't mean he *doesn't* like to get the chills once in a while. "That's like saying, 'Do you like ice cream, or don't you? Do you like sandwiches, or don't you?' I like certain kinds of sandwiches, like peanut butter and bacon." (The latter cuisine choice is a passion Bell shares with the late great Elvis Presley.)

"I wasn't interested in being frightened in theaters," he said. "As a child, it wasn't what I was drawn to. That being said, there are many different kinds of horror films. There are quality horror films and there are horror films that are not so quality. You can accomplish the same thing in horror that you can accomplish in any other genre; you just have to be determined to do it.

"I have a great respect for the genre of horror. If you have a wonderful story, and for part of the story, there's fear for the viewer, I'll take that ride. The viewers, especially the *Saw* viewers, are an edgy and smart crowd of people, looking for stuff to be first-rate."

Even Jigsaw's death at the end of *Saw III* didn't stop him, as he returned in flashbacks in the next *four Saw* installments—but this time, apprentice Det. Mark Hoffman (Costas Mandylor) was carrying on the tutor's teachings.

"Hoffman learned from the master," says Mandylor, whose career horror debut came as the dark-hearted detective. "He passed him the baton, so to speak, and you see that he's a much more mature creature over what he does. He gets into a little bit of trouble and thinks he loses his way, which makes it a little bit exciting. [Jigsaw] did his best. He gave Hoffman all the advice and warned him. I just think that it just makes it a touch different that Hoffman is a fool. He's not as smart as his mentor."

As Hoffman first went evil in the closing moments of *Saw IV*, Mandylor got quite a bit of outside assistance from those who'd been there before. "I've always gotten great help from the directors because they're so involved," he recalls. "When I first got there, I was just trying to stay out of the way. But the directors always keep track of everything. And I get phone calls, late at night, from Tobin."

But could he, could *anyone* with at least an outside grasp upon the strange world known as reality, ever actually witness, let alone perform any of the Saw-man's deeds? How can such a thing even be imagined?

"The most important thing for me was you can have the idea of wanting to take revenge and do terrible things to people," Mandylor says. "But the reality of it is something completely different. As soon as you see that, it's just sickening and nauseating—unless you're just completely dissociated and a mental sociopath or insane, I guess.

"It's like, 'I have to sell that reality and try to make it as real as possible.' That was it. Like I said, if a painting of Jesus is just so-so, the detail isn't really there, then I'll pass it and look at the Statue of David. But if the detail is specific and it's done correctly, then you are looking at the real thing. If the violence is disturbing as opposed to cartoonish or something—and that includes the emotional state of the people who are watching it or who it's being done to—that's where I think it's important to be able to get those specifics right."

He and Jigsaw would push things all the way to the lucky number of seven *Saw*s; of course, the horror world being what it is, a later sequel or remake would not be earth-shatteringly shocking.

"With each of these films, we get to fill in a new piece of the puzzle," Bell says. "*Saw* fans are remarkably vigilant when it comes to paying attention to detail, so every time we have a chance to fill in one of the pieces of this intricate puzzle, that's a great thing."

Up until 2004, Bell was known for showing up as one-shot deals on everything from *The Sopranos* to *Seinfeld*. He also had small parts in *Goodfellas* and *In the Line of Fire*, and got an earlier shot at real-life horror, playing Unabomber Theodore Kaczynski in a 1996 TV movie biopic. Bell hasn't quite grasped (willingly) the fans' concept of legendary uber-villian.

"I don't know what a horror icon is!" he says with a laugh. "I'm playing a guy named John Kramer, and I try to bring as much as I can bring to this guy's dedication and commitment to what he's doing. The most interesting people in our whole lives are the people that have a lot of different parts to them, like Renaissance people. That's what John Kramer is. He's a mechanical engineer. He's a genius, interested in science, art, and music. Hopefully we see that in his eyes—the depth of who he is, and what he does."

Even if it's scaring the hell out of us.

Saw II and *III* gave viewers a sense of John's personality: The only escapee of Jigsaw's torment in the first film was a young beauty named Amanda, who'd managed to tear her mind off the jaw-trap threatening to split her skull long enough to rip the key out of a fellow captive's stomach and get away. Call it the epitome of a "scared straight" technique, or some serious Stockholm Syndrome: By the end of the second flick, she'd be siding with the man who nearly killed her.

When Shawnee Smith first checked over the first film's script, "I was horrified," she recalls. "I said, 'Please don't make me live this out for a day.'" Her reps and the film crew insisted she take a second look, recalling her past in the area (she'd done *The Blob* and *The Stand*), and she reluctantly agreed.

Still, as Amanda was pretending to save herself and the others throughout the second film, Smith says that even she didn't know she would end up the bad girl. "That ending was kind of discovered almost at the end of the shoot, which is probably part of the success with the *Saw* movies, the flexibility with the script," she says. "No one settles until the film is in the can. There's just this continuous search for truth, and that goes on until filming is done."

In the third *Saw*, Amanda, now in full-blown evil mode, kidnapped a nurse and forced her to restore John to health, while a man trapped in Jigsaw's world searched for clues in the death of his son.

"Usually you don't get a lot of female villains that aren't the spawn of someone else," says Smith, who'd played the unwilling accomplice of real-life serial killer Christopher Wilder in the 1986 TV movie *Easy Prey*. "It's almost like a true marriage between Jigsaw and Amanda, which are two halves to a whole. Some people might say monster. I saw ... their intentions are more noble, but that's because I'm on their side.

"Acting is like a game of tennis. The better your opponent, the better you're going to play. I've had some of my best tennis matches with Tobin; he's relentless about truth."

Amanda would get waxed near the end of *Saw III*, but still show up in flashbacks as the series continued, mainly to show the audience that the interaction between Amanda and Jigsaw was of the instructor-student type, rather than anything serious.

"Basically, our rehearsal is just this sort of walking and talking," Smith says of her work with Bell. "You know, we just left marks on the sidewalks of Toronto, walking and talking. And then we'd sit down at some café, because we figured that's what John and Amanda did."

As Matthews' search for his son drove him even more nuts than Jigsaw himself ever was in the second *Saw*, a fellow detective was there, his backup on a search for a madman. Over the next few films, the man would step into protagonist mode.

Lyriq Bent watched the first flick to get ready to try out for the second. He recalls, "I wasn't a big fan of the crazy torture stuff, but the writing was clever, and the concepts of the torture, the traps, it made sense. It wasn't gratuitous violence." Still, when he went in for part two, Bent was ready to dish out some violence of his own: He was looking to become Xavier, the captive who torments his fellow prisoners to selfishly sneak home before Daniel and Amanda take him out. Things didn't work that way.

"I thought I gave a great audition," Bent says. "It happens in projects when you do a great audition, but you come back with something small in size. It turned out to be a great opportunity." Indeed, he was offered the role of Daniel Rigg, the detective who sees one colleague after another fall victim to Jigsaw (Franky G became Xavier).

"I started to visualize the character in the scenarios and situations of the story. I started to paint a picture of this character and what he was feeling. It's an expression of the body, and I figured that for me to express it to the audience, they needed to fully understand what my story was and what I was trying to accomplish in the thick of things. That was me believing in what I wanted to do with the character, taking my plans, and creating it with a very well-written film."

Bent had a quick chat with director Bousman. "I asked to leave the camera on my character for an extra two seconds, to keep the storyline going, have the audience wonder what was going on with that character, that there was something up with him," he says. "It really helped draw that underlying story into the main script, and it led to *Saw III* and *Saw IV*."

As John and Amanda took center stage in the third film, Rigg was back for the same tiny bit of background, with all of Bent's scenes knocked out in a day.

"*Saw IV* came about because Rigg was a consistent character that people related to and got to know," Bent says. "Whether like or dislike, they had a relationship with him."

Informed that his friend (well, as it seemed then) Hoffman has become Jigsaw's next target, Rigg's sent on his own hunt. He saves a woman's life, then is forced to clock her when she attacks him. He forces a serial rapist into another trap, then helps an abused wife escape her beater. But he barges in too soon to save Matthews, and Hoffman, now revealed as behind it all, escapes.

"You want to be honest with whatever is placed in front of you, with the character, the situation, and the scenario, and just really focus and listen to what's happening around you, based on the other characters," Bent says. "I surrendered to that idea."

John Kramer's wife, Jill (Betsy Russell), carried on her late husband's work through the last few *Saw* movies.

Saw III gave us a new aspect of John's personality, one that truly showed that Jigsaw was more than just a monster, or at least hadn't always been one. But it wasn't until the next film that we really got a stronger glimpse of his main woman, the perils that they'd faced together, and the effect that she had on his life.

"I decided I wanted to be an actress at around eight years old," recalls Betsy Russell, who played Jill Tuck. "My favorite TV show was *I Love Lucy* and I imitated her 24 hours a day. I wanted to be Lucy! If I wasn't acting out Lucy episodes, I was pretending to be old silly men or Marlo Thomas from *That Girl* or Cher from *The Sonny and Cher Show*."

"Horror films aren't my thing," admits Russell, more of a romantic comedy fan. "But I saw [the first two *Saw* films] and respected their originality and their message. As the fans grew and became so devoted, I really got that this was going to be a franchise that would continue to grow, surprise and impress the fans … so I became a fan as well."

As fans came to see if Jigsaw could escape once again—not only from his pursuers, but from the cancer that had wracked his body through the first two films—*Saw III* found him mostly playing his deadly games from a bed and reminiscing about his past crimes, his early life, and, very briefly, Jill.

"When I got the role, it was three seconds of Jill with John in a park having a loving moment," Russell says. "I knew nothing of our background, so I invented it. I wanted her to be light (thus the light hair), bright and loving, someone that the audience as well as John could fall in love with."

In the fourth *Saw* installment (2007), Russell got hold of a true character to play in Jill. While Jigsaw's protégé Hoffman secretly continues his trainer's work, Jill's called in for some interrogating. Like many of her colleagues, Russell prepared by sitting down with an acting coach and writing the autobiography of a life she'd act out on screen.

"We dissect every detail of the character's life," she says. "We create a character biography that rounds out her life and creates her emotional and behavioral background. Through improvisation we add more dimension and layers to the character, so I know what my thoughts are between the lines. On the set before every scene I do relaxation, substitution personalization, and effective memory work if needed. I also find music to be incredibly helpful in creating the right mood for each scene."

She and John had a great marriage, but something went horribly wrong: During a robbery at the clinic where Jill worked, a man crashed through a door and slammed her between it and the wall, causing her to miscarry the child the couple had already named Gideon.

"I spent about three days sobbing while we were filming and I really thought Jill's pain came across on screen," Russell says of the scene. "I had so many crew members who were shocked to find out after the scene was done that those were all my own tears." The robber would become one of John's victims ... but, like almost everything else about the *Saw* series, little was what it seemed.

When *Saw V* came to theaters, Hoffman was hailed as a hero for stopping the baddies, but Jill was still around, and she wasn't going to let anyone take her man's spotlight. Though she and John had grown apart and divorced before his death, all too often the case when couples lose a child, their love never left, and it pushed Jill forward.

"As the role grew, so did Jill's depth," Russell says. "Not only is she strong and devoted to her husband through thick and thin, but her desire to help others through their pain is a quality I know we can all learn from."

In a scene that would soon mean much more, Jill gets a box from John's lawyer, with a message from John saying everything there was important. From the look on her face, we knew he was right—but not quite why, as she got up and left without showing the contents to anyone. Jill had a secret.

That secret was revealed in *Saw VI*: Jill, now something of a seductress straddling the line between good and evil (like John himself, except for the seductive part), learns that John's assistant Amanda was involved with the robbery that killed her child, and Hoffman was in on it too. Channeling the spirit of her dead hubby, Jill plants Hoffman in one of his own traps.

He escapes, nabs her with the same trap, and appears to have gotten away with everything once again. But as 2011's *Saw 3D* comes to an end, Dr. Gordon reappears to get everyone's revenge; by now, even the fans are cheering for the man who once terrified and sickened them. It shows that *Saw* had a connection with its audience, one that brought them into the storyline farther than just about any other series. By now, the *Saws* were almost all about flashbacks and inside jokes, but our hero Jigsaw, or John, had a decent heart and a gorgeous woman who stuck around to live with it.

"For the first five movies I couldn't watch the gory scenes," Russell remembers, "but by [part] six I watched every frame. I think I've gotten used to it, which in itself is pretty scary. I believe the *Saw* movies are exceptionally well made. They have a story with a heart and a message. They look wonderful and they really accomplish what they set out to do, which is make the audience experience so many emotions! I really love the message in *Saw* as well. Coming from a Spiritual Psychology background, I understand the message to be about appreciation and accountability for our actions. Those are two things that are important to me in my life! Of course I also believe it to be a love story, but isn't everything?"

"Actress Shawnee Smith Featuring 'Saw 3.'" *Killer Reviews*. 2013. Retrieved Sept. 9, 2013, from http://www.killerreviews.com/dispinterview.php?intid=1598.
Bell, Tobin. Phone interview. May 28, 2008.
Bent, Lyriq. Phone interview. July 24, 2013.
JimmyO. "Interview: Shawnee Smith." *Arrow in the Head*. Nov. 18, 2008. Retrieved Sept. 9, 2013, from http://www.joblo.com/horror-movies/news/interview-shawnee-smith-02&order=popular.
Murray, Rebecca. "Shawnee Smith Returns as Jigsaw's Partner in Crime in 'Saw III.'" *About*. 2013. Retrieved Sept. 9, 2013, from http://movies.about.com/od/saw3/a/saw3ss102306.htm.
Russell, Betsy. E-mail interview. Aug. 1, 2010.
Wayland, Sara. "Tobin Bell and Costas Mandylor Interview *SAW VI*." *Collider*. Oct. 17, 2009. Retrieved Feb. 2, 2011, from http://collider.com/tobin-bell-and-costas-mandylor-interview-saw-vi/9429/.

•••••••••••••••••••••••••••••

Susan Swift: *Audrey Rose*

She'd sold tinfoil cookies door to door with the rest of the local Girl Scouts. She'd worked her hands through clay figures and tried to avoid the evils of paint stains in art classes. The balance beam and uneven bars had been just a bit too uncomfortable.

Typical "young girl activities" just weren't appealing much to the Houston elementary schooler. Cinematically terrifying a nation, though ... that would be interesting.

"My mom and dad would provide different activities for us growing up," remembers Susan Swift. "The rule was that you tried it for a certain amount of time, and if you didn't like it, you could stop it." As is usually the case for those her age, the attention span didn't

A terrified Audrey Rose (Susan Swift) tries to find the secret of the tormentor living within.

stretch far through her first few pastime shots. Then her mom heard about a local acting school.

"She asked would I like to sign up for it," Swift says. "I said only if I could get out of it. I didn't want to get stuck in it." A trial run of a month was struck, and she headed off to the stage.

"I enjoyed it," she says of the school. "I just kept going. It wasn't a career goal; it was just like any other extracurricular activity, like piano or soccer, or something else to do."

After she'd been there for about a year, the school director got a call from a film crew member looking to bring a new story to the screen. A fellow named Frank De Felitta had written a novel about the darkness of reincarnation. Now director Robert Wise and his crew were moving the story to the screen. A young girl was the title character, if not the protagonist, but this was no kids' movie.

"They had gone through different talent from Los Angeles, and had not found anybody," Swift says. "They'd literally begun a nationwide hunt, calling studios and schools around the country." Her teachers were told to pick a select few to try out.

Wise and a few others showed up. Swift rose to the occasion. "I did my best," she recalls. "I suppose he liked me—he arranged for me to fly to L.A. to do the screen test. Then he offered me the part." She'd play the title role—or at least partially. Ivy Templeton would appear to be a normal preteen girl in a normal neighborhood with normal parents. But on the inside, there's a dark secret, one that she doesn't even know about—and it arrives in the form of a mysterious stranger. Prowling outside her school, following her home, seemingly the type that should be showing up on *To Catch a Predator*, the stranger keeps getting closer and closer, but not close enough that the cops can make a move. It's up to Ivy's parents to try to take justice into their own hands…

With little training, Swift sat down with an acting coach to get ready to play her role. They worked on relating to the aspects of memorability to which so many of us can relate—the way a girl her age would react to things she'd never seen before but would always remember, and the ways she'd interact with people. "She taught me the method of just closing your eyes and meditating, although it's not meditation," Swift says. "It's a creative kind of thinking where, in the beginning, she would help me remember the feeling of sunshine on my face. Can you recall what that feels like, the sunshine striking your leg or your face? You get more attuned to your sense that way. We're very visual creatures, and we're overloaded visually, and sometimes ways to connect emotionally are not visually stimulating. What does a rose smell like? Do you remember the smell of your girlfriend's perfume? Then you gradually work your way with imaginative clay. That can even be expanded into your clothing. If you wear a certain type of clothing, it can make you feel differently. You create the feelings, and then you manifest them outwardly."

The story Ivy's parents could not possibly believe comes from a fellow named Elliot Hoover. It's the tragedy of the sudden loss of his wife and daughter in a car accident. It's the tale of two psychics who told him that the young girl's spirit was still around. And it's the shocking conclusion that his daughter, Audrey Rose herself, lives on in Ivy.

Hoover was played by an up-and-coming Anthony Hopkins.

"I got to visit with him, just a tiny bit," Swift recalls of the man who'd turn Hannibal Lecter into a legend. "He'd take copious notes, make out many, many notes on the script to get his character there. There was something about him, so much energy. For me, just as a child nearby, every time I would come near him, I was so touched emotionally that I would cry—not out of fear or whininess or sadness, but tears of empathy, of feeling discreet. It's just a tenderness. I was just quiet around him, and touched by his emotional energy."

Slowly, a poison appears to enter Ivy: storming around the family apartment, screaming, oblivious to her surroundings, ignoring those desperately calling for her. Hoover is the only one who can calm her down, but there's suddenly burns all over her hands, and fire was nowhere near. It's what killed Audrey, and what still remains of her.

Many people compare *Audrey Rose* to *The Exorcist*, but that's unfair. They're both stories of young girls who lose control of their bodies, but who exactly is running the show here draws a canyon-sized distinction between the two. Like Regan McNeil, Ivy's not inherently evil. Like Regan, she's been overtaken from the inside out. But while Regan, and so many others who have become Satan's playgrounds in world cinema, are being possessed by evil, Ivy's remote controller is a scared soul who just wants to move on to a better place.

Ivy's behavior starts to go downhill. Nightmares torment her sleep, and reality isn't much better. Memories of a life she never would have had the time to live start to emerge, and she discusses things she has never seen and places she's never been. Hoover is about the only one who can get her to calm down enough to return to being Ivy.

To stay in character, the actress and her coach continued to create her own imagined memories.

"I would just close my eyes and remember a couple of the things that my acting coach had talked about," Swift says. "There are always events in one's life that one can remember and encapsulate the emotion of the event. For instance, the first kiss. You remember your first kiss, where you were and when you were. You also remember the last goodbye, of someone you lost from death. If you remember that, it doesn't take just one little thought, a permission, to mourn that. And you can cry as much as you want, because that memory is just as fresh as if you were standing there the other day, and you do it with specificity, such as recalling very specific things in the room, sometimes even the pattern on the sheets. It brings you back into that moment and reminds you of the emotions that you had, and all you have to do is put it into the emotions that you have."

Hoover's on trial for trying to abduct Ivy, and the reincarnation become a worldwide topic of discussion. Soon Ivy's in a hypnotist's office, ready to prove once and for all whether she's the only one inside.

Way under, she regresses to one of her first birthdays. Ivy's speech starts to change, and also her vocabulary. She mentally shrinks back to infanthood.

Then the doctor looks for Audrey. The convulsions start again, and Ivy tumbles off the table. But the jolt doesn't knock her into "reality." She's back at the wreck. Hoover was telling the truth all along.

"To some degree, we choreographed how the scene would go," Swift remembers. "Then it goes into reliving the car crash. I was thinking in the back of my head, is he going to call 'cut'? I'm supposed to fall off the table. I wasn't sure what the plan was, but I went right off the table. I thought that they were not ready for me to come off the table. They continued going, and they were worried that I had hurt myself, but I didn't want to mess up the scene."

The doctor and observers desperately call for Ivy, but Ivy's no longer there. Hoover reaches out for his daughter once more, but it's too late even for him. Heartbreakingly, Audrey takes Ivy where Audrey hasn't yet gotten to visit: Heaven.

"People die every day," Swift says, "and that's where the real trauma and the real tragedy is, not in movies. I never was confused. In the movie, the point was, is there such a thing as reincarnation? That's a pretend question. It's a dramatic pretend question to get some people thinking. It's a philosophical question."

By the time adulthood arrived for Swift in the late 1980s, Swift switched careers, heading to law school. She was soon working in litigation. "Education, as my parents explained," she says, "is the one thing they cannot take away from you. They can tax everything. They can take your home, your car, but they cannot take what you know. They cannot take what is packed between your ears. That is something you have forever."

Soon, marriage and motherhood arrived. Seven became her lucky number of children.

"I got a promotion!" she proclaims proudly.

Still, she wasn't quite done.

Persuaded by her family to let them see her in action, Swift took a small role in 1995's *The Curse of Michael Myers*, the sixth installment in the *Halloween* series. She got sacrificed early in the flick.

"It was a small part that I liked very much," she says. "I was just pretending to be horrified during this human sacrifice ritual. Any normal person would be scared during this.

"I think acting is, quite simply, the ability to pretend openly, to embrace something that you are not, or that you want to be, or who you are," Swift says. "Children do it very naturally. The author creates the words; the actor just brings the pretend, the play, and puts them on the words, and you just believe. It's as easy as that. That's what I found."

Swift, Susan. Phone interview. July 11, 2012.

·····························

Pat Tallman: *Night of the Living Dead*

Imitation may be the sincerest form of flattery, but one of the best things about acting is that it gives performers their own way to pay tribute.

When she was gearing up to play a role in 1990s *Night of the Living Dead*, Pat Tallman knew that, as effectively as Judy O'Dea had made Barbara into a damsel in distress in the George Romero original, Tallman had a chance to put her own mark on the role. Whether it would be better was in the eye of the beholder (or the ticket buyer), but at least it would be her own.

Rather than having Barbra turn and run, as O'Dea had, Tallman went hardcore on the offensive. Sure, she might start off a bit petrified of the zombie critters, but this was her world, and you didn't come back from the dead and get her in this one. By the time special effects legend Tom Savini's 1990 *Dead* remake was done, Barbara (in all her rugged, bare-armed, biceped glory) had iced many as the zombies.

"I just constructed a character based on the script," she recalls of getting ready to become the second Barbara. "The writer puts the black on the page, I fill in the white. I never wanted her to be the same as the original. What would be the point in that? The original was so perfect as it was!"

The setup was about the same; Barbara and her brother Johnny are in a cemetery, when they're suddenly attacked by a weirdo who kills her bro. Barbara takes off and soon finds herself in a house with Ben, the Cooper family, and others.

Once again, Ben and Cooper battle for control. But this Barbara's not content to be a spectator; she's locked, loaded, and ready for battle. Barbara and Ben are a tag team that would terrorize World Wrestling Entertainment, and their finishing maneuver involves a couple of Magnums.

At the start, Tallman says, "[Barbara] was a wimpy little mousy schoolteacher person, not very powerful. But she starts to change. She becomes more real, a believable woman trying to survive, whipping around guns bigger than herself."

As for Tony Todd, the new movie's Ben, she says, "Tony was the most serious guy, and he'd often just kick back while we were waiting for a setup, and often, we just couldn't let him get away with that! The guy who lived in the house we shot in, I believe really did have a hobby in taxidermy. The whole place was filled with real stuffed animals! Animals that were once alive. We used all of them in the movie. All the ones on the wall were already there and they were really creepy. So, anyway, I would find a stuffed alligator or something and stick it on Tony while he was trying to sleep. But he was really a good sport about it. You go a little nuts when you're shooting all night, every night, six days a week. You just need some sort of comic relief."

Perhaps not knowing exactly what he was in for, a local who'd managed to finagle a role in the play got in character by playfully threatening and stalking "Barbara." "He was just so scary to me, and he really got into it ... following me around and whispering about how he was going to get me. Oh yeah ... it was fun being me.

"I can understand why Tom made Barbara's character more commanding," says Tallman. "Women were asserting their strength and equality in so many ways and venues in the 90s. It seems quite acceptable that Barbra should be so much more a leader and vanquisher in this version. I don't compare the two versions. Each stands on its own merit in its own time."

Two years later, Tallman followed Todd to the dark side of horror–sci-fi: In *Army of Darkness,* she was the possessed, tenth-degree black belt–holding

Pat Tallman became the new and much more physical Barbra in the 1990 remake of *Night of the Living Dead.*

witch with whom Bruce Campbell's heroic Ash is forced to suddenly do battle. "Bruce is a hunk," Tallman says. "I wish I wasn't in so much pain at the time so I could have really enjoyed it." That's because her war with Ash and shotgun death at his hands might have been the simplest part of filming. "I was in makeup for over 17 hours," she recalls. "[I] had horrible contact lenses in, so I couldn't see, couldn't eat or pee, and was working two stunt jobs at the same time. I really wanted him to shoot me for real and get it over with."

In the 1968 *Night of the Living Dead*, as O'Dea's Barbra runs for her life after her brother loses his own to a zombie, she runs into passerby Ben, who takes her into a house and assures her that she'll be okay as long as he's around.

This guy was the flick's hero. He was also black. At the time, this was almost unthinkable in horror films. As audiences of the time and afterward watched Ben work to protect a group of people he'd never met before, it mattered less and less that he was black. It didn't matter to the characters, so it didn't to the audiences.

"Ben didn't really have a biography," Duane Jones recalled. "Where was he coming from? He was just passing through. That's how it worked out. That's my destiny. I never was sorry that I did [the film]. I did it knowing what it was. I did it knowing the people, I did it knowing some of the risks, and I've never been sorry."

"There was a wonderful feeling of camaraderie, good humor, and good will," said Jones. "I really do appreciate it. I've never taken that for granted, because I wouldn't want anyone to think that I am so arrogant as not to be grateful for the acclaim they have given me for the film, and it should never be misconstrued that the enigmatic, mysterious persona that I have in some instances deliberately created just to have a space, just to have a private life is a lack of gratitude. It is my absolute insistence that I be seen as a full person, rather than Ben."

The person he became had a quarter-century teaching career, including as director of New York's State University College's Old Westbury's Maguire Theater. It's now named after Jones, who was working on his Master's in Communication from New York University during *Dead* filming. Years after the film came out, a group of students informed him of their practice of watching Ben's work to take the edge off during the hell week of final exams

"It was then that I came to have another kind of appreciation and respect for the movie," he said. "As artists, isn't that what we're trying to do—lighten people's lives and

Duane Jones became one of horror's earliest heroes as Ben, who did what was right just because it was right, in *Night of the Living Dead*.

give them entertainment? That's when I started to overcome my sensitivity, insecurity, embarrassment, whatever you want to call it, about the genre. These young people really had a special fondness for me and for the film. We helped them through some rough times."

Jones says of the movie's shocking ending, "I convinced George that the black community would rather see me dead than saved. I have said that it would have a wonderful O. Henry ending to have the character killed fortuitously. The heroes never die in American movies. The jolt of that and the double jolt of the hero figure being black seemed like a double-barreled whammy."

ArchivesOfTheDead. "Night Of The Living Dead Duane Jones Interview." *YouTube.* Jan. 27, 2009. Retrieved on Jan. 22, 2014, from http://www.youtube.com/watch?v=DZSQxiZ-df8.
Ferrante, Tim. "A Farewell to Duane Jones." *Fangoria* 80 (Feb. 1989): 14–18, 64.
Interview with Patricia Tallman. *Icons of Fright.* June 2005. Retrieved May 26, 2010, from http://www.iconsoffright.com/IV_Pat.htm.
Kuhns, Rob, Dir. *Birth of the Living Dead* [DVD]. New York: Predestinate Productions, 2013.

Tony Todd: *Candyman* films

Researching the work of Tony Todd, I was surprised to find out how many parallels there were between Todd and Duane Jones of *Night of the Living Dead*. Both of them got started in horror, even launching from the same role, although Todd stayed in the business longer. Both took some major steps in the horror world for African American performers, with Jones being one of the first to lead the way through the frightening genre and Todd becoming the first to play a recurring persona.

And it's just my opinion, but it appears that both very much would like to be remembered for more than just being frightening. I definitely got that impression researching Jones' thoughts on the matter.

"I hate being pigeonholed," admits Todd, who, like Jones, taught school between acting gigs. "The worst comment that I hate is when I'm bothered at a supermarket and they say, 'You're the guy from *Candyman*. Are you still working?' I work constantly and, for some reason, people galvanize around that part. I respect it, but I'm also resentful of that obscurity."

As George Romero prepared to remake *Night of the Living Dead* in 1990, Todd was lucky enough to be in Pittsburgh. He took a breather from *Criminal Justice* (alongside his *Bird* costar Forest Whitaker) to visit the *Dead* crew. "When I got there, I said, 'You know, I think I bear a fleeting resemblance to Duane Jones…. You gotta read me. I'm here. I love the movie. I want to do it.' And I was told that the sessions were over and they were very close to casting. So I refused to leave."

Tom Savini, whose own work in the horror field would eventually rise to legend, happened to stroll by. Todd snared him—perhaps not literally, which, going by Todd's size and build, might be quite unpleasant!

"Thanks to his humanity and patience he allowed me to intrude on his Saturday," Todd recalls. "Next thing I know, I get a call on Monday saying that the role was mine. It was one of those huckster moments. It was one of those times where artists stand up for themselves and the consequences are accurate."

Tony Todd felt and dished out the torture as the title character in the *Candyman* series.

Ben may have been the leading good guy in *Living Dead,* but two years later, Todd got a shot to go the other way in horror, and put his legendarily deep, haunting voice on full display.

A decade before, horror household name Clive Barker had penned a tale of a slave from decades past, murdered for allowing intelligence, education, and, eventually real love to find strong places in his life. Then his spirit found a way back to the present, and it was time for some payback.

To go back even farther than Barker's tale, Candyman's origins had taken form in one of the oldest and most well-known urban legends in history. Standing in front of a mirror and slowly repeating the name of a spirit—usually Bloody Mary or the ghost of a loved or hated one—will summon it. It's how, early in the tale, grad student Helen Lyle (Virginia Madsen) and her friends come to jokingly call for Candyman one night in the midst of studying.

Impressed by his work in the 1990 TV film *The Ivory Hunters,* Barker and director Bernard Rose had called on Todd to play the psychic creation (Barker produced the film). Candyman was once Daniel Robitaille, a New Orleans slave with a penchant for art and study. Boasting of a few college degrees himself (a Master's in theater being one), Todd was already relating to the human side that Daniel hadn't gotten enough time to display.

"That's what I attribute everything to," he says of his education. "I had wonderful, fantastic teachers that took time and allowed me the room to fail. Part of graduate school in the theater field is doing all kinds of things that you would never do again in life, walking on the [high wire] and not being afraid to fail, as long as you try. It's because of that I was able to have the huckster in me to challenge [Savini] into considering me for casting and in subsequent roles that I've done." Like this one, for example.

"It was very important for me to justify why he was a specter, why he was a ghost," says the performer. "He was a painter. He was an artist. His father was a shoe cobbler. His greatest crime was falling in love with the wrong woman."

Falling in love with a rich white man's daughter—the two had an affair and a child—the young man was hunted and tortured to death by an angry mob, a sadly factual situation that played itself out far too many times during the dark days of slavery.

"We didn't want to make him just some generic bogeyman. Bernard and I wanted to make sure he was steeped in a kind of gothic American racial history. We mutually decided that he was an artist, and from that came the idea of the painting, and once we had that, we knew it was going to be *Phantom of the Opera*. Once I had all that, I knew how to make him human, in spite of the fact that he's a ghost. Having grown up in America just as the civil rights movement started, I could completely relate to him."

On a hunt for more of Candyman's story, Helen soon stumbles upon the "real" thing that she'd originally called for. Soon people are bloodily dying around her, and cops and shrinks (along with the audience, not sure what's going on here) are feeling *she* might just be behind it. Equipped with a hook to replace the hand that the mob chopped off, Candyman keeps appearing out of nowhere. Helen's fascination with him is too strong for her to understand. Pathetically, the film had to be changed and delayed at times because certain people above the crew were apprehensive about bringing love, and potentially lovemaking, into a story of a black man and white woman.

Todd's Master's degree, he says, "taught me a way of way of working, a way of preparing, and a way of staying true. At that time, I was doing things like sketching books. When I got an impression, I put it in [the film]: a leaf, color, poem, apple." He and Madsen took horseback riding lessons, dancing, even fencing lessons together.

As Helen gets ready for trial, Candyman helps her escape, his power over her similar not to a strong husband over a devoted wife, but more of a cult leader over a follower. With him, in Jim Jones fashion, ready to sacrifice her to feed his tale, the two are trapped in a huge fire, left to live on back in urban legend.

We learned a bit more about Candyman three years later in 1995's *Farewell to the Flesh*, which Barker also wrote and produced. The phenom stalks his own great-granddaughter through New Orleans, looking to sacrifice her to ensure their safety in the afterlife. *Day of the Dead* (1999) would have him doing the same thing, except now to his great-great-granddaughter.

"I knew he was unique," Todd says. "He was this powerful, demented force of nature. But I loved his elegance too. We wanted him to walk with pride."

The next year, Todd kicked off another horrifying series trek with the first of his four appearances in the *Final Destination* series. A year after putting a new spin on the old tale on both sides of *The Strange Case of Dr. Jekyll and Mr. Hyde*, he'd ironically head back to Candyman's Big Easy hangout for the *Hatchet* films as Clive Washington, masquerading as Rev. Zombie. Like Candyman, he believed in the value of human sacrifice to succeed afterward.

"He's a charlatan, he's a salesman," Todd says. "He's just one step from being a used car salesman, and he makes quite a living selling tourism, selling trinkets. But I think he's done it so long that he actually believes his own hype, which can be kind of interestingly, sardonically humorous, in spite of the grave things that are going on. And also he's the storyteller. I'm the guy that has to tell the exposition, that hopefully I do in a way that's not too boring."

Frappler, Rob. "Interview with Horror Icon Tony Todd." *Screen Rant*. 2013. Retrieved on June 14, 2013, from http://screenrant.com/tony-todd-interview-hatchet-final-destination-robf-80905/all/1/.
Neumyer, Scott. "Exclusive: Tony Todd Talks 'Night of the Living Dead,' 'Candyman,' and That Iconic Voice." *Fear Net*. Oct. 10, 2012. Retrieved June 14, 2013, from http://www.fearnet.com/news/interview/exclusive-tony-todd-talks-night-living-dead-candyman-and-iconic-voice.
Todd, Tony. Personal interview. May 2, 2012.

Dee Wallace: *The Howling, Cujo* and *The Frighteners*

Have you ever hear of a performer being accused of playing "themselves," in every role they play? Ever checked out a film and hear someone say, "Oh, he/she just plays the same role in every film"?

Dee Wallace goes the other route. When camera time gets near, the actress who took a brief break from horror to become America's favorite mother in *E.T.* just stands back and waits for her new role to take over—and it's taken her everywhere. "I don't 'prepare,'" she asserts. "I become. I prefer to just learn the lines and then let the character channel through me."

After a quick jaunt through the world of high school teaching, Wallace charged into the cult film setting—literally—in the mid–1970s, being pursued by cannibals in 1978's *The Hills Have Eyes* and werewolves in *The Howling* two years later.

In *The Howling*, she was newscaster Karen White, the target of a serial killer's obsession. Upon learning that the fellow has a few tendencies of the wolf-turning type, Karen and her husband Bill (Christopher Stone, Wallace's real-life hubby) are sent to a psychiatric camp. But it's much worse than they could have dreamed; not only is the killer there, but it's a haven for other shapeshifters. "I happened to love the character," Wallace says of Karen. "There was a lot of emotional ride there. In retrospect, in my life, I've always been interested in that conflict of dark and light, in good and evil."

Karen and her friend Chris (Dennis Dugan, who'd thrill younger generations a decade later by directing *Happy Gilmore* and other such films) manage to escape the camp, but hardly unscathed. As they start to drive away, a new wolf leaps into the car and takes a bite out of Karen. The wolf is shot, and reverts to human form: it's Bill, who begs Karen to spread the word.

"The whole film was tough to do," Wallace recalls, "working three days during the day, then turning around into nights. Energetically, we never had a day off. All we did was work and sleep. Any time there's a film with that many special effects, it's a constant emotional output. On the other hand, we had an amazing amount of fun."

Back on TV, Karen tries to tell the story, but something's wrong. She goes off script, then starts to scream. But it's not any leftover trauma from her encounter with the killer: she becomes a werewolf in living color, and then in death, as her sad pal Chris is forced to shoot her.

"It's a technique based on really, extremely high energy," Wallace says. "You get your energy up and you channel the character. As an actor, it's your job to really believe that you're in every moment, whether it's with a monster, or with a little alien from outer space. It's your job to make yourself believe that every moment is real. The approach is the thing. Whether it's a light comedy or a horror, you just have to take the moment and submit to it."

Then, in 1981, she helped Steven Spielberg and a lovable alien steal the planet's heart as Elliot's mom Mary in the story of Earth's newest visitor. "I was attracted to the heart of the entire piece [*E.T.*]," she says, "and Mary was one of the first single mothers on screen. She reminded me a lot of the strength, fortitude and love of my mom. It was a real homage to her."

As one of the few adults with a prominent role in the first half of the film, Mary's often the comic foil for Elliot and his sister Gertie (Drew Barrymore) as they try to hide their

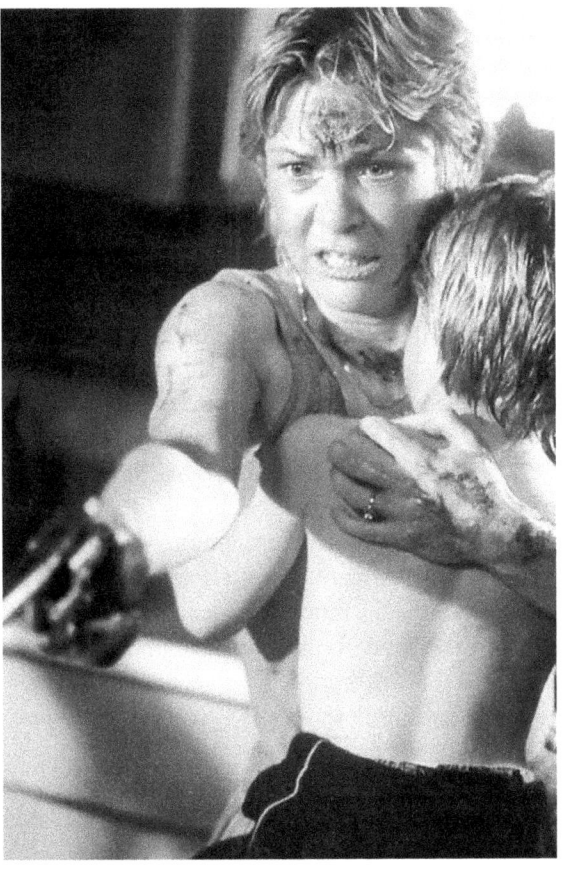

Donna Trenton (Dee Wallace) protects her son Tad (Danny Pintauro) from the four-legged title character of *Cujo*.

new friend from the mean, prying eyes of adults. Mary accidentally whacks the alien with a refrigerator door, tries to assure her young fellow that he never actually saw E.T., and gets fooled by the creature in drag at Halloween, a hilarious scene where she peeks in the closet and misses E.T. hiding amongst a group of toys (Wallace called the dining room scene and the Halloween outing two of her favorites).

With the story, Wallace says, "I became everybody's mom. Before *E.T.*, I played call girls, hookers, Senators, astronauts. Then *E.T.* came out, and all of a sudden I'm everybody's mom, because the movie was so powerful, the part was so powerful."

In the end, a mother's love, a child's loyalty, and an alien's magic turned *E.T.* into one for the generations, as the film was the highest grossing in history until *Star Wars* was re-released in 1997. "I knew it was special the minute I read it," Wallace says. "It is a heart picture that reminds us of the truthfulness of love and consciousness. Like *The Wizard of Oz*, those messages endure through all generations."

Back in the horror world a year later, Wallace blended Mary's motherly love with terrifying toughness in the film adaptation of Stephen King's *Cujo*, as her Donna Trenton protects her young son from a rabid Saint Bernard. "I purposely didn't read the book before filming because I didn't want to 'fill in' what wasn't in the script." The film had several differences from the book, the biggest of which arguably being the youngster's literary death; he survives in the movie. "Donna was a tour de force role for a woman," she continues. "Again, it was that mother's unconditional love for her child that hooked me: my mother's strength and love."

Putting together an earlier scene when Donna, an adulteress in an unhappy marriage, is nearly raped by her lover Steve Kemp would be almost as tough as anything with the dog, largely because Steve was played by none other than Christopher. "It was one of the weirdest things I've ever done, because there we were, sitting in the bedroom, saying, 'Okay, how are we going to do this? We can't do it like we *really* do this!' It's almost like having your mother in the bedroom with you. Then we got on the set and Christopher was so protective of how I was going to be [filmed], and if everything was going to be in as good taste as it could be. That got a little weird because you're not just dealing with technical acting any more."

Wallace didn't have things as bad as her stunt double, who was inadvertently chomped by the dog after a missed cue during filming. She still had to delve into the darkest part of love during a scene where she hysterically shouts at her youngster. "It was real," she said of the scene. "I fought to keep it in. The producers were afraid people might not like me, [but] it was the most noted scene by reviewers, in a positive way." King called *Cujo* the best screen adaptation of his work, trumpeting that Wallace should have been up for an Oscar. *Cujo* marked the first of *six* adaptations of King's work to hit the big screen in less than four years; viewers would also see *The Dead Zone, Christine, Firestarter, Silver Bullet,* and *Cat's Eye* by the end of 1985.

Wallace's status as one of the film world's longest-reigning scream queens continued through the next few decades, as she appeared in *Critters, Popcorn,* and a multitude of other flicks, most of them made for television. "I'm a good screamer, and vulnerable and strong," she says, "A perfect medium for the girl!"

Then, in 1996, she finally decided to go on the evil offensive in the Peter Jackson–Michael J. Fox ghost-chasing *The Frighteners,* in which she plays Patricia, an innocent schoolgirl-type who turns out to be an evil serial killer. "I got to play this amazing arc of weak victim to bold killer," says Wallace. "What a ride! I think the picture is amazing."

Tragically, Christopher suddenly died of a heart attack during filming. "Peter Jackson is an amazing, kind, and obviously talented director," she says. "I was loved and supported by everyone [during filming] through a very difficult time."

While very few of us will ever be chased by cannibals, werewolves, ghosts, zombies, sharks, alligators, aliens, or anything else that so often terrorizes us on the film screen, Wallace, like many in her profession, urges budding performers to look within while looking for a place to start their own careers.

"Know yourself," she says. "Be yourself. Love yourself. Everyone will tell you you have to be different. [But] all they really want is the authentic you."

We want to believe Wallace's character in *The Frighteners.* We spend over an hour hoping that her Patricia Ann Bradley may have been just an innocent pawn in the game of Jake Busey's Johnny Bartlett, who took a dozen lives during his life and now steals them from the hereafter. But as more bodies pile up, we realize that she was in on it all along, the willing Manson family member to his Charles, the Bonnie to his Clyde.

We see Wallace as evil as never seen before. But when the film flashes back to the murders done alive, we meet the woman Patricia once was, the young girl who was never innocent, the youthful personification of her evil.

"I think I was too young to fully comprehend what an amazing opportunity the role gave me," remembers Nicola Cliff, the younger Patty. "At that age, I was just having fun doing what I loved doing. The role of Patricia was so alluring because it was dramatically dark and moody, with the chance to fire big shotguns—something that was far removed from my normal everyday teenage life in New Zealand!"

In a scene that's become far less entertaining since the mass shootings that ravaged America through the early 2000s, Patty and Johnny turn a hospital into a target practice range, remarking that they just want to set a new record when it comes to lives taken, a popular motive theory as to why these real-life tragedies keep occurring. "I've always believed in intuition when it comes to playing acting roles," Cliff says. "You either have a natural talent or you don't. I believe you can give people the tools to unlock abilities, but that can only go so far. I do play scenes out in my mind though as if I'm watching them on screen when learning lines, and have always tried to understand motives and empathize with the characters I play. I also listen to the director, and try to take their vision on board as much as I can, so it pays to be flexible."

Cliff calls a love scene with Busey on a mortuary slab, chopped from the final film, one of her toughest. "Peter Jackson used a real mortuary slab (with bars for drainage!) and a whole lot of fake blood," she recalls. "It was a closed set, and Jake Busey and I were basically directed to 'just go for it.' I ended up cutting a gash in my finger and having to get a tetanus shot straight afterwards."

According to Cliff, it's always important to remember realism. "Be as natural as you can to be as believable as you can," she says. "Ignore the cameras, director, crew, and immerse yourself in the scene. Pull your performance right in, and just say the lines for whoever you're acting with. Horror scenes seem to be much more thrilling when the performance is understated."

Cliff, Nicola. E-mail interview. August 14, 2013.
Rogak, Lisa. *Haunted Heart: The Life and Times of Stephen King.* New York: St. Martin's Press, 2008.
Szebin, Fred. "Dee Wallace-Stone." *Filmfax* 112 (Oct/Dec 1996): 71–73, 119.
Wallace, Dee. E-mail interview. July 30, 2009.
Wallace, Dee. Phone interview. July 16, 2010/March 28, 2013.
Wiater, Stanley, Christopher Golden, & Hank Wagner. *The Stephen King Universe.* Los Angeles: Renaissance Books, 2001.

Virginia Welch:
Prosecuting Casey Anthony

It's never been hard for America to find reasons for fury. Hundreds of innocents died at Oklahoma City, and the perpetrators never gave us the slightest reason. We'll never know why so many people in the wrong place at the wrong time died at Virginia Tech, in Connecticut, Arizona, and Colorado. Why so many people stood silently by while Jerry Sandusky victimized one child after another.

Sometimes the TV news is scarier than anything at the cinema. But in the movies, we can at least take solace in the bad guy or girl almost always getting their just deserts. Back home in reality, that doesn't always happen.

About twenty years ago, O.J. Simpson committed about the most obvious case of double murder in history, then laughed in our faces as our system let him walk away. The cretin's later armed robbery conviction for stealing a box of worthless crap in a Las Vegas hotel was both darkly hysterical and some pretty strong proof of karma.

In the last days of 2008, Florida, and eventually the nation, was shocked and saddened by the discovery of a young girl who'd never get the chance to live. But shock soon turned to anger. First, anger that a child was dead. Anger because Caylee Anthony's body had been thrown into the woods and brutally torn to shreds by animals.

And most of all, anger at the mother who'd partied away the days and weeks after her daughter was killed. Who did everything in her power—lying to cops, lying to her family—to stop people from learning the truth. Anger because she'd been the one who tossed her little girl's body out like a bag of trash, then apparently and gleefully forgotten that she'd ever existed.

Prosecutors put her on trial for the murder everyone knew she'd committed. Up until that fateful day in July 2011, millions hoped that the girl whom Casey Anthony had both given and stolen away life would get justice. But like the twelve who helped Simpson get away, another group stole justice away from Caylee, and we were left to wonder how these horrifying things can occur.

As is commonplace in America, it was only a short time before the story hit the small screen.

Rather than focusing much on the murder itself, *Prosecuting Casey Anthony* was more about the battle between those trying to put her away and those trying to help her *get* away. But the film would never have worked without a hell of an effort from someone entrusted with one of the most unenviable of acting tasks.

Who would have ever thought that bearing a physical resemblance to one of the world's most hated humans could come in handy? For one young actress, it did.

"I found my way into theater through talent shows at school," remembers Virginia Welch. "I had been choreographing dance routines and discovered I loved the feeling of being on stage and capturing the imagination of an audience. I started auditioning for school musicals and plays

Virginia Welch explored the realistic side of evil in the title role of *Prosecuting Casey Anthony*.

and from there was hooked." The Texas native calls the renowned Minnesota acting school Interlochen Arts Academy "my own personal Hogwarts!"

Regarding her big-screen debut, stage veteran Welch recalls getting the script for 2009's *Pandorum* very shortly before her work on the movie began.

"It was a mad dash," she recalls. "I was lucky to work with a great cast and crew and play on a fantastic set.

"After the mad scramble to memorize lines, the character work begins. Sometimes I build characters first through their speech patterns and vocal quality, sometimes it starts with their movements—the way they hold their body or how they sit in their clothing."

By the time the infamous Casey Anthony role came her way, Welch was a bit more used to running straight into character. "There is a lot of research either way to flesh out a character," Welch says, "but with actual people you have to honor any information that is already out there. I'm definitely more of a technical than method actor. I work from the outside in, letting physicality or costume or vocality influence me first. I do also sit down and figure out line by line the thoughts the character is, having to make her say each bit of dialogue."

Then there was the second hurdle to cross: portraying arguably America's most evil acquitted killer. But like those who played Simpson in TV movies about his case, those who have carried the lead in biographical films of every serial killer from Ted Bundy to Aileen Wuornos and everyone in between, she knew the role wasn't there for justification or explanation, just exploration.

"Most of my prep work for *Prosecuting Casey Anthony* was watching hours of courtroom, news, and jailhouse footage," she recalls. "Because I was portraying an actual person with minimal dialogue, I wanted to make sure that I could nail down all her mannerisms and facial expressions. Then I did some journaling as the character—I needed to find a way to connect with her. You can't get caught up in any judgments about who you are playing or you come off as false."

Once again, the film was more about the lawyers than the defendant. Rob Lowe was Jeff Ashton, confident he and his team would help Caylee find justice. Oscar Nuñez of *The Office* took a break from comedy to become Anthony's protector Jose Baez. Still, Anthony's eerily stoic face and ice-cold smile that still make her look like the Mona Lisa's evil twin showed up throughout, and her acquittal moment, a sad landmark in America legal history, brought Welch a new challenge.

"It was the first time I ever had to cry on screen," she says, "and the waterworks just had to keep on flowing! Journaling really helped in this particular area because it focused me and helped me create her reality and mindset for myself. Hours and hours of having to stay in a heightened emotional state was exhilarating but also exhausting. I would have to go on a run or watch a feel-good romantic comedy to let myself mentally check out and relax after each day wrapped."

Welch, Virginia. E-mail interview. Nov. 8, 2013.

Ian Whyte: *Aliens vs. Predator* and *Requiem*

For nearly two decades, Ian Whyte outshot, blocked, and intimidated fellow basketball court combatants around the world (being over seven feet tall gives one quite the advantage in that department). Cager fans in France, Belgium, Portugal, Greece, and America watched him vanquish one opponent after another.

But no athlete can ever really defeat the opponent known as time: In his 30s, Whyte knew that the basketball career that had enveloped so much of his life was coming to an end.

Finishing up his sporting career back in his English homeland, he tried to think of new outlets.

"I was going through a very personal process of introspection and evaluation of what I was going to do next with my life, after I stopped playing," recalls Whyte, who hung up his high tops in 2002. "Boredom had set in and I had already made the decision to look for something else to light a fire beneath me."

A phone call from a casting agent gave him the chance to battle an enemy far more dangerous than any point guard or power forward.

"Quite simply, the Predator is one of the most iconic monsters in movie history," says Whyte. "I didn't have to think twice about it." He quickly signed on to become the new version of the space critter that ambushed Arnold Schwarzenegger in 1987 as two sci-fi icons went claw to claw in 2004's *Aliens vs. Predator*.

A longtime fan of the first two *Predator* movies, Whyte took a stroll down movie memory lane.

"I sat down and watched, frame by frame, the first two Predator films," he remembers,

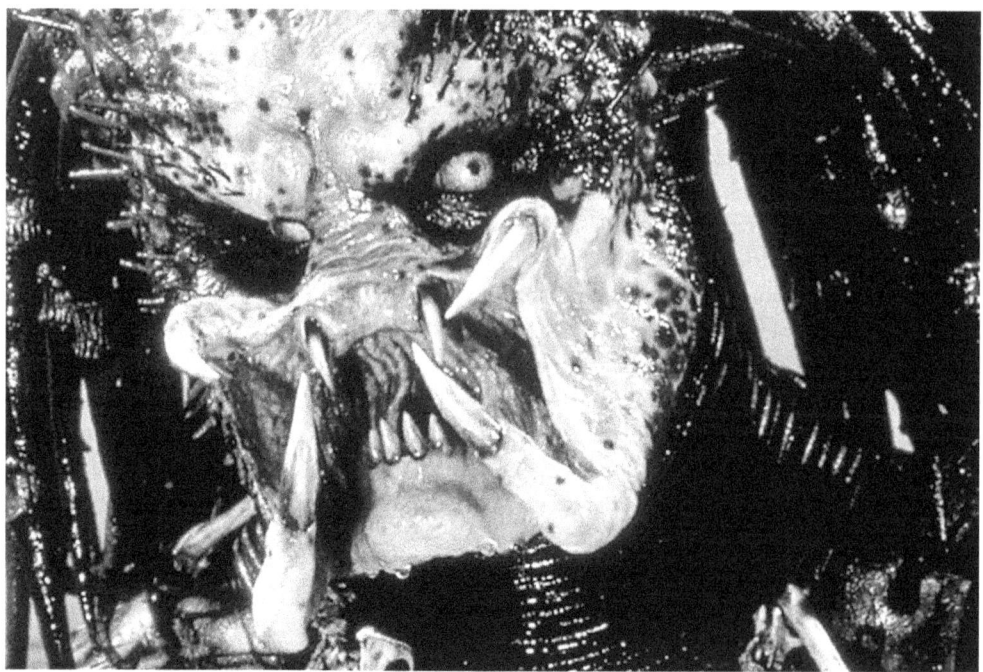

As of early 2014, the Predator travelled across outer space to find its prey through five films.

"so that I could extrapolate some sort of movement, a character reference from the original performance. Had [original Predator Kevin Peter Hall] been around to ask questions of, I probably would have spent a lot of time picking his brains on the rudiments of the role in particular and costume performance in general."

After over 15 years of basketball court action, Whyte figured his body could withstand just about anything. Little did he know that his new "uniform" would dwarf any attire he'd previously put on.

"I had trained as a basketball player since the age of 15," he says, "but the physical requirements of actually acting through the costume, and indeed the weight of the costume itself, was a sharp wakeup call." To develop his Predator prowess, Whyte trained with a combat vest weighted down with bricks for over a month before filming began.

Tom Woodruff, who worked on the special effects of the last three *Alien* films—winning an Oscar for his work in 1993's *Death Becomes Her*—helped familiarize Whyte with the part.

"The costume and mask provided a luxury that few actors actually have and in effect it was a doubled-edged sword," Whyte explains. "On the one hand, I could completely let go of my inhibitions. Underneath the mask, I'm doing all the facial expressions, but the camera only sees the mask, and the helmet and the facial expressions are radio-controlled by expert puppeteers, so as long as you can correlate your movement and emotional timing with your puppeteers, everything should go fine."

Still, he couldn't allow the costume and mechanics to get *all* the attention. Even without his voice, visible face work, or a great deal of body language, Whyte had to give his creation some personality, and used his past training in martial arts to speak without his mouth. "That is when body language comes into play. A simple tilt or nod of the head, movement in the shoulders, fingers, the forming of a fist, the slightest movement becomes all-important to convey exactly what the face would be conveying if it were on camera."

Before the six months of filming ended, Whyte knew he'd want to put on the outfit again, and just hoped he'd get the chance. He says that playing the Predator "got me in the best shape of my life. I knew after the first one that I didn't want to see anyone else in the Predator costume if I had anything to do with it." Three years later, film fans got a gory Christmas present with *Aliens vs. Predator: Requiem*. Utilizing the same martial arts techniques that had helped him do the job in the first place, Whyte had a second chance to hunt down some aliens.

The first flick had been tough to put together, and the reunion was much more difficult. "The whole thing was shot in three months and we managed to squeeze twice as much Predator action into the film as before. On top of that, the film was shot almost entirely in the rain on location in British Columbia, which, although beautiful, is very far removed from being a tropical paradise. When the freezing cold rain was not pouring down from massive rain towers onto my head, I was up to my waist in freezing water or on many occasions completely submerged."

The parts when guns blazed and bodies fell in the sewer, thermal plant, and hospital are Whyte's favorite scenes. "All were wet and cold, and all required a great deal of commitment to get right," he says. "The whole entire film was tough to do, [but] that's what made it so enjoyable! I'm a bit of a martyr to it: The tougher the part, the harder I work and the more rewarding the end result."

In 2005, Whyte and Frances de la Tour teamed up to become Madame Olympe Maxime, the giantess headmistress of Beauxbatons Academy that brings some of her students to take on Harry Potter and his Hogwarts colleagues in *Harry Potter and the Goblet of Fire.*

"Some of the creature effects artists working on *Aliens vs. Predator* had previously been involved in the *Harry Potter* films," he says. "They suggested I contact the Harry Potter creature designer for when *Aliens vs. Predator* finished and was invited to come and see him."

Things worked out quickly, and Whyte went about developing his ultra-feminine side.

"I had never been on stilts before," he says, "and never been a woman before, let alone a lady as sublime as Frances, so [I had] four months of stilt training, studying footage of Frances' feminine wiles, posture training, Pilates, dance choreography and learning the lines ensued before I even set foot in front of a camera."

While de la Tour handled much of Maxime's close-up work, Whyte was the wide-shot person, with de la Tour always there to help him out. "Frances was on set to offer advice, which is a luxury that doubles do not enjoy," he says. "If a double is employed to deliver a performance, it is usually because the main actor is not available or a stunt performer is required. Because this character was so specialized, it really required a team effort."

One morning during filming, the acting veteran walked up to her partner in performing. "Darling, you're acting," she told him.

"Yes," Whyte said. "How am I doing?"

De la Tour had one simple piece of advice.

"Stop acting," she demanded. "Be yourself!"

It's counsel that he still takes to every audition. "Don't become disillusioned if you fail to get parts, or spend a great deal of time wondering where the next part is coming from," Whyte tells upcoming actors. "The list of parts that I have dearly wanted, but lost out on, grows by the day and far exceeds the great projects that I have been involved in. To be able to deliver a performance and bring joy to an audience is a privileged position and deserves hard work."

When another round of predators came to do their thing in 2010's *Predators,* the situations were, well, somewhat altered. Now, the homo sapien prey was on the creatures' homeland, and Arnold Schwarzenegger, Jessie Ventura, and Carl Weathers had been replaced by Adrian Brody, Alice Bragg, and Topher Grace.

And just as he had resurrected one superhuman horror icon the year before in *Friday the 13th,* Derek Mears became another super–non-human this time around, playing the alien king.

"It is fucking cool!" says Mears. "My fanboy mind has been blown. This time around they have some new Predators and there are different races. They are a little taller, a little leaner, a little darker and their technology is a little more advanced. When I saw the new designs, I thought that they were really, really cool."

Aside from checking out the first few *Predator* flicks, Mears got in the same shape he'd been in as Jason Voorhees. "I knew I was going to be zipped up in a giant monster suit," he says. "I did a lot of endurance training. I was trying to figure out with the character how to make it more fluent and animalistic. When I didn't wear the battle helmet and just had a mask, they had to glue black rubber donuts over my eyes for padding. Then put my contacts in, so that took a little extra time."

Still, even getting into the Predator suit required between an hour and ninety minutes a day, he continues. "The first thing I thought was, 'Where is the zipper?' so in case I have to go to the bathroom, I can relieve myself," he says. "I was really excited when I put the outfit on because the way it felt and moved, it was made for my body. Sometimes when you wear different prosthetics and monster suits you have to over-exaggerate what you are doing. With this it was so super thin and skin tight."

Just as with Mr. Voorhees, he'd have to scare without face or voice. "People might think 'Oh, you're just a big guy, so you just put on a big mask and roar!' But that's not me. Language is only ten percent of communication. Mentally, you make your character, who that character is in the blueprint of the script. The energy transfers through the makeup in whatever you're doing on camera."

Early on in the original *Predator*, and several times throughout the sequel and other films, the flicks made sure to point out that the title character, or characters, weren't malicious, not just there because they liked to hurt people. They were hunters, there for the sport, not the death. In the first film, a Predator passes over an innocent women to square off with a bunch of Marines. In the second, the Predators battle armed police officers, drug dealers, and soldiers to the death, but not only allow the elderly and unarmed to escape, but award a human who manages to bump off one of their predatory colleagues.

Fresh off playing Bigfoot in *Harry and the Hendersons* (a role he'd reprise in the film's TV show spin-off), Kevin Peter Hall was getting ready to become the alien in the first film—and he was looking to create a being of the hunt, not the slaughter. Only this time, the humans would be on the hunted defensive.

"This Predator is really wonderful, because of the character, the hunting," Hall remembered. "There's already the incentive to get into it, because you're going to get to be going after Arnold Schwarzenegger. But on top of all that, there's creating a personality that the audience can relate to, because without it, then it's just something from somewhere else, whereas this is a real conflict, and this is real important in this movie that the audience get a sense of who it is."

Like Whyte and Mears, Hall was left without facial features, human characteristics, and a voice (well, his own, as the Predator's speech belonged to Peter Cullen, who'd later voice Optimus Prime in the *Transformers* movies). This character's inside would have to come out physically, and after years of basketball, martial arts, and even ballet, he knew all about outer expression.

"Every part you take on poses some challenges," explained Hall, "and being in a suit makes more challenges, because you wonder how much of your performance is actually going to come through. Most people think that when you prepare for a role like this, it's mostly just physical, just jogging and pushups and movement, and all of that's very important, because it's really rough work. But there was also a lot of thought into what kind of movement, what kind of plane he came from. You work on the inner things that are going on in the character, just as you would any other character. I like the spark, the life inside. Without that, you just have a suit." He did accidentally clock Schwarzenegger in the head during filming.

After spending so much of the film trying to kill the Marines, Hall also played the helicopter pilot who came to help rescue them at the end.

He'd reprise the Predator role in the film's 1990 sequel. Tragically, he passed away the next year after contracting AIDS from a blood transfusion.

"What's great about playing the Predator is that he is the star character, and the movie hinges on him," Hall said of part two. "Early in my career I felt like I was just another guy in a suit. Now I know that whether or not this movie works depends on whether audiences believe this creature."

Gencarelli, Mike. "Interview with Derek Mears, Pt.2." *Movie Mike's*. July 9, 2010. Retrieved Feb. 1, 2011, from http://moviemikes.com/2010/07/interview-with-predators-derek-mears/.
Mears, Derek. Personal interview. May 10, 11, 2013.
Kevin Peter Hall. Dec. 23, 2009. Retrieved Jan. 16, 2010, from http://kevinpeterhall.com/.
McTiernan, John, Dir. *Predator* [DVD]. Los Angeles: Davis Entertainment.
Shapiro, Marc. "'Predator 2' Stalks the Urban Jungle." *Fangoria* (Dec. 1990): 37–40, 62.
Whyte, Ian. E-mail interview. Jan. 17, 2012.

References

"Actress Blythe Auffarth Featuring The Girl Next Door." *Killer Reviews*. 2009. Retrieved Oct. 18, 2011, from http://www.killerreviews.com/dispinterview.php?intid=1572.

"Actress Shawnee Smith Featuring 'Saw 3.'" *Killer Reviews*. 2013. Retrieved Sept. 9, 2013, from http://www.killerreviews.com/dispinterview.php?intid=1598.

Aloisi, Michael & Kane Hodder. *Unmasked*. U.S.: Dark Ink, 2011.

ArchivesOfTheDead. "Night Of The Living Dead Duane Jones Interview." Youtube. Jan. 27, 2009. Retrieved on Jan. 22, 2014, from http://www.youtube.com/watch?v=DZSQxiZ-df8.

Argyis, Michelle. E-mail interview. June 14, 2013.

Askew, Desmond. E-mail interview. July 19, 2013.

Auffarth, Blythe. E-mail interview. Oct. 18, 2011.

BackStageCasting. "'Paranormal Activity' Cast Interview." Nov. 6, 2009. Retrieved May 19, 2010, from http://www.youtube.com/watch?v=kHK-RjW_lpM.

Bain, Whitney Scott. "Interview: Pollyanna McIntosh, Star of 'THE WOMAN.'" *Starburst Magazine*. Oct. 31, 2011. Retrieved Sept. 17, 2012, from http://www.starburstmagazine.com/features/feature-articles/1246-interview-with-pollyanna-mcintosh-star-of-the-woman.

Baiss, Bridget. *The Crow: The Story Behind the Film*. London: Titan Books, 2004.

Balaski, Belinda. Phone interview. June 11, 2010.

Balme, Timothy. E-mail interview. Oct. 8, 2012.

Bank, Ashley. Phone interview. April 24, 2010.

Barker, Clive, Dir. *Hellraiser* [DVD]. Cinemarque Entertinment BV.

BarryAce. "Kane Hodder Interview." Youtube. Nov. 27, 2008. Retrieved Dec. 12, 2010, from http://www.youtube.com/watch?v=8o9Z0gOSRD4.

"Behind the Mask with George P. Wilbur." *Horror Bid*. n.d. Retrieved July 11, 2011, from http://www.horrorbid.com/forum/viewtopic.php?f=210&t=3028.

Beeler, Michael. "Valentina Vargas Raises a Little Hell." *Femme Fatales* 3 (Spring 1995): 4, 24–31, 61.

Bell, Tobin. Phone interview. May 28, 2008.

Bent, Lyriq. Phone interview. July 24, 2013.

Berryman, Michael. Phone interview. March 20, 2013.

BillyBushShow. "Paranormal Activity—Katie Featherston and Micah Sloat—Part 1." Youtube. Nov. 2, 2009. Retrieved May 20, 2010, from http://www.youtube.com/watch?v=lX5uU1Q-Z9k&feature=related.

Bogdanovich, Peter. *Who The Hell's in It*. New York: Alfred A. Knopf, 2004.

Bradley, Doug. *Behind the Mask of the Horror Actor*. London: Titan Books, 2004.

Bradley, Doug. Personal interview. May 10, 11, 2013.

"Brandon Lee's Final Interview." *The Crow: Believe In Angels*. 2002. Retrieved on April 15, 2010, from http://inner_mercy.tripod.com/Last_Int.html.

"Brandon Lee's Last Interview." *EW.com*. 1994. Retrieved April 15, 2010, from http://www.ew.com/ew/article/0,,302196,00.html.

Breck, Jonathan. Phone interview. April 3, 2010.

Brewer, Jamie. Phone interview. Jan. 5, 2014.

Brooker, Richard. *Richard J. Brooker*. 2007. Retrieved Dec. 12, 2010, from http://www.richardjbrooker.com/index.html.

Carle, Chris. "Comic-Con 2005: IGN Interviews Sid Haig." *IGN.* July 15, 2005. Retrieved June 5, 2012, from http://www.ign.com/articles/2005/07/17/comic-con-2005-ign-interviews-sid-haig.

Carlton, Hope Marie. E-mail interview. May 17, 2011.

Carpenter, John (Director). *Halloween* [DVD]. U.S.: Compass International Pictures, 1978.

Chbosky, Stacy. E-mail interview. Dec. 9, 2013.

Clark, Sean. "Dash, Steve ('Friday the 13th Part 2')." *Dread Central.* 2006. Retrieved May 29, 2010, from http://www.dreadcentral.com/interviews/dash-steve-friday-13th-part-2.

Cliff, Nicola. E-mail interview. Aug. 14, 2013.

Coe, Terry. "Nick Principe." *The Horror Asylum.* Dec. 1. 2010. Retrieved Aug. 14, 2012, from http://www.horror-asylum.com/interview/nick-principe/interview.asp.

Coet, Noelle. E-mail interview. Jan. 16, 2014.

Cunningham, Lora. E-mail interview. Oct. 1, 2010.

Dan. "An Interview with Danielle Harris." *GeekaDelphia.* Feb. 24, 2011. Retrieved Sept. 11, 2012, from http://geekadelphia.com/2011/02/24/hatchet-2-an-interview-with-danielle-harris/.

Dash, Steve. E-mail interview. Nov. 30, 2013.

Davis, Rochelle. Phone interview. March 20, 2013.

"DEADPIT Interviews: Ari Lehman aka First Jason!" Youtube. March 28, 2008. Retrieved April 4, 2010, from http://www.youtube.com/watch?v=nkfQGHfza6I.

Dean, Lezlie. E-mail interview. April 25, 2010.

Dekker, Fred. *The Monster Squad* [DVD]. Santa Monica, CA: HBO, 1987.

Demme, Jonathan, Dir. *The Silence of the Lambs* [DVD]. U.S.: Orion Pictures, 1991.

Dourif, Fiona. Phone interview. Dec. 1, 2013.

Eichenbaum, Rose. *The Actor Within.* Middletown, CT: Wesleyan University Press, 2011.

Elmstreetgirl22. "Original Halloween Q&A Panel at Monster Mania 13." Youtube. Aug. 24, 2009. Retrieved Jan. 16, 2014, from http://www.youtube.com/watch?v=ju1T7ccawiw.

Eramo, Steve. "Savage Instinct: Interview with *The Woman*'s Pollyanna McIntosh." *The Morton Report.* Nov. 16, 2011. Retrieved Sept. 17, 2012, from http://www.themortonreport.com/entertainment/film/savage-instinct-interview-with-the-womans-pollyanna-mcintosh/.

"Exclusive—Interview with Dan Yeager." *Horror Pilot.* 2013. Retrieved Sept. 10, 2013, from http://www.horrorpilot.com/exclusiv-interview-with-dan-yeager-texas-chainsaw-massacre-3d/.

Faraci, Dennis. "Exclusive! The New Jason Speaks." *Chud.* Feb. 12, 2009. Retrieved Dec. 12, 2010, from http://www.chud.com/articles/articles/18143/1/exclusive-the-new-jason-speaks-derek-mears-interview/Page1.html.

Farinella, Tony. "Danielle Harris of Halloween 4 and 5 Interview." *Matchflick.* 2013. Retrieved Sept. 10, 2012, from http://www.matchflick.com/column/1498.

Farrands, Daniel. *His Name Was Jason: 30 Years of Friday the 13th* [DVD]. Masimedia, 2009.

Farrands, Daniel, and Andrew Kasch. *Never Sleep Again: The Elm Street Legacy* [DVD]. 1428 Films, 2010.

Felton, Bruce, and Mark Fowler. *The Best, Worst, and Most Unusual.* New York: Galahad Books, 1976.

Ferrante, Anthony C. "Hellraiser IV: Bloodline." *Fangoria* 141 (April 1995): 40–45, 69.

Ferrante, Tim. "A Farewell to Duane Jones." *Fangoria* 80 (Feb. 1989): 14–18, 64.

Fierman, Hannah. E-mail interview. Dec. 18–19, 2012.

Frances, Laura. "Interview: Director John Luessenhop and Leatherface Actor Dan Yeager on 'Texas Chainsaw 3D.'" *Screen Crave.* Jan. 3, 2013. Retrieved Sept. 10, 2013, from http://screencrave.com/2013-01-03/interview-director-john-luessenhop-leatherface-actor-dan-yeager-texas-chainsaw-3d/.

Frappler, Rob. "Interview with Horror Icon Tony Todd." *Screen Rant.* 2013. Retrieved June 14, 2013, from http://screenrant.com/tony-todd-interview-hatchet-final-destination-robf-80905/all/1/.

Freeman, Royce. "Kane Hodder." *Pit of Horror.* n.d. Retrieved Dec. 12, 2010, from http://www.pitofhorror.com/main/hodder.html.

Galluzzo, Rob. "FRIGHT INTERVIEW—Nick Principe (Chromeskull of 'LAID TO REST')!" *Icons of Fright.* Oct. 27, 2011. Retrieved Aug. 14, 2012, from http://iconsoffright.com/2011/10/27/fright-interview-nick-principe-chromeskull-of-laid-to-rest/.

Garentano, Christopher P. "An Interview with Sid Haig." *Icons of Fright.* 2006. Retrieved June 4, 2012, from http://www.iconsoffright.com/IV_SidAYG.htm.

Gencarelli, Mike. "Interview with Derek Mears, Pt.2." *Movie Mike's*. July 9, 2010. Retrieved Feb. 1, 2011, from http://moviemikes.com/2010/07/interview-with-predators-derek-mears/.

Goodson, William Wilson. "A Tribute to Brandon Lee: Martial Arts Legends. Brandon Lee's Last Interview." n.d. Retrieved April 15, 2010, from http://stickgrappler.tripod.com/articles/brandonlast.html.

Graham, C.J. Phone interview. Jan. 6, 2014.

Grossman, Naomi. E-mail interview. Jan. 6, 2014.

Haig, Sid. Personal interview. Nov. 11, 2012.

"Halloween: Daeg Faerch and Tyler Mane Interview." Cinema.com. 2011. Retrieved July 11, 2011, from http://www.cinema.com/articles/5193/halloween-daeg-faerch-and-tyler-mane-interview.phtml.

Halloween II Retrospective. *Halloween Movies*. Oct. 31, 2006. Retrieved July 11, 2011, from http://www.halloweenmovies.com/h2retro/dickwarlock_lobby.html.

Harris, Danielle. Personal interview. May 2, 2012.

Harris, Will. "Done Raising Hell?" *The Virginian Pilot*, May 9, 2013, p. 4.

Hayward, Sarah. Phone interview. July 9, 2013.

Hodder, Kane. Personal interview. Nov. 11, 2012.

Hoffman, Leslie. E-mail interview. May 9, 2013.

Hogan, Erin Marie. Phone interview. Feb. 19, 2010.

Horror News.net. 2008. Retrieved Jan. 16, 2010, from http://www.horrornews.net/.

"Horror News Podcasts: Camille Keaton." *Horror News*. Sept. 19, 2010. Retrieved March 27, 2011, from http://horrornews.net/podcasts/09.19.10_Horrornews.net_podcast.mp3.

Hutchinson, Stefan. *Halloween: 25 Years of Terror* [DVD]. Paramount Pictures, 2006.

"Interview: Michael Bailey Smith." *Movie Hole*. Feb. 24, 2006. Retrieved July 25, 2013 from http://moviehole.net/20068417interview-michael-bailey-smith#JGGYF3StCtrcmt6B.99.

"Interview with Patricia Tallman." *Icons of Fright*. June 2005. Retrieved May 26, 2010, from http://www.iconsoffright.com/IV_Pat.htm.

"Interview with Sid Haig." *Badmouth*. 2012. Retrieved June 10, 2012, from http://badmouth.net/interview-sid-haig/.

"Interview with Warrington Gillette." Fright Exclusive Interview. *Icons of Fright*. June 2004. Retrieved on May 29, 2010, from http://www.iconsoffright.com/IV_Jason2.htm.

Jar385. "Horror on the Boulevard 2012: Tim Interviews Kim Myers and Mark Patton." Youtube. March 1, 2013. Retrieved July 25, 2013, from http://www.youtube.com/watch?v=d1blzro4R-0.

"JASONS (FRIDAY THE 13th) CINEMA WASTELAND." Youtube. Dec. 3, 2008. Retrieved April 4, 2010, from http://www.youtube.com/watch?v=DPQdtGcMVjc.

JimmyO. "Interview: Shawnee Smith." *Arrow in the Head*. Nov. 18, 2008. Retrieved Sept. 9, 2013, from http://www.joblo.com/horror-movies/news/interview-shawnee-smith-02&order=popular.

Johnson, Bill. Phone interview. March 25, 2012.

Jones, Stephen. *Clive Barker's A-Z of Horror*. New York: BBC Books, 1997.

Joseph, Jackie. Phone interview. Feb. 12, 2014.

Joy, Robert. Personal interview. April 3, 2013.

Juvinall, Michael. "More Horror Exclusive: Interview with Captain Spaulding Himself: Sid Haig." *More Horror*. 2013. Retrieved June 5, 2012, from http://www.morehorror.com/More-Horror-Exclusive-Interview-with-Captain-Spaulding-Himself-Sid-Haig.

Juvinall, Michael. "More Horror Exclusive: Interview with Michael Berryman." *More Horror*. 2013. Retrieved July 25, 2013, from http://www.morehorror.com/More-Horror-Exclusive-Interview-with-Michael-Berryman.

Kane, Paul. *The Hellraiser Films and Their Legacy*. Jefferson, NC: McFarland, 2006.

Kara, Patricia. E-mail interview. Aug. 4, 2013.

Karnow, Michael. Phone interview. Feb. 17, 2010.

Kassir, John. Personal interview. May 25, 2013.

Katz, Alex. "Interview: Pollyanna McIntosh, The Woman." *Flixist*. Oct. 13, 2011. Retrieved on Sept. 17, 2012, from http://www.flixist.com/interview-pollyanna-mcintosh-the-woman-205170.phtml.

Keaton, Camille. Personal interview. April 20, 2012.

Keehnen, Owen. *Racks and Razors*. n.d. Retrieved April 4, 2010, from http://www.racksandrazors.com/arilehman.html.

Kerswell, J.A. *The Slasher Movie Book*. Chicago: Chicago Review Press, 2012.

Kevin Peter Hall. Dec. 23, 2009. Retrieved on Jan. 16, 2010, from http://kevinpeterhall.com/.

King, Adrienne. E-mail interview. Oct. 11, 2013.

King, Adrienne. Personal interview. Nov. 11, 2012.

King, Adrienne. Phone interview. April 22, 2009.

King, Nick. Phone interview. Sept. 18, 2013.
Kirzinger, Ken. E-mail interview. Jan. 15, 2014.
Kuhns, Rob, Dir. *Birth of the Living Dead* [DVD]. New York: Predestinate Productions, 2013.
"L.A. Screening: Clare Foley." *Trailer Addict*. 2012. Retrieved Sept. 22, 2013, from http://www.traileraddict.com/trailer/sinister/la-screening-clare-foley.
Lanier-Bramlett, Suze. E-mail interview. March 27, 2013.
Laurence, Ashley, interview. *Monsters from the Basement*. n.d. Retrieved Aug. 6, 2013, from http://monstersfromthebasement.com/interviews/ashley-laurence/.
Lawton, Adam. "Interview with Tony Moran." *Movie Mikes*. Jan. 6, 2011. Retrieved July 11, 2011, from http://moviemikes.com/2011/01/interview-with-tony-moran/.
Layne, Staci. "Nick Principe in 'ChromeSkull: Laid to Rest 2'—Exclusive Interview." *Horror*. Sept. 9, 2011. Retrieved Aug. 14, 2012, from http://www.horror.com/php/article-3664-1.html.
Locke, Peter. Phone interview. April 9, 2013.
Luessenhop, John. *Texas Chainsaw 3D* [DVD]. U.S.: Lionsgate, 2013.
Lyne, Adrien, Dir. *Jacob's Ladder* [DVD]. U.S.: Carolco Pictures.
MacKay, Michael Reid. Phone interview. May 30, 2013.
Mallory-McCree, J. Phone interview. May 3, 2013.
Mane, Tyler. Phone interview. Jan. 13, 2014.
Manzetti, Alessandro. "The Woman: Interview with Pollyanna McIntosh." *Mezzotints*. April 11, 2011. Retrieved Sept. 17, 2012, from http://postonero.blogspot.com/2011/04/woman-interview-with-pollyanna-mcintosh.html.
Marcigliano, Alexa. Phone interview. March 12, 2013.
Martin, Todd. "Interview: Michael Berryman (Below Zero)." *HorrorNews*. Aug. 19, 2012. Retrieved July 25, 2013, from http://horrornews.net/55889/interview-michael-berryman-below-zero/#fbJT60cWpkut7idX.99.
Mauro, Eve. Phone interview. Feb. 19, 2013.
McGinn, Chris. Phone interview. June 28, 2012.
McIntee, David. *Beautiful Monsters*. England: Telos, 2005.
McTiernan, John, Dir. *Predator* [DVD]. Los Angeles: Davis Entertainment.
Mears, Derek. Personal interview. May 10, 11, 2013.
"Michael Bailey Smith." *Pit of Horror*. Retrieved July 25, 2013, from http://www.pitofhorror.com/newdesign/interviews/baileysmith.htm.
"Michael Myers." *Chasing the Frog*. Retrieved Jan. 16, 2014, from http://www.chasingthefrog.com/unmasked/michaelmyers.php.
Mihailoff, R.A. Phone interview. March 9, 2012.
Mondozilla. "Michael Berryman." *Horrorpedia*. March 12, 2013. Retrieved July 25, 2013, from http://horrorpedia.com/2013/03/12/michael-berryman-actor-article-and-interview/.
Morton, Eugene. "Paranormal Activity Interview with Katie Featherson & Micah Sloat." *Attack of the Show*. Oct. 28, 2009. Retrieved May 19, 2010, from http://g4tv.com/attackoftheshow/moviesandtv/68884/paranormal-activity-interview-with-katie-featherson—micah-sloat.html#ixzz0oRGRHE00.
Murray, Rebecca. "Shawnee Smith Returns as Jigsaw's Partner in Crime in 'Saw III.'" About.com. 2013. Retrieved Sept. 9, 2013, from http://movies.about.com/od/saw3/a/saw3ss102306.htm.
Natty. "Fright Interview with Scream Queen/Hatchet III Star Danielle Harris." *Icons of Fright*. Aug. 8, 2013. Retrieved Aug. 17, 2013, from http://iconsoffright.com/2013/08/08/fright-exclusive-interview-with-scream-queenhatchet-iii-star-danielle-harris-2/?utm_source=rss&utm_medium=rss&utm_campaign=fright-exclusive-interview-with-scream-queenhatchet-iii-star-danielle-harris-2.
Naylor, Zoe. Phone/E-mail interview. August 26, 2011.
Nemiroff, Perri. "'Texas Chainsaw 3D' Interview: Dan Yeager's Leatherface is a Family Man." *Screen Rant*. Jan. 2013. Retrieved Sept. 10, 2013, from http://screenrant.com/texas-chainsaw-3d-interview-dan-yeager/.
Neumyer, Scott. "Exclusive: Tony Todd Talks 'Night of the Living Dead,' 'Candyman,' and That Iconic Voice." *Fear Net*. Oct. 10, 2012, Retrieved June 14, 2013, from http://www.fearnet.com/news/interview/exclusive-tony-todd-talks-night-living-dead-candyman-and-iconic-voice.
Newgen, Heather. "Interview: Halloween II's Scout Taylor-Compton." *Shock Till You Drop*. Aug. 26, 2009. Retrieved July 11, 2011, from http://www.shocktillyoudrop.com/news/topnews.php?id=11532.

Noe, Denise. "The Torturing Death of Sylvia Marie Likens." *TruTV*. 2012. Retrieved Oct. 19, 2011, from http://www.trutv.com/library/crime/notorious_murders/young/likens/1.html.

Nutman, Philip. "King Talks." *Fangoria* (Dec. 1990): 22–26, 59.

Otherin-Girard, Dominique, Dir. *Halloween 5* [DVD]. U.S.: Magnum Pictures, 1989.

Owen, Lyla Hay. Phone interview. January 9, 2011.

Palmer, Betsy. Phone interview. Jan. 23, 2009.

Park Lincoln, Lar. Personal interview. May 11, 2013.

Parker, Katie. Phone/E-mail interview. May 2,3, 2012.

Pednaud, J. Tithonus. "Rondo Hatton—The Creeper." *The Human Marvels*. 2012. Retrieved Feb. 12, 2013, from http://thehumanmarvels.com/850/rondo-hatton-%e2%80%93-the-creeper/disfigured.

Pena, Elizabeth. Phone interview. Dec. 3, 2009.

Perera, Fia. Phone interview. March 2, 2010.

Principe, Nick. E-mail interview. June 9, 2012.

"Q&A with Ari Lehman webisode 1: Friday the 13th content and surprise." Youtube. July 12, 2008. Retrieved April 4, 2010, from http://www.youtube.com/watch?v=k66KUJxPUv0&feature=related.

"Q&A with Ari Lehman webisode 5: How he got the part." Youtube. July 12, 2008. Retrieved April 4, 2010, from http://www.youtube.com/watch?v=EoR9SRZW5yc&feature=related.

"Q&A with Ari Lehman webisode 7: Compares New Jason and old Jason." Youtube. July 12, 2008. Retrieved April 4, 2010, from http://www.youtube.com/watch?v=gtXLEpD6jeg&feature=related.

"Q&A with Ari Lehman webisode 8: Jason and influences." Youtube. July 12, 2008. Retrieved April 4, 2010, from http://www.youtube.com/watch?v=3zHD_b-X7JI&feature=related.

"Q&A with Ari Lehman webisode 9: favorite Jason." Youtube. July 12, 2008. Retrieved April 4, 2010, from http://www.youtube.com/watch?v=r4vQtK613DU&feature=related.

Raimi, Sam, Dir. *Drag Me to Hell* [DVD]. U.S.: Universal Studios, 2009.

Raver, Lorna. Phone interview. Dec. 16, 2011.

Ray, Fred Olen. "Rondo Hatton: Monster Man." *Midnight Marquee* 37 (Fall 1988): 87–93.

Red Carpet News. "Danielle Harris Interview: Halloween and Action Stars." Youtube. July 9, 2012. Retrieved Sept. 10, 2013, from http://www.youtube.com/watch?v=47PksSy6344.

Reinåmo, Silje. E-mail interview. January 10, 2013.

Reynolds, Simon. "Katie Featherston interview: 'I still find "Paranormal Activity" scary.'" *Digital Spy*. Oct. 18, 2012. Retrieved March 14, 2013, from http://www.digitalspy.com/movies/interviews/a431704/katie-featherston-interview-i-still-find-paranormal-activity-scary.html.

"Rob Zombie Interviews Danielle Harris." *AMC*. 2007. Retrieved Sept. 10, 2012, from http://www.amctv.com/videos/rob-zombie-interviews-danielle-harris.

Robg. "Fright Exclusive Interview." *Icons of Fright*. Oct. 2004. Retrieved July 11, 2011, from http://www.iconsoffright.com/IV_Brad.htm.

Robg. "Fright Exclusive Interview." *Icons of Fright*. Oct. 2005. Retrieved July 11, 2011, from http://www.iconsoffright.com/IV_Don.html.

Robinson, Julianna. Phone interview. March 18, 2013.

Rogak, Lisa. *Haunted Heart: The Life and Times of Stephen King*. New York: St. Martin's Press, 2008.

Rollans, Scott. "Angela's Slashes." *Fangoria* 262 (April 2007): 66–69.

Rose, Felissa. Personal interview. April 20, 2012.

Russell, Betsy. E-mail interview. Aug. 1, 2010.

Schwartz, Missy. "A Shocking Hit." EW.com. Oct. 30, 2009. Retrieved May 24, 2010, from http://www.ew.com/ew/article/0,,20316189,00.html.

Shapiro, Marc. "Hodder Than Ever." *Fangoria* (Jan. 2007): 31

Shapiro, Marc. "'Predator 2' Stalks the Urban Jungle." *Fangoria* (Dec. 1990): 37–40, 62.

Shapiro, Marc. "The Women of Crystal Lake." *Fangoria* 83 (June 1989): 18–21.

Shinas, Sofia. *The Crow—A Dead Man Visits You*. 2007. Retrieved April 15, 2010, from http://deadman.crowfans.com/crow_shinas.html.

Smith, Nigel. "Meet Pollyanna McIntosh, The Woman Behind 'The Woman.'" *IndieWire*. Oct. 11, 2011. Retrieved Sept. 17, 2012, from http://www.indiewire.com/article/interview_pollyanna_mcintosh_the_woman_behind_the_woman_on_sundances_most_c.

Smith, Richard Harland. "Everybody Talks About Rondo, But Nobody Does Anything About Him." *Movie Morlocks*. Feb. 24, 2009. Retrieved Feb. 12, 2013, from http://movie

morlocks.com/2009/02/24/everybody-talks-about-rondo-but-nobody-does-anything-about-him/.

SmithAcitivity. "Paranormal Activity Actors Interview—Stars of Paranormal Activity—Katie and Micah." Youtube. Oct. 27, 2009. Retrieved May 19, 2010, from http://www.youtube.com/watch?v=dcpQAKbAeLg.

Steel, Amy. Personal interview. Nov. 11, 2012.

Swift, Susan. Phone interview. July 11, 2012.

Szebin, Fred. "Dee Wallace-Stone." *Filmfax* 112 (Oct/Dec 1996): 71–73, 119.

"Talking with the Dead: 13 Questions with Barbie Wilde." *Horror Society.* June 4, 2013. Retrieved Aug. 6, 2013, from http://www.horrorsociety.com/2013/06/04/talking-with-the-dead-13-questions-with-barbie-wilde-female-Cenobite-and-the-venus-complex-author/.

Thambounaris, Amanda. "Interview with Pollyanna McIntosh." *The Celebrity Cafe.* Oct. 31, 2011. Retrieved Sept. 17, 2012, from http://thecelebritycafe.com/feature/interview-pollyanna-mcintosh-10-31-2011.

TheRoadtoFear.com. "Chris Durand." Youtube. Feb. 18, 2009. Retrieved July 11, 2011, from http://www.youtube.com/watch?v=7weSXp2lEts.

Tibbets, John C., and James M. Welsh. *The Encyclopedia of Novels into Film.* New York: Facts on File, 1998.

Todd, Tony. Personal interview. May 2, 2012.

Tribute Movies. "Katie Featherston—'Paranormal Activity 4' Interview with Tribute." Youtube. Nov. 2, 2012. Retrieved March 14, 2013, from http://www.youtube.com/watch?v=cNoQbs7XeoQ.

"Video Interview with Danielle Harris." *Halloween Movies.* n.d. Retrieved Sept. 10, 2012, from http://www.halloweenmovies.com/DanielleHarris/DH.html.

Wallace, Dee. E-mail interview. July 30, 2009.

Wallace, Dee. Phone interviews. July 16, 2010, and March 28, 2013.

Wayland, Sara. "Tobin Bell and Costas Mandylor Interview *SAW VI.*" *Collider.* Oct. 17, 2009. Retrieved on Feb. 2, 2011, from http://collider.com/tobin-bell-and-costas-mandylor-interview-saw-vi/9429/.

Welch, Virginia. E-mail interview. Nov. 8, 2013.

White, Ted. Phone interview. Dec. 14, 2013.

Whyte, Ian. E-mail interview. Jan. 17, 2012.

Wiater, Stanley, Christopher Golden, and Hank Wagner. *The Stephen King Universe.* Los Angeles: Renaissance Books, 2001.

Wieand, Dick. Phone interview. Dec. 20, 2013.

Wilbur, George, interview. *Bloody Good Horror.* Sept. 4, 2007. Retrieved July 11, 2011, from http://www.bloodygoodhorror.com/bgh/interviews/09/04/2007/george-wilbur.

Wilcox, Lisa. Phone interview. March 7, 2009.

Wixson, Heather. "Interview with Adrienne King." *Dread Central.* 2006. Retrieved May 31, 2010, from http://www.dreadcentral.com/interviews/king-adrienne-final-girls.

Wooley, John. *Wes Craven: The Man and His Nightmares.* Hoboken, NJ: John Wiley & Sons, 2011.

Worland, Rick. *The Horror Film.* Malden, MA: Blackwell Publishing, 2007.

Wyss, Amanda. E-mail interviews. April 8, 11, 2010.

Index

Absentia 3, 149–151
Adams, Amy 1
After the Fall 48, 49
Aja, Alex 21
Alien 52
Aliens 193
Aliens vs. Predator 22, 52, 192
Aliens vs. Predator: Requiem 193–194
An American Crime 8
American Graffiti 130
American Horror Story 36–41
American Psycho 155
Aniston, Jennifer 1
Argyris, Michelle 5–7
Askew, Desmond 24–25
Audrey Rose 177–180
Auffarth, Blythe 3, 7–9, 140

Bacon, Francis 151
Bacon, Kevin 1, 71, 168
Baker, Blanche 8
Balaski, Belinda 9–11
Balme, Tim 14
Banderas, Antonio 148
Bank, Ashley 14–17
Barker, Clive 27, 28, 184, 185
Bassett, Angela 40
Bates, Kathy 40
Bell, Ashley 5, 6
Bell, Courtney 149–150
Bell, Tobin 169–177
Bent, Lyriq 174
Berryman, Michael 17–26
Bettis, Angela 142
Bird 183
Blade Runner 155
Blair, Linda 5, 6
The Blair Witch Project 41, 59, 61, 62, 64
Blood Night: Legend of Mary Hatchet 101
Blythe, Janus 20

Boldin, Jo Edna 46
The Book of Eli 46–47
Bradley, Doug 26–32
Brando, Marlon 114, 171
Breck, Jonathan 33–35
Brewer, Jamie 36–41
Britton, Connie 37, 38
Brooker, Richard 73
Bryniarski, Andrew 134–135
Burns, Marilyn 133
Busey, Jake 188, 189
Byrd, Dan 23

Cagney, James 81
Candyman 28, 103, 183–186
Cannonball 10
Carlton, Hope Marie 54–55
Carpenter, Jennifer 43
Carpenter, John 41, 93, 94
Carrie 3, 11, 37, 71, 78, 85, 89
Castle, Nick 94, 97
Cat's Eye 188
Chbosky, Stacy 41–44
Children of the Corn III 1
Child's Play 47–50, 113
Christine 188
Cliff, Nicola 189
Cloned: The Recreator Chronicles 3, 128–129
Clooney, George 1
Cloverfield 43, 62
Coet, Noell 3, 44–45
Collins, Stephan Smith 32
Conroy, Frances 37, 40
Craven, Wes 19, 20, 21, 23, 25, 47
Critters 188
Critters 3 1
Cruise, Tom 148
Cujo 186, 187–188
Cullen, Peter 195
Cunningham, Lora 46–47

Cunningham, Noel 79
Cunningham, Sean 70, 71, 79, 84, 85
Curry, Tim 114
Curtis, Jamie Lee 1, 94, 96, 99, 100

Damon, Matt 52
Dante, Joe 10
Dash, Steve 72–73, 88
Davis, Rochelle 3, 123–125
Dawn of the Dead 13, 164
Dead Alive 11–14
The Dead Zone 188
Dean, James 81
Dean, Lezlie 57
Death Becomes Her 193
Deep Blue Sea 146
de la Tour, Frances 194
DePalma, Brian 11
Depp, Johnny 1, 57
Devil 43
Devil Seed 5–7
The Devil's Rejects 91, 92, 97
Diamonds Are Forever 90
Di Caprio, Leonardo 1
Douglas, Kirk 17
Douglas, Michael 17
Dourif, Brad 47, 49
Dourif, Fiona 47–50
Dowdle, John Erick 41, 43
Drag Me to Hell 157–160
Durand, Chris 96

Eastern Promises 132
Englund, Robert 32, 47, 52, 53, 56, 57, 79, 103, 155, 158
E.T. 73, 186, 187
Evil Dead 13, 158
The Exorcist 5, 66, 179

Faerch, Daeg 93, 97, 98
Farmiga, Taissa 37, 38, 40
Farnsworth, Richard 126
Fatal Attraction 15, 16
Featherston, Katie 58–61
Feldman, Tamara 103
Field, Sally 84
Fields, Karen 168
Fierman, Hannah 68–70
Final Destination 185
Fincher, David 126
Firestarter 188
Fisher, Carrie 11
Foley, Claire 119
The Food of the Gods 9, 11

Ford, John 73, 81
Fox, Michael J. 114, 188
Freeman, Morgan 126
Friday the 13th 1, 3, 41, 53, 70–89, 103, 133, 153, 166, 167, 168, 194
The Frighteners 186

Gibson, Mel 86, 87
Gillette, Warrington 72, 88
Gilligan, Zach 103
The Girl Next Door 7–9, 140
Glover, Danny 171
The Goonies 16
Graham, C.J. 75–76
Grease 51
Greene, Ellen 107, 109
Gremlins 9, 10, 103, 109
Grizzly II 1
Grossman, Naomi 36–41

Haig, Sid 90–93, 104
Hair 84
Hall, Kevin Peter 193, 195–196
Halloween 1, 3, 35, 41, 62, 91, 93–103, 133, 153, 180
Hanks, Tom 1
Hansen, Gunnar 130, 131, 132, 134, 135
Harris, Danielle 3, 95, 97, 99–104, 154, 157
Harry Potter and the Goblet of Fire 194
Hatchet 79, 100, 103
Hatchet II 154
Hatton, Rondo 104–107
Hawke, Ethan 117
Hayward, Sarah 32
Haze, Jonathan 107
He Knows You're Alone 1
Hell Harbor 105
Hellraiser 3, 26–32, 65
Henriksen, Lance 32
Herzog, Werner 111, 112
Highway to Hell 126
The Hills Have Eyes 17, 19–25, 186
Hiltzik, Robert 166–167
Hitchcock, Alfred 47, 113
Hodder, Kane 47, 71, 77–79, 103, 153
Hoffman, Leslie 51–52
Hogan, Erin Marie 62–64
Hopkins, Anthony 2, 138, 178
Hopper, Dennis 130
House of Horrors 106
House of 1000 Corpses 90
Houston, Robert 21
The Howling 9, 186–187
The Hunchback of Notre Dame 105

I Spit on Your Grave 114–117
Incident at Loch Ness 110–112
Interview with the Vampire 147–149
It 62

Jacks, Robert 133
Jackson, Peter 14, 132, 188, 189
Jacob's Ladder 151–153
Jaws 2, 14, 81, 94, 112, 145, 146
Jeepers Creepers 33–35
Johnson, Bill 130–132
Jones, Doug 43, 150
Jones, Duane 182–183
Jones, Tommy Lee 171
Jordan, Neil 148
Joseph, Jackie 107–110
Joy, Robert 22–23

Kara, Patricia 31
Karnow, Michael 110–112
Kassir, John 112–114
Keaton, Camille 3, 114–117
Keaton, Michael 114
King, Adrienne 71, 82, 83–87
King, Henry 105
King, Nick 117–119
King, Stephen 3, 55, 62, 187, 188
Kirby, Grace 28, 29
Kirzinger, Ken 76
Knight, Tuesday 55
Krakowski, Jane 168
Kunis, Mila 46

Laid to Rest 43, 101, 155, 156
Lange, Jessica 37, 40
Langenkamp, Heather 47, 50, 52, 55
Lanier-Bramlett, Suze 21
The Last Boy Scout 102
The Last Exorcism 5
The Last House on the Left 19
Laurence, Ashley 28, 29, 31, 32
Lee, Brandon 119–125
Lee, Bruce 119, 122
Lehman, Ari 70–72, 85
Lemmon, Jack 81
Leprechaun 1
Letterman, Dave 86
Levine, Ted 22, 136–139
Little Shop of Horrors 107–110
Locke, Peter 19, 20, 21
Lohman, Allison 158, 159
The Lord of the Rings 14, 132
Loree, Brad 97
Lucas, George 11

MacKay, Michael Reid 125–128
Maeve, Stella 128
Mallory-McCree, J. 128–129
Mandylor, Costas 172–173
Mandylor, Louis 67
Mane, Tyler 97–98
Manhunter 16
Marcigliano, Alexa 144–145
Massee, Michael 121, 122
Mauro, Eve 64–67
McConaughey, Matthew 133
McDermott, Dylan 37
McDowell, Malcolm 97, 102
McGinn, Chris 136–137
McIntosh, Pollyanna 3, 139–145
Mears, Derek 76–77, 194–195
Men in Black II 22
Messmer, Ben 42
Mihailoff, R.J. 103, 132–133
Miller, Dick 109
Mischief Night 44–45
Mister Roberts 81
Monster 1, 78
The Monster Squad 14–17, 126
Moore, Demi 114
Moran, Tony 94
Moranis, Rick 109
Mortenson, Viggo 132
Murphy, Ryan 40
Murray, Bill
Myers, Kim 52

Naylor, Zoe 145–147
Neeson, Liam 15
Nicholson, Jack 18, 108–109
Nifong, Alex 128
Night of the Living Dead 2, 13, 163, 164, 180–183, 184
A Nightmare on Elm Street 1, 2, 22, 31, 50–58, 65, 70, 113, 133, 168
967-Evil 57
No Country for Old Men 46
Noonan, Tom 16

O'Dea, Judy 180, 182
O'Hare, Denis 40
Office Space 46
Offspring 140, 141, 142
One Flew Over the Cuckoo's Nest 17–19, 25, 37
Ordinary People 86
Ortiz, Laura 23–24
Owen, Lyla Hay 147–149
Oz 31
Oz, Frank 109

Page, Ellen 8
Palmer, Betsy 3, 80–83
Paltrow, Gwyneth 86
Paranormal Activity 3, 41, 43, 58–61, 117
Paranormal Entity 62–64
Park Lincoln, Lar 89–90
Parker, Katie 149–151
Patton, Mark 52
The Pearl of Death 106
Peli, Orin 41, 59–61
The Pelican Brief 87
Pena, Elizabeth 151–153
Perera, Fia 62–64
The Perks of Being a Wildflower 41
Pet Sematary 3
Philadelphia 87
Pintauro, Danny 187
Piranha 9, 10
Pirates of the Caribbean 77
Pitt, Brad 52, 114, 126, 127, 147, 148, 149
Pleasence, Donald 94, 100
Poltergeist 65, 90
Popcorn 188
The Poughkeepsie Tapes 41–44
Predator 133, 192
Pretty in Pink 51
Principe, Nick 103, 153–157
Prosecuting Casey Anthony 189–191
Psycho 2, 50, 102, 167
Psycho Beach Party 1

Quarantine 43, 62

Rabe, Lily 37, 40
Raiders of the Lost Ark 14
Raimi, Sam 158
Rathbone, Basil 105–106
Raver, Lorna 157–160
Red Dragon 106
The Reef 145–147
Regehr, Duncan 15, 16
Reinåmo, Silje 160–163
Return of the Killer Tomatoes 1
Return to Horror High 1
Robbins, Tim 151
Robinson, Julianna 163–166
Romero, George 164, 180, 183
Rose, Felissa 166–169
Russell, Betsy 175–177

Saldana, Theresa 86
Saturday Night Fever 84
Saw 3, 169–177
Schaeffer, Rebecca 86

Schwarzenegger, Arnold 114, 192, 194, 195
The Scorpion King 97
Scream 21, 52, 96
Serling, Rod 113
Se7en 125–127
Shanks, Don 95–96
Shaun of the Dead 164
Shinas, Sofia 121
The Shining 3
The Silence of the Lambs 2, 22, 136–139
Silver Bullet 188
Sinister 117–119
616: Paranormal Incident 64–67
Sixteen Candles 8
Skarsgård, Alexander 160
Sleepaway Camp 166–169
Sloat, Micah 59–61
Small Soldiers 11
Smith, Michael Bailey 22, 25
Smith, Shawnee 169, 173–174
Spacey, Kevin 127
Spielberg, Steven 60–61, 187
The Stand 55
Stand by Me 16
Star Wars 187
Steel, Amy 87–89
Stiller, Ben 126
Stiller, Jerry 126
Stone, Christopher 186, 188
Stump, Spencer 76
Swanson, Kristy 126
Swift, Susan 177–180

Tales from the Crypt 112–114
Tallman, Pat 180–182
Taylor-Compton, Scout 97, 98–99, 102
The Texas Chainsaw Massacre 2, 3, 79, 91, 92, 133
Thale 3, 160–163
Theron, Charlize 1
The Thin Blue Line 41
Tilly, Jennifer 48
Todd, Tony 103, 181, 183–186
Transformers 195
True Blood 48, 160
Turchetto, Ivana 24

Urban Legend 102

V/H/S 68
Vargas, Valentina 30

W. 33
Wahlberg, Donnie 171

Wallace, Dee 10, 21, 186–189
Warlock, Dick 94–95
Washington, Denzel 46
Wasting Away 3, 163–166
Welch, Virginia 189–191
The Werewolf at Woodstock 9
Whannell, Leigh 170, 171
What's Eating Gilbert Grape 1, 87
Whitaker, Forest 183
White, Ted 73–74
Whyte, Ian 192–194
Wieand, Dick 74–75
Wilbur, George 95
Wilcox, Lisa 52–57
Wilde, Barbie 29
Winters, Dean 31

The Wizard of Oz 187
The Woman 139–145
World Trade Center 77
Wyss, Amanda 50–51

X-Men 97

Yeager, Dan 134–136
Yeager, Kevin 113

Zarchi, Meir 114–115, 116
Zellwger, Renee 133
Zeta-Jones, Catherine 86
Zombie, Rob 91, 93, 97, 98, 100, 102
Zombie, Sheri Moon 91, 97

www.ingramcontent.com/pod-product-compliance
Ingram Content Group UK Ltd.
Pitfield, Milton Keynes, MK11 3LW, UK
UKHW050527150426
5217IPUK00026B/1833